THE CREATIVE CLAS[S]

the elementary experience

THIRD EDITION

M000086804

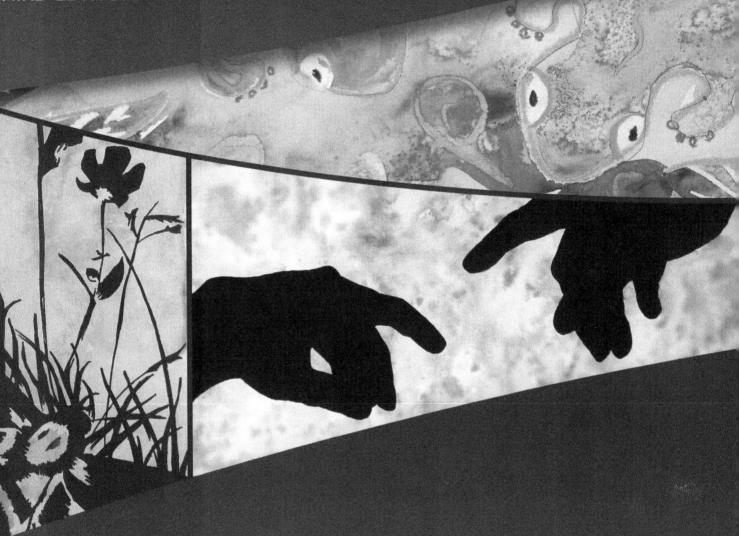

Kay Devine | Marsha Judd

WITH CONTRIBUTIONS BY:

JIM DAHL, JOHN L DEVINE, JULIE DUNN, ELIZABETH HOLSTER,
DRU MAURER & MELANIE VOGEL

Kendall Hunt
publishing company

Cover design & graphics created by Hannie Waldron
Cover art work created by Crystal Martinez, Melody Nunez, and Marsha Judd
With design contributions by Crystal Martinez, Melody Nunez, and Richard Wallace
Graphic insets designed by Tara Simonds
A very special thank you to our logophile proofreader Julie Dunn. Thank you for your keen eye and sharp pencil.

Kendall Hunt
publishing company

www.kendallhunt.com
Send all inquiries to:
4050 Westmark Drive
Dubuque, IA 52004-1840

Copyright © 2009, 2012, 2013 by Kendall Hunt Publishing Company

ISBN 978-1-4652-2488-0

All rights reserved. No part of this publication may be reproduced,
stored in a retrieval system, or transmitted, in any form or by any means,
electronic, mechanical, photocopying, recording, or otherwise,
without the prior written permission of the copyright owner.

Printed in the United States of America
10 9 8 7 6 5 4 3

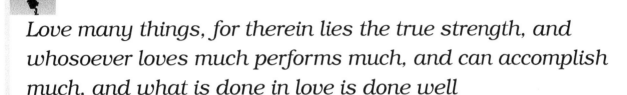

Love many things, for therein lies the true strength, and whosoever loves much performs much, and can accomplish much, and what is done in love is done well

VINCENT VAN GOGH

This text is meant as a tool offering both theoretical ideas and practical applications for pre-service and practicing educators. It is a work in progress.

Contents

Preface

As I write this preface, the California State government faces financial challenges, possible cuts to education, and other readjustments to State spending. As someone who prepares future educators to teach Visual Arts, I am certain to be asked in the coming weeks, "Why bother when there appear to be diminishing opportunities for careers in the field?" More to the point, why do the Visual Arts still matter, if the whole fabric of education is threatened? In these few paragraphs I propose that the Arts not only matter, they are central to understanding teaching and learning as an engagement with challenges we all face in the 21st century. In other words, the course you are about to undertake enables preparation of an intelligent response, demanding alert participation, to comprehend the many choices necessary for quality education.

Our crossroads resembles that faced by the art education writer, Herbert Read, who sought to deepen understanding of how the Visual Arts contribute the mindfulness needed to comprehend and defeat the threats to civilization. While writing *Education Through Art* (1947) during the bombing of London during World War II, Read argued that through the Arts people participate in a life connected meaningfully to threads of their past, present and future. He did not see the Arts as a form of entertainment or escapism from the serious threat to democracy posed by the Nazis. Rather, he articulated a rationale for Arts learning as a means of supporting critical reasoning, of discernment and respect for diversity. Read's point of view contrasts with the perception that the Arts offer expressive release.

The processes for learning about art and art education are straightforward, yet not simplistic. An often stated cliché, "thinking out of the box," confuses the goal of arts learning as preparation for a release from conformity. The Arts, the capital letter referring to subjects Music, Dance, Theater and Visual Arts, provide understandings through the deepening of abilities to discern, describe and experience the meaning of the box itself, the potential to live with or modify the box, and the value of a "one size fits most" mindset. Through the Arts in education comes the possibility of real critical thinking, the "wide-awakedness" of being that philosopher Maxine Greene intimates in *Art and the Imagination* (1994).

The promise of learning in the Arts is not simply the rehearsal of factoids about the famous artists, movements or cultures through activity by the classroom teacher or parent. It's more about assembling habits of mind that comprehend a lived experience of culture, to borrow John Dewey's words from *Art and Experience* (1934), a culture of empowerment that moves away from empty rituals of redefining. The process involves not only gaining new insights into artmaking, but also framing new understanding of what *learning* means. This demands self-reflection to build one's own set of understandings, not simply adapting, adopting and regurgitating the ideas *conveyed* during coursework.

The process of learning is especially difficult in the Arts because of common pre-conceptions held about the Arts as merely being expressive activity. Through exploring the meanings of visuals, one goal of this book is to recognize the practical ways that the Arts contribute to a whole education. Some readers reasonably ask, *"Why not* see the Arts as an entertainment, a sweetening of the bitter pill of knowledge building?" This is only one step back from the notion that the Arts are merely a vehicle for learning more important lessons, and therefore something not essential, saved for Friday afternoon or anytime when nothing of importance occurs in the classroom. The Arts *are* often fun; they necessarily involve release from the drudgery of learning facts and processes for the big test. Arts classes might be the only time during the day when students share conversations, when the outcomes are not all fit into the same form, and when the process, not the product, takes over. One unfortunate consequence of seeing the Arts as entertainment is the notion that the Arts should be easy, or that practicing the Arts is dependent upon talent. How many of our students avoid joining in because they fear being judged harshly?

There is as yet no mandated assessment for Arts learning, although we do have laws that state every child must have Arts in public school education. The influential Arts educator, Victor Lowenfeld, argued persuasively that teaching of the Arts should be part and parcel of a child's unfolding maturity. He detailed a stage theory adapted from Piaget and he devised a theory of stages in which increasing graphic sophistication demonstrated children's affective and cognitive capability. Lowenfeld saw these domains as intertwined, cognitive and emotional understanding both being part of the mind's ability to make sense of the world. The stages of growth still are used as a means of understanding children's artistic development, although they were never intended to serve as rigid indicators of levels of maturity. A common misinterpretation of Lowenfeld's ideas is that developmental teaching means not interfering with children, that anything goes in the art classroom, and that it ignores the idea that the good teacher provides guidance and responsive presence.

Developmental pathways thus not only describe a change in children's thinking, they also describe paradigms for thinking. Educators use understandings of growth for insights into how children think. Developmental understandings also provide insights for responsive conversations, as well as learning objectives. By deepening pre-service understanding of child maturation processes through Visual Art, educators can comprehend the meaning made possible through lesson activity and ultimately, the curriculum. In a broader view, understanding a child's growth through art enables discernment of aesthetic ideas, which are at first kinesthetic sensations, and gradually more like the representations of concepts.

Deepening the process of reflecting about art involves students in the discerning of works of art. This supports seeing, and the various languages that are used to describe personal experiences. The work of learning in the Arts is valuable because so many different responses are appropriate. Some of the learning occurs because the students and the teacher must accommodate diversity, and see more clearly the multiple languages that must be used to communicate. Though there are many arts activities that involve marshalling factoids ("I see a red balloon"), most learning in the Arts involves making comparisons and evaluations ("I prefer the red balloon to the yellow one because . . ."). Thinking in the Visual Arts involves complex preparation of multiple skill sets. Ultimately, the aesthetic process connects us to what we cannot articulate, even to recognizing the miraculous. "Wow!" is a valid comment in the Arts.

Many abilities, including what begins to look like well-roundedness, come into play through greater experiences in the Arts. This is a process of personal development, a pathway towards teaching, but also a journey towards a fuller, more human life.

To recapitulate, learning in the Arts contributes value to education because knowledge building demands individual creation through the medium of self. All learning in the Arts contributes to developmental growth, where meaning-making is at the core, because students actively investigate. This involves work by both teachers and learners. The pleasure of the Visual Arts lies in their capacity for renewing linkages of perception, culture, and the environment. Supporting learning in the Arts demands a vital, responsive person, someone who may know the answers, but takes greater delight in the inquiry.

Jim Dahl, *Assistant Professor Art Education, CSUF*

Why Art Is Essential to a Child's Learning and Growth

"Great teachers empathize with kids, respect them, and believe that each one has something special that can be built upon."

—Ann Lieberman

The aim of education should be to teach us how to think, rather than what to think—rather to improve our minds, so as to enable us to think for ourselves, than to load the memory with the thoughts of other men.

— JOHN DEWEY

Although debates as to the purpose of education continue to exist in this century, few disagree that education is purposeful. We create curricula for both general and specific intents. Few challenge the view that education is to prepare our children for the future. "Such is the intent of education: to allow students to attain certain understandings, skills, or attitudes or to gain a receptivity to participate in the world current and future, in particular ways, and even to design their means of interactions."

Forrest W. Parkay and Glen Hass

In these dynamic times, this statement is perhaps more significant than when Dewey first made it. Education is a journey, and our intentions must be to ensure that each student is equipped with the knowledge and skills necessary to enable him or her to proceed to the next level of learning. As Dewey commented, "Ends are, in fact, literally endless, forever coming into existence as new activities occasion new consequences." *John Dewey*

While attempting to answer why art is essential to a child's education, one must first determine what the ultimate purpose of educating our children is. As a teacher, what is the most important objective of the educational process? Is it the ability to read? Or the ability to add, subtract, multiply and divide? Could it be to promote the love of learning? Write down a few goals that you as a teacher might have. . . .

_____

_____

_____

_____

It is vital that one realize that these goals are not unique to the United States; rather, there are many universal themes presented when discussing the goals of education. Below are listed some of the goals presented in the The National Curriculum Framework of 2005 of India:

Siksha Satra

1. Education should provide an environment and opportunity for children to exercise their natural desire for self-expansion and growth.

2. Education should provide skills in art, science and business to assist in self-preservation of individuals.

3. Education should prepare individuals to operate effectively in the field of human service and citizenship. It should inculcate in individuals the capacity to understand and sympathize with their neighbors and hence function as a decent member of the human society. Through education of children, entire neighborhoods can be rejuvenated for active self-governance.

4. Education, through art, should assist the individual in self-expression and imagination. It should provide the ability to expand the horizon through this imagination for spiritual abstraction and human welfare.

http://ulavu.blogspot.com/2007/12/aims-of-education.html

In the United Kingdom, "The aim of education in general is to develop to the full the talents of both children and adults for their own benefit and that of society as a whole. It is a large-scale investment in the future." *uz.ref. uz/download.php?id=3457*

Perhaps the ultimate aim of education is to produce the most successful and effective individuals men and women who aspire to improve the world, operate effectively in today's communities, and have the ambition to grow and become more aware of their individual talents and gifts. If this is the case, how then is the use of the visual arts essential in attaining these goals?

Why is Art Essential to a Child's Education?

Harry S. Broudy, a well-regarded author and scholar on the philosophy of education, believed that imagery had an important, even central, role in a child's ability to form ideas, standards and communication skills. It is this connection between imagery and the learning process that makes art an important element of general education. Art is an essential component in a balanced educational program, providing different ways to know and interpret the world.

Art offers a variety of experiences that are otherwise ignored or neglected. It promotes cultural awareness, enabling children to experience and celebrate everyday experiences and at the same time expressing their own feelings and attitudes to the adults around them. Art allows for creative problem solving and the knowledge that with art there is no one correct answer. The study of works of art heightens a child's awareness of not only art, but of the world around them. Integrated learning experiences allow children who may not otherwise experience success in the classroom to learn concepts in a new, more informal manner. This approach provides an alternative to the standardized test for students to express their knowledge. These are just a few reasons that art plays such a significant role in the education of our children.

Personal Communication and Self-expression

The visual arts are unique in their ability to allow children to develop and express their own personal dimension of sensitivity and self-expression. Children are able to develop an idea that brings meaning and pleasure to themselves and those around them. Through

a child's art, the adults around him are able to glance into the thought processes and ideas that are uniquely his own. Today's world is becoming focused on standardized, mechanical processes, and the loss of individualization and creative thinking is eminent. Throughout the ages, mankind has found it necessary to produce art; an art program that enables a child to make qualitative judgments about his own artwork is ensuring that its citizens will be more able to take a responsible and productive role in society.

A Heightened Awareness of the World Around Them

Not only does the study of the visual arts enable a child to observe the world around him more thoroughly, it also enables him to express what he sees more clearly. Scientists need the ability to observe minute details and changes when completing experiments. A doctor needs the ability to look closely and observe changes in his/her patients to determine the correct diagnosis. A police officer needs citizens who are capable of careful observations when recording a witness's statement. The ability to closely observe things is not restricted to the arts, but is necessary to many diverse careers.

The visual awareness of the world around them should not be limited to artworks alone. By viewing costumes, artifacts, and everyday items, children develop an awareness of other cultures and societies. By viewing the artwork of others, a child becomes aware of the thoughts and feelings of the artists and develops insights into perceiving others and the world around him. Frank Wachowiak stated in *Emphasis Art* that "art is an international language, universally accessible even to those who know little about how art was used in a culture. It communicates meaning without words" (p. 3). When looking at an Aztec calendar, a child becomes aware of not only a sculptural piece depicting the measurements of days, months, and cosmic cycles, but also this ancient culture's knowledge of astronomy and mathematics. Through this knowledge, the Aztecs become more than just a lost people, but a culture with diverse values, beliefs, and ideas.

Creative Problem Solving

When presented with the problem of creating a container that would safely allow a raw egg to be dropped from a great distance using only construction paper, today's college students look to the teacher for the correct answer. Children who have experienced problems such as this in their elementary educational program do not have such restricted mind sets. They realize that there are numerous solutions—and some solutions that have never been thought of before. They meet the challenge with enthusiasm and deliberation. When questioned if a person will ever use an algebraic formula in everyday life, a math teacher may respond that they are trying to teach a child to think. Art allows for an even greater degree of rumination. With art, there is never only one correct answer. The possibilities are endless. Why would a school district choose to eliminate such a constructive and beneficial tool?

Thematic Based Approach to Teaching

One of the greatest challenges that today's schools face is low-attendance and the high dropout rate of students. If a teacher is able to provide a classroom where a child is allowed to explore, experiment, and even fail at times, that teacher is allowing the child a safe opportunity for growth. If our children are not continually facing failure, poor grades, and chastisement, they are more likely to have a positive self-image and ultimately better able to face the world. Teaching is not for the faint-hearted. In fact, if you have no love of children, do yourself a favor and change majors now. Today's schools need teachers who want to guide children in an exploration of their talents and abilities—teachers who are dedicated to providing the best education for ALL

of their students, not just the gifted or high achievers. The visual arts provide children with ways of expressing their knowledge in ways other than the standard form of tests. The arts allow children to grow when working together in group projects. The arts allow children the ability to succeed even if they are not "book smart."

Thematic based approach to teaching is using all of the subject matters to enhance the learning of each other. This will be further explained in the following chapters. Some children may find history to be dry and boring especially when asked to read a portion of a textbook and to take the test the following day. The use of visual arts can help alleviate this problem. By using art in a thematic based approach, a teacher is able to present material from another subject matter in a new and exciting manner. At times, the children will not even know that they are learning. But as a child hears about the Egyptian method of embalming mummies and tries that process out on a chili pepper, he or she is often unaware of the learning that is taking place. As those same children create a sarcophagus in which to entomb their mummified pepper, they will be closely looking at examples from ancient Egypt and learning the historical significance of that culture. Sometimes the best learning is done when the children are not aware that they are learning.

In conclusion, art needs to be looked at as a viable and productive part of the curriculum. When presented in a qualitative and thoughtful manner, it can enhance a program and stimulate a child's learning and desire to grow. As with all subject matter, art must have a relevant and thoughtful presentation requiring the teacher to encourage the children to produce artwork that is in turn both original and shows a great deal of thought. Art must not play a subordinate role to the other subjects, but must be thought of as having merit both in a cognitive, social and creative dimension.

Education is life itself.

—JOHN DEWEY

"Interdisciplinary understanding (i.e., the ability to integrate knowledge from two or more disciplines to create products, solve problems, or produce explanations) has become a hallmark of contemporary knowledge production and a primary challenge for contemporary educators." *http://www.pz. harvard.edu/Research/GoodWorkIS.htm*

It is indisputable that art should ultimately be taught as an integral part of the core curriculum of every educational program, but with budget cuts and the overwhelming focus on standardized tests, schools are finding it increasingly difficult to offer a quality education to their students. Instead of cutting the arts from the program, the visual and performing arts can be excellent tools in the effective presentation and assessment of educational theories. A holistic approach to education does not eliminate areas, but rather focuses on everything that the learner needs to know in order to become an effective, successful citizen.

In the fifth component of the California State Content Standards called Connections, Relationships, and Applications, it is stated, "Students apply what they learn in the visual arts across subject matters. They develop competencies and creative skills in problem solving, communication, and management of time and resources that contribute to lifelong career skills." Teachers throughout the years have employed this concept. A ***thematic-based*** approach to education merely means that the teacher is using a central theme throughout the subjects. For example, a third grade teacher felt that her social studies program was exceptional; therefore, the class would start out each day with a social studies unit. One of the chapters was based on the Oregon Trail and the western movement in North America during the 1800s. When it was time for language arts, she might have the children write a journal portraying what they thought it would be like to be a child riding in

a covered wagon on the Oregon Trail. The children may be involved in reading, *I'm Sorry, Alimira Ann,* a book about a young girl traveling west with her parents by covered wagon to California. So far, this would be easy planning and preparation for the third grade teacher. But what would the lessons be for math and science? Both should be centered around the Oregon Trail theme. Although this could be thought out and presented, the time to create such lessons would be immense and often teachers would give up.

When faced with this dilemma, many teachers feel that the ***interdisciplinary approach*** is a better choice. Interdisciplinary merely means that two or more subject matters will enhance the learning of each other. In the above case, social studies and language arts could easily work together to make the children's learning more effective and fun. The teacher is then able to go on to the unit of study in other areas such as math and science without the constraints of focusing on a specific theme. An example of an effective interdisciplinary lesson plan would be the insect lesson plan found at the end of this chapter. While learning about the physical characteristics of an insect such as the head, thorax, abdomen, antennae, and so on, a teacher may assign reading the chapter on insects in the science book. The average teacher would then lead a discussion in class on the readings and test the children's knowledge with a quiz, chapter exam, or such. Many children are not adept at taking tests or imparting their knowledge in such a limited manner.

Today, our children are facing an ever-changing world—one that is demanding creative use of knowledge and advanced thinking. Students will always need to know the basics, but in order for our country to advance and progress, the need to develop citizens who are able to think critically, to analyze situations and problems, and make quality decisions is paramount. Assessment procedures of that knowledge must also change. For example, by using the lesson plan on insect designs, a teacher will be able to ascertain the degree of a child's understanding of the physical characteristics of an insect without the normal examination process. Paper and pencil tests do not measure a child's creativity nor does it measure their ability to use knowledge of real-life situations. Tests tend to promote the instruction of less important skills and passive learning. Instead, a quality teacher will offer a variety of methods for their students to present their comprehension and competencies. The Insect Design Lesson Plan would allow children to show their grasp of the variety of physical characteristics of an insect without the stress or anxiety of being assessed.

The Insect Design

Scientific Concepts to be learned:

An insect is a small animal that has very specific physical characteristics:

They are invertebrates (they have no backbone).

They have an exoskeleton, or a hard covering on the outside of their body much like a shell.

They have three main body parts: head, thorax, and an abdomen.

They have a pair of antennae. Moths have simple, thread-like or feathery antennae, and butterflies have a thickened club or hook on the tip of theirs. Dragonflies have two small antennae since they rely more heavily on sight, smell and touch.

They have three pairs of legs used for walking or jumping.

They have two pairs of wings. Moths hold their wings flat when resting, and butterflies hold them together above the body.

At this time, would you rather take a test to measure your knowledge **OR** create an Insect Design described next?

Butterfly Kaleidoscope

Jaclyn Erselius
Art 380, 1pm

Time: Approx. 3–4 hours (1 hour periods)   **Age:** 4th–6th grade

Goals:

General Goal:

Children will learn about . . .
—The anatomy of a butterfly and will be able to differentiate between the head, thorax, and abdomen.
(5.0 Connections, Relationships and Applications)
—Symmetry. (1.0 Artistic Perception)
—Contrasting colors. (1.0 Artistic Perception)
—Emphasis. (1.0 Artistic Perception)

These three additions will remind the students of the standards that each fulfills. All that is needed is to put the standard in ( ) behind each step.

Specific Goal:

Children will . . .
—Create an original symmetrical designs with four butterflies (each with a head, thorax and abdomen) that are connected at the upper wings.
—Trace their design with the fine point Sharpie and will add emphasis by making some lines thicker.
—Color their designs with crayons or colored pencils. They will select contrasting colors.
  (2.0 Creative Expression)

Motivation:

Show the children photographs of different types of butterflies and ask them to point out specific colors they see on the butterfly's wings. Use creative movement to pretend you are a heavy caterpillar, then a tight cocoon and finally beautiful butterfly. Bring in a butterfly collection to show children and inspire their designs.

Vocabulary:

Abdomen   Contrast   Emphasis   Head   Insect   Symmetry   Thorax

Materials:

Per child . . .
—Photographs of butterflies with their wings open*
—1 #2 pencil
—Colored pencils
—1 black fine point Sharpie
—Masking tape*
—1 gum or kneaded eraser*
—1 5.5" X 5.5" piece of tracing paper
—1 11" X 11" piece of white drawing paper

*The teacher may want to supply these items for the whole class.

Procedure

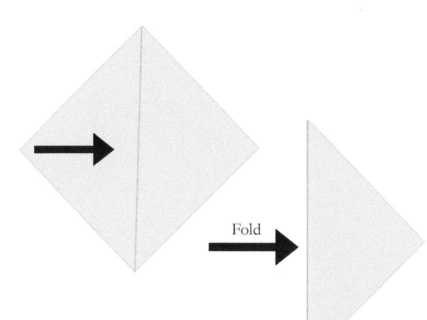

1. Fold the tracing paper (5.5" X 5.5") in half to form an isoceles triangle.

2. Using a pencil, draw half of the butterfly's head, thorax and abdomen on the fold of the tracing paper.

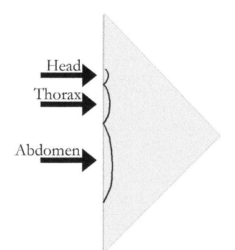

3. Draw the upper wing partially off the tracing paper. Draw the lower wing completely on the tracing paper. Both wings should be attached to the thorax.

4. Looking at your butterfly photographs for ideas, add details to your butterfly. Do not add too many details because you are going to draw this butterfly four times. (It is desirable that the students add more than the two circles in the diagram. Each student will create a unique design.)

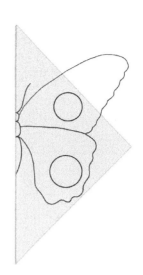

5. Turn the tracing paper over. With a pencil, trace the other half of the butterfly.

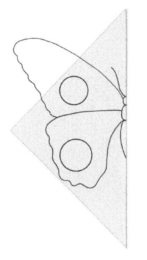

6. Open the tracing paper to a square. You now have a symmetrical butterfly.

7. Place the tracing paper in one corner of the drawing paper (11" X 11") with the pencil side down and the "open" upper wings toward the center. Use masking tape to hold the tracing paper in place.

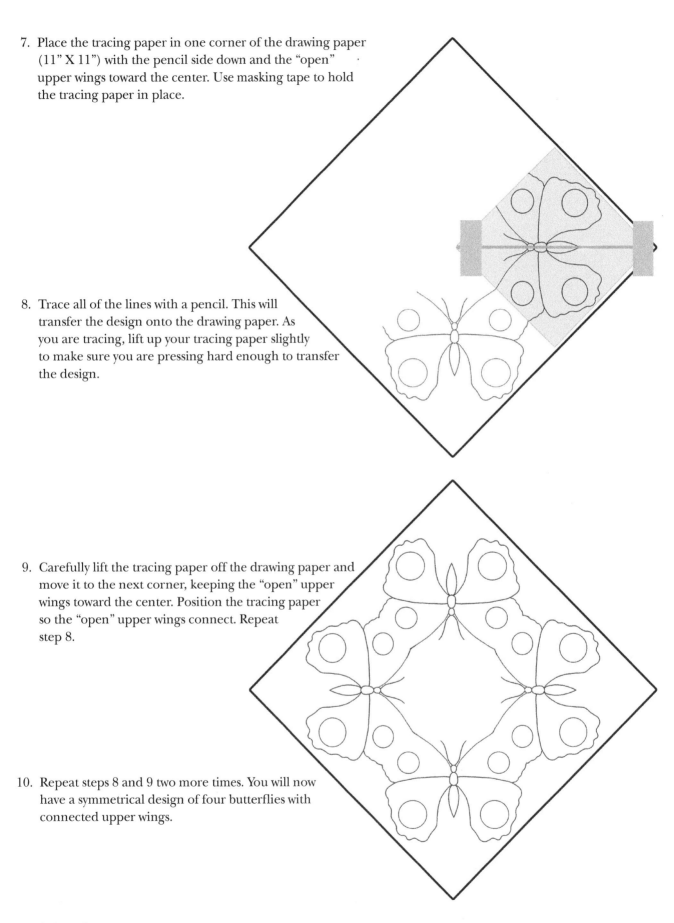

8. Trace all of the lines with a pencil. This will transfer the design onto the drawing paper. As you are tracing, lift up your tracing paper slightly to make sure you are pressing hard enough to transfer the design.

9. Carefully lift the tracing paper off the drawing paper and move it to the next corner, keeping the "open" upper wings toward the center. Position the tracing paper so the "open" upper wings connect. Repeat step 8.

10. Repeat steps 8 and 9 two more times. You will now have a symmetrical design of four butterflies with connected upper wings.

11. Trace over the pencil lines with the fine point Sharpie.
    Erase all the pencil marks.

12. Emphasize a few parts of your design by using your fine
    point Sharpie to make some lines thicker.

13. Choosing either colored pencils or crayons, select contrasting colors.
Test your colors on a separate piece of paper first to see how
they look.
Color your butterfly!

Evaluation

Children will . . .

—have a symmetrical design with four butterflies (each with a head, thorax and abdomen) that
are connected at the upper wings.

—have colored their design with high contrasting colors using colored pencils.

—have all of the lines traced with Sharpie and some thicker lines to emphasize certain areas.

—have used good craftsmanship.

ACTIVITY: What role will art play in your future classroom?

Can you relate an activity during your elementary education that was thought provoking, exciting and made you want to come to school? Describe that activity.

Please watch YouTube video on Ellen Dissanayake: Ritual, Art and Ethology

---

Further reading:

Emphasis Art by Frank Wachowiak and Robert Clements

Children and Their Art by Al Hurwitz and Michael Day

Art for Life by Tom Anderson and Melody K. Milbrandt

Parkay F.W., Hass G. *Curriculum Planning: A Contemporary Appraoch.* 7th ed. Boston: Allyn and Bacon, 2000.

Dewey J. John Dewey on Education. In: *Selected Writings.* New York: Random House, 1964.

What is Art For by Ellen Dissanayake

"Teach the young people how to
think, not what to think."
—*Sidney Sugarman*

2

Teaching the Visual Arts

Art is the colors and textures of your imagination.

—MEGHAN, LOS CERROS
MIDDLE SCHOOL, 1999

I found I could say things with color and shapes that I couldn't say any other way—things I had no words for.

—GEORGIA O'KEEFFE

Someone once said that everyone smiles in a universal language; art is very much the same. Art is often considered an international language which merely means that an idea, feeling, or opinion can be expressed and understood no matter what the viewer's language may be. Since the communication of ideas is a vital and necessary part of all educational programs, it is incompressible that so many schools are cutting the arts when visual art provides such a wonderful and effective tool for children to present their thoughts and ideas. In this section, the art terms that will be explored are simple enough for kindergarten, yet complex enough for college level. The ability to discuss and share ideas using art vocabulary should be an integral part of our children's education. This aptitude is a vital part used in the following discussion and critique of visual arts. Art is the place where all subjects converge, and the study of art gives students a more comprehensive awareness of the world around them, allowing them to function successfully in the world.

Most art educators begin their study with an investigation of the Elements and Principles of Art. While these are usually presented separately, they are intertwined. The Elements of Art are the basic *tools* the artist uses to create artwork while the Principles of Art are the *tools* for composition. When viewing a work of art, one cannot help but have the two blend and merge together. Not all works illustrate each and every term, but rather each piece needs to be analyzed and viewed as original and unique.

The Elements of Art

Art can be made for a variety of reasons, including communicating an idea or a feeling, or just for the joy of creating. When verbally expressing their feelings and ideas about their art or the art of others, people are able to communicate more effectively when they use the same terms or visual vocabulary. These basic terms that are used are called **The Elements of Art** and include line, shape, color, value, texture, space, and form or mass.

Line is a man-made invention that cannot be found in nature, but is our perception of an edge—for example, the stripes on a zebra, or supports on a suspension bridge. *Line is the path of a moving point.* The character of line is thought to convey different messages. For example, line may be used to portray the outline, or contour line of an object.

Line can create a feeling of movement, emphasis, or a pattern. The direction of line can express or suggest emotions. Horizontal lines promote a feeling of calm or stability, while diagonal lines portray action or unease. The line quality ultimately creates the overall emotional impact of the work of art.

Visual 2:1

Shape is a two-dimensional area that is created when a line intersects itself. Shapes may be geometric or organic. Geometric shapes are sharp, angular, and are usually found in man-made objects such as tables, chairs, buildings, and bridges. Organic shapes are soft, rounded, and irregular and more often found in nature; examples could be clouds, potatoes, and even animals. The variety of shapes is endless and each has a personality and feeling of its own ranging from the basic, unwavering square to a fanciful curvilinear abstraction dependant only on the individual's response.

Exercise: The variety of line is endless as is the media used to draw it. Fill the area below with a variety of lines and strive to use an assortment of media ranging from the useful pencil to a stone picked up outside. Be creative!

16-26
Element

EXERCISE: Shapes have expressive and emotional characteristics. Below are several words. In the space directly above each word, draw a shape that reflects the word. Then, come up with three words of your own and draw those respective shapes.

| Stability | Carefree | Complex | Silly | Sad |

| Playful | Serious | Active | Strong | Flashy |

Why do two *colors*, put one next to the other, sing? Can one really *explain* this? No. Just as one can never *learn* how to *paint*.

PABLO PICASSO

Color is the reflection of light; without light, one could not perceive color. If a light strikes the surface of a red apple, all of the colors of that light are absorbed in except for the red rays that are reflected back to the eye. Current understanding of color may be directly related to the experiments of Sir Isaac Newton. In the late 1660s, Newton set up a prism by a window and proved that light was responsible for color. He came up with a circular representation of the arrangement of colors and thus the concept of the color wheel was born (*www.webexhibits.org/colorart/index.html*).

Visual 2:3 Color Wheel Example

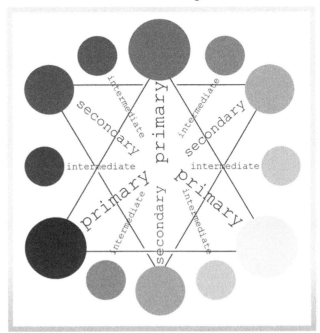

Visual 2:2 Color/Reflection of Light

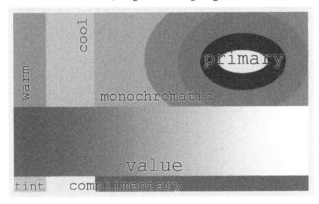

Most artists use pigments rather than light to create their work. When working with pigments, there are three *primary colors*—colors that cannot be obtained by mixing any other colors. They are red, blue, and yellow. *Secondary colors* are created when two primary colors mixed; such as red and yellow which, when mixed produce orange. Mixing a primary color and a neighboring secondary color produces a *tertiary* or *intermediate* color such as blue-green or red-orange with the name of the primary color coming first. Below is a simple color wheel that illustrates this color theory in a manner that even a preschool child could grasp.

Colors create emotional or psychological responses. *Warm colors*—red, yellow, and orange—give the illusion of moving forward in space and evoke lively, exciting moods. *Cool colors*—blue, green, and violet—tend to recede into the background and are used to suggest emotions such as calm, loneliness, and even apprehension.

There are a variety of color schemes which are combinations of colors thought to achieve special effects. *Complementary colors* are colors that are opposite to each other on the color wheel and are the most contrasting. The following are complementary color pairs:

Red and Green
Blue and Orange
Violet and Yellow

Schools often select complementary colors to achieve psychological domination. When their team runs out onto the floor or field, they stand out more because of the bold color scheme. Another color scheme is *analogous colors*. Analogous colors are three colors that are side by side on the color wheel and include at least one tertiary or intermediate color and only one primary color; these colors relate closely to each other much like a family does. Red, red-orange, and orange are analogous colors. Another color scheme is *monochromatic*; *mono* is a prefix that means one and chroma means color. Using one color such as blue and adding only white and black to achieve a variety of tints and shades may achieve a monochromatic painting. Tint is the term for any color plus white while shade is any color with black. Pink is not a color, but rather a tint!

Color has three properties: hue, intensity, and value. Hue is the name of the color, value denotes the lightness and darkness of a color, and intensity is the saturation of a color. The purest color is one that has nothing added to it. The less that is added to a color, the more intense it is. For example, pink, a tint, is less intense than the original color red.

Color has the most universal appeal and is the element that the majority of people appreciate most. The emotional characteristics of color are both individual and universal, but the symbolic meaning of color may vary from culture to culture. While red is a warm color that often denotes power, sin, or courage, an individual may respond more favorably to another color. For example, Nathaniel Hawthorne used the *red* letter "A" sewn onto their clothes to mark women who were being publicly punished for their sins in his book, *The Scarlett Letter*. The appreciation or perception of a color may also be cultural. The Chinese people have positive feelings for red which is associated with honor, success, fortune, fertility, and happiness. It is also the color of choice for most Chinese weddings with many traditional brides wearing red and gifts being offered in red envelopes.

Color combinations can create emotional responses that differ from person to person. Vincent Van Gogh took pieces of yarn and laid them next to each other in order to decide what colors to use in his paintings. Children delight in the smells and colors in a new box of crayons. The key to the successful use of color is to understand all of these qualities and then make an informed decision in order to accomplish the desired effect.

EXERCISE: Using your crayons or colored pencils, illustrate the following terms:

Analogous   Complementary

Monochromatic   Tint

Shade   Intermediate

Value is the lightness and darkness of a color. Using a monochromatic color scheme can create a variety of values. Another way of creating values may be through the use of shading—a technique used to produce light and dark tones. Blending, crosshatching, or a process called stippling can also produce the effect of shading. A line alone can portray a variety of values as the artist changes the amount of pressure placed upon the drawing utensil. An illusion of three-dimensional shape can be created by the use of value. There are also several expressive uses of value by artists. One of these is *chiaroscuro*—a technique of using light and shade in a piece that creates a dramatic contrast. Rembrandt was a master at using chiaroscuro in his paintings. *Nightwatch*, one of his most famous paintings, depicts a musketeer branch of the Dutch civic militia. In this painting, a group of men are portrayed, but the focus is placed on two men and a lady; these three are much brighter with the rest of the group being placed in the shadows.

Visual 2:4

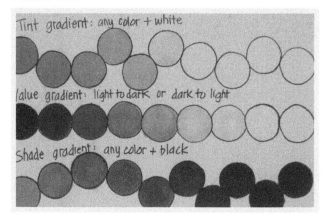

EXERCISE: Look up *Nightwatch*. How can you tell what era this painting portrays? What is the mood of the painting? How did Rembrandt achieve this? Why is this a good representation of chiaroscuro? Can you give another example of an artwork that uses chiaroscuro?

The way the surface of an object feels is called **texture** and can be real or simulated. Textures range from silky and smooth to rough and course. Although texture is more commonly found in weavings, sculptures, and three-dimensional media, a palette knife can add texture to a painting. Repeated use of texture can affect our reaction to a number of things: sweaters, socks, chairs, car seats, and even foods. Children are extremely tactile beings and are greatly attracted to a variety of textures. Sometimes a viewer can be so tempted by the tactile quality of a piece that they have trouble refraining from touching the artwork. The series of sculptures by Rodin called *Danaid* is an excellent example of this. This sculpture portrays a woman emerging from a rough, hewn piece of marble. The contrast between the coarse, scratchy stone and the soft, smooth line of the woman's back may tempt the viewer to steal just the lightest of touches. In contrast, Van Gogh's *Irises* displayed at the J. Paul Getty Museum in Los Angeles tempted the audience so much that the museum was forced to place the oil painting behind glass. The artist's thick, textural brushstrokes almost appeared to still be wet and the guards were repeatedly forced to ask people to step back and refrain from touching the painting.

Visual 2:5

Space is often hard for children to understand and may be better understood in regards to positive and negative space. Positive space is the area taken up by the objects found in a piece of art; negative space is the empty area surrounding the positive space. Space is often referred to as foreground, a middle ground, and a background. Illusions of this type of space can also be depicted through the use of overlapping of objects, using warm colors and contrasting values in the foreground and having the objects become cooler or duller as they recede, or by showing less detail as they recede into the background. A process called linear perspective creates the illusion of three-dimensional space on a flat piece of paper through the use of converging lines, a vanishing point, and a horizon line.

An excellent example of an art project that plays with positive and negative space is the *notan*, which is the Japanese art of balancing the positive and negative space in a composition. Notan is the Japanese word for "dark—light." The Western cultures commonly emphasize the positive spaces while the Eastern seeks a more balanced, harmonious use of space. One of the most common notans is the expansion of the square. Note how the piece that is taken from the square is place directly across and in reverse.

Lao Tse

We put thirty spokes together and call it a wheel;
But it is on the space where there is nothing that
the utility of the wheel depends.
We turn clay to make a vessel;
But it is on the space where there is nothing that
the utility of the vessel depends.
We pierce doors and windows to make a house;
and it is on these spaces where there is nothing that
the utility of the house depends.
Therefore, just as we take advantage of what
is, we should
recognize the utility of what is not.

Visual 2:6 Space

EXERCISE: Take a 5-inch square of black (or a dark color) paper. Cut a shape from each side.

(It should be noted that not all artists consider space to be an element of art; many feel more comfortable with it used in conjunction with the principles.)

Finally, **mass** (or **form**) is three-dimensional shape. Mass/form has height, width, and depth unlike two-dimensional shape which does not have depth. Sculptures, ceramic pieces, and weavings can readily be seen as having form or mass, but two-dimensional art can also portray form/mass. Geometric shapes such as squares and triangles can be shaded and will take on the appearance of three-dimensional objects as are shown below.

Visual 2:7 Examples of Shapes Changed to Forms

Three-dimensional images may be reliefs, three-quarter works, or freestanding pieces. Reliefs are depictions of three-dimensional images that are raised out of a flat, two-dimensional piece. Michelangelo's *Battle of the Centaurs* is an excellent example of relief, as is the portrayal of past presidents on United States coins. A three-quarter work, such as Jean Baptiste Carpeauz's *The Dance*, can be viewed on three distinct sides. A free standing piece allows the viewer to walk around the artwork in its entirety.

Three-dimensional images can also be portrayed on a flat two-dimensional surface through a technique called linear perspective. Linear perspective is a mathematical system that originated in Florence, Italy, in the early 1400s that uses a horizon line, a vanishing point, and a series of straight lines to create the illusion of three dimensional images.

Visual 2:8 Linear Perspective Examples

The Principles of Art

The guidelines for the visual organization of design are called the Principles of Art and consist of: emphasis, balance, variety, pattern, repetition, rhythm, and unity. The principles of art are the concepts used to organize or arrange the elements in a piece of art which ultimately affects the expressive and emotional nature of a piece of art. Knowledge of these terms will enable one to speak more effectively and succinctly about artworks, but it will also prove invaluable in everyday life situations such as decorating a room, creating a scrapbook, landscaping a yard, or presenting an aesthetically pleasing meal. Not every principle or element is used in each piece of art, but these terms are an excellent start when beginning an art dialogue.

Emphasis is merely the creation of one object, color, or element that has dominance in a piece, thus creating a focal point. This is often created by an artist to ensure that the viewer's eye is immediately drawn to that area first and may return to it over and over again. Objects that have emphasis may also be placed in the foreground or center of a piece creating a focal point. Contrast is another way an artist adds emphasis to a piece; this may be achieved by making something larger, brighter, darker, or just different from the surrounding area. Emphasis is a vital tool in a work of art, but should not be overdone. When using emphasis in a piece, an artist is calling attention to a specific area or shape and giving visual clarity and direction to the viewer.

EXERCISE: Draw three examples of emphasis.

Balance is the feeling of equality in a piece of art and may be symmetrical or asymmetrical. Symmetrical balance, or formal balance, is often called mirror-like balance. If one were to draw a line down the center of the piece, all of the objects on one side would be mirrored on the other. A snowflake is symmetrical as is a butterfly. Asymmetrical balance is achieved when the elements in a piece are placed unevenly, but the overall effect is harmonious and the visual weight feels even. An imaginary fulcrum may be placed in the center of an artwork. If both sides intuitively feel even, then that piece is asymmetrically balanced. Leonardo da Vinci's *Mona Lisa* is asymmetrically balanced. A third type of balance is called radial balance and is created when objects or lines radiate out from a center point. Examples of this might be a bicycle wheel, an Aztec calendar, or a mandala. Radial symmetry is achieved when the elements are mirrored both vertically and horizontally to each other. The center of an artwork such as this becomes the focal point with the lines or shapes radiating out.

EXERCISE: Name three things that have symmetrical balance.

Now try to draw one. How can you overcome any difficulty in drawing symmetrical objects?

Visual 2:10a Symmetrical Balance

Visual 2:10b

Many of the principles of design are so connected that it is difficult to explain one without delving into a discussion of another. **Variety** is often called the spice of life, and with art it is no different. An artist may use variety to add interest to a piece or draw the viewer's eye to a certain part of the art. Variety is often created subconsciously and is often counterbalanced with repetition.

Visual 2:11

Repetition, using a color, shape, or line repeatedly, often gives a piece a sense of unity and can lessen the chaotic sense that too much variety can create. Repetition and rhythm are normally felt to be inseparable.

Rhythm is the visual beat or sense of motion that pattern can create and is the ultimate result of repetition. Rhythm and pattern often occur simultaneously and create interest in a composition and as well as a sense of motion.

Pattern is created when a shape is repeated in a uniform, consistent manner and can be found in quilts, rugs, and tessellations. Regular patterns are the most common types such

Visual 2:13

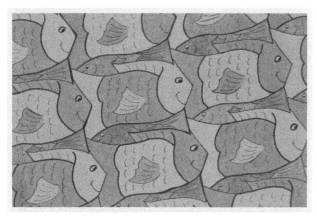

as ABC ABC ABC. Examples of alternating patterns are ABA CBC ABA CBC or ABC abc DEF def. **Unity** is achieved in a composition when all of the objects feel as though they "belong," and nothing appears to be competing for the viewer's attention and is a cornerstone in the creation of a strong composition. Composition is defined as the combination of multiple parts melding into a unified whole. In art it is the way an artist organizes space. There are many ways to create the sense of unity. One of these methods is grouping objects closely together to give the illusion that they belong. Another method is using an element or concept repeatedly throughout the composition. Finally, using continuation of an

Visual 2:14

element throughout the piece will give the illusion of unity such as line or an object.

Visual 2:15

The principles of design are varied and may differ from state to state and artist to artist, but ultimately they are used in both the creation of art and the dialogue about art. Through the discussion and critique of artwork, children as well as adults explore the communication of ideas both visually and verbally. Critical thinking, analysis, and the process of sharing ideas are just some of the results of this process and will be discussed later on in the book when Aesthetic Awareness is discussed.

Formalist, Contextualist, and Media Approaches

Frank Wachowiak in his book, *Emphasis Art* (p. 19 8th edition), states that there are three distinct approaches to teaching art in the classroom: formalist, contextualist, and media centered. He explains that in order to provide a quality program to the students, teachers must have cohesive lessons with clear objectives for each lesson. These approaches may be used separately or in combination and are often expected to be centered on the national or state standards for the visual arts.

When a teacher uses the elements and principles of art to create the main focus of a lesson plan, this is considered a *Formalist Approach*. The children may be learning about symmetrical balance during the lecture and may observe, discuss, and analyze several examples of symmetrical design such as a rose-stained glass window in a church, a wheel spoke, or an Aztec calendar. The teacher would then present a demonstration as to how to create a symmetrical design, leaving the children to come up with their own individual creations. The formalist approach is perhaps the oldest method of teaching art and focuses on the theory that, as stated by Wachowiak, "Art's job is to be beautiful."

The second approach to teaching art is one that is especially suited to the public school classroom. The *Contextualist Approach* to teaching art is centered on the content or statement that the artwork is making. This may be a political statement, an idea that would be beneficial to the school, or a reflection on a feeling that the artist may wish to portray. The main goal of art in a contextualist approach is to improve the society. There are a great many artists who created their art for just such a purpose. Diego Rivera, a famous Mexican muralist, felt that society should be able to view his art for free and began creating murals on the sides of buildings so that anyone passing by could see his work. He also had very strong feelings that the communist belief was superior to other political views at that time. Diego expressed some of these feelings when he portrayed the dignity of the working class in paintings such as "El Venedor de Alcatraces," "The Flower Vendor," and the infamous "El Hombre al Cruce."

Finally, the third approach to teaching art is the *Media-Centered Approach*. In this approach, the teacher would demonstrate a technique using a specific media, have the children practice that process, and then create an original piece of art using that technique. Ultimately, there would be no direction with subject matter—just the process. Suggestions or guidelines may be an excellent addition to this approach ultimately ensuring a better product. Many children and adults need more direction for their artwork to be successful and evocative.

Teaching Color and Color Theory

Color is arguably the most complex of the Elements of Art and it can be difficult to teach color in a way that covers the range of possibilities and concerns afforded by its use. In the U.S. color is most often taught through use of the basic color wheel and there are many varieties of color wheels on the market, all arranged with their emphasis in different areas. For teaching color at the elementary level, stressing the simplicity and logic of the basic color wheel arrangement will give students a confidence in their ability to understand and use color in their work.

Yellow Is on the Top

An excellent way to teach color theory is by helping students to fill in the color wheel by asking a series of questions. Drawing a blank color wheel, announcing that yellow is on the top and asking why, can start this process. Why IS yellow on the top of the color wheel? Students will guess that it is the brightest color, or it is up high like the sun, and someone will eventually guess that it is the lightest color. This gives the teacher a chance to talk about the difference between brightness and lightness, and to introduce the important term, **value**. If yellow is the lightest color and it is at the top, then what will be at the bottom? They will immediately guess that it must be the darkest color. Some students will wonder if the darkest color might be black, which gives the teacher an opportunity to point out that white, black and gray are NOT found on this color wheel (and to explain to older children that they ARE included in other color study systems). If black is not the answer, someone will soon see that purple or violet is the darkest color. Ask the students at this point what the difference is between purple and violet. They will usually say that purple is more red in color and violet is more blue in color, and are very surprised to learn that violet and purple are both names for the same color! To further confuse this issue, colors in the U.S. are not named logically, but are instead named for foods or current trends—all things that do not help students understand the relationships between colors. This holds true even for the names on color crayons! This gives the teacher an opportunity to point out that there is a naming system for colors, the **hues**, and in art we use these special art terms.

Color Diagram 2.1 Blank color wheel

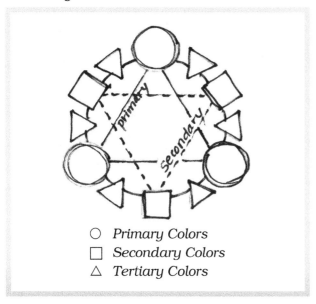

○ *Primary Colors*
□ *Secondary Colors*
△ *Tertiary Colors*

There Are Three Primary Colors

Once yellow is in place at the top of the color wheel, two more color circles, forming a triangle, are added. These two colors are red and blue. After telling students that these are the **primary** colors, ask them what they think this might mean. This gives the teacher an opportunity to talk about the words prime and primary, so students understand that all colors are mixed from these three colors, but mixing colors together cannot make the three primary colors.

Color Diagram 2.2 Color wheel: Label the three primary colors with Yellow on the top

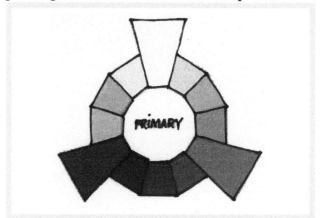

There Are Three Secondary Colors

The three blank circles between the primary colors are filled in by asking students if they know what happens when you mix red and blue primary colors together, when yellow and blue are mixed, and when red and yellow are mixed. Showing students that the secondary color is made by mixing two primary colors, and that the secondary color is situated between those two primary colors on the color wheel reinforces the logic behind the color wheel. Some students will already know that blue and yellow make green, red and yellow make orange, and blue and red make violet; the organization of the color wheel will help the rest of the students learn to mix secondary colors.

Color Diagram 2.3 Color wheel with 3 secondary colors labeled

Color Diagram 2.4 Color wheel with tertiary colors labeled

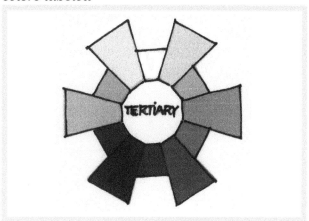

There Are Six Intermediate (Tertiary) Colors

In between the primary and secondary colors there are **intermediate** colors. These are sometimes called **tertiary** colors. Again, looking at the color wheel and asking students what colors belong between the primary and secondary colors will yield answers that give the teacher the chance to talk about the proper names of colors and how these hue names help one to know how to mix colors. An **intermediate**, or **tertiary**, color is created by mixing neighboring primary and secondary colors. So, for example, red and orange mixed together make red-orange. Many students will answer with orange-red allowing the teacher to point out that these colors always use the name of the primary color used to mix the first, with the secondary color listed second after a hyphen. Students readily see the logic in this. Asking students whether there IS a color named orange-red opens the door to discussing the colors in between the **intermediate** colors that will not be shown on the color wheel but do exist. It is much easier to understand that the color orange-red has more orange than red in it when the students can see the visual example of the color wheel.

Primary and Secondary Triads

Once the colors have been properly placed around the color wheel, the primary colors can be connected by one equilateral triangle and the secondary colors can be connected by another equilateral triangle. Both of these triangles are **triads**, or triangle composed of three equally spaced colors on the color wheel.

Color Diagram 2.5 Color wheel with primary and secondary triads drawn and labeled

Complementary Colors

Colors opposite each other on the color wheel are called **complementary** colors. Point out to the students that this word is spelled with an e and not an i, and is a special art term. Complimentary refers to things that look good together, while complementary refers to things that when put together complete each other. One way for students to understand this is to talk about what happens when all three primaries are mixed. Many students, and even adults, think that this mixture will make brown or gray but that is not the case. The mixture made is referred to as mud by water-colorists, and beginning painters are often warned about muddying their colors by mixing all three primaries. Brown is a distinct color that will be discussed later. Following this logic, then ask students what happens when they mix two complementary colors. Either by discussion or demonstration students will see that two complementary colors also make mud. When asked why it takes them a while looking at the color wheel to see that when mixing complementary colors one is actually mixing all three primaries. For example, violet and yellow are complements and create mud when mixed together because yellow is a primary color and violet is a secondary color that is made out of the remaining two primaries, red and blue. Knowing this is very important in order to be able to mix the colors students want without muddying or dulling the hues.

Color Diagram 2.6 Color wheel with pairs of complementary colors labeled

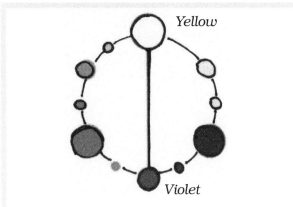

Yellow

Violet

Label the other pairs of complementary colors

Color Schemes

A **color scheme** is the way an artist limits their colors. Very young children may not see any need to limit colors and instead may want to use everything they can find. As they get a bit older they become familiar with the idea of coordinating colors, especially as they choose their clothes for school, or as they notice the way rooms in their home are decorated. There are many different color schemes but making students aware of how and why artists choose to limit their colors is more important than knowing all of the variations. There are some basic color schemes that have art terminology names and it is important for students to learn the language of art.

A **complementary** color scheme is self-explanatory, and students can think of a number of these color schemes when they think about the professional sports teams that their family members may root for. For example, the Minnesota Vikings team colors are Violet and Yellow. Sports teams often choose complementary colors because when these colors are seen next to each other there is a high amount of contrast, drawing attention and appearing to be very dynamic. Other important color schemes include analogous, monochromatic, and triadic.

Analogous color schemes are composed of neighboring colors on the color wheel, starting at one primary and going up to, but not including, the next primary. In an analogous color scheme there is one color that is included in every other color. For example red, red-orange, and orange would be an analogous color scheme, with every color including some red. A **triadic** color scheme includes any three evenly spaced colors on the color wheel. Primary and secondary triads are the two most commonly used.

A **monochromatic** color scheme is made up of one color and all of the tints, tones and shades of that color. In this case, tints, tones and shades are specific art terms and are important for students to learn in order for them to be able to mix colors easily.

Tints Tones and Shades

Tints are made up of a color plus white, **shades** are made up of a color plus black, and **tones** are made up of a color plus gray. Creating tints, tones, and shades are one way to change the **value** of a color. In the U.S. we give special names to some of the most commonly used tints tones and shades. Pink is a tint of red, and brown is a shade of orange. Students are often curious about why white, black and gray are not included in the simple color wheel. Some have even been told that white and black aren't colors. A better way to refer to white, black and gray is by calling them **neutral colors**. When students ask about black, white and gray, it gives an opportunity to show students where the neutral would be if they were included in the color wheel. White would be above yellow, since it is lighter in value than yellow, while black would be placed below violet, since it is darker than violet. Gray would be placed in the center of the color wheel, signifying the value halfway between white and black. Some printed color wheels come with gray in the center and some

people have erroneously deduced that gray is placed there because it is what you get when you mix all of the colors together. The actual meaning is that the colors blue-green, and red-orange are mid-range values, equal to gray, halfway between black and white in value. After students have practiced creating colors in a variety of mediums they do very well when challenged to match something in the real world by mixing colors.

Color Diagram 2.7 Diagram showing formation of tints tones and shades

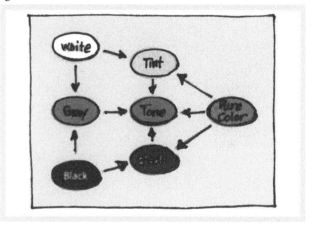

Color Diagram 2.8 Value scale

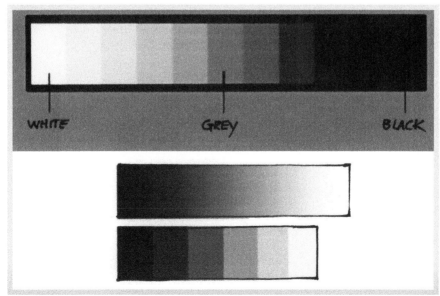

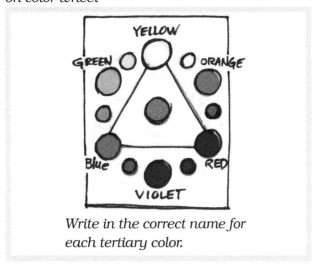

Write in the correct name for each tertiary color.

Values

Another way to change the value of a color is by mixing it with a color that is lighter or darker. For example, violet mixed with any color above it on the color wheel becomes lighter in value. Yellow mixed with any color below it on the color wheel is darker. Orange is a lighter value than red, and green is a lighter value than blue. Reminding students that all of the colors on the color wheel are placed with the lightest color, yellow, at the top and the darkest color, violet, at the bottom will help them to see relative values.

Color Temperature and Relative Color

The color wheel can be divided in half with the colors on one side (red, yellow and orange) designated **warm** colors, and those on the other side (blue, green and violet) as **cool** colors. The warm and cool color categories can be used in a number of ways including creating the illusion of three-dimensional space on the two-dimensional surface. In the real world we perceive colors that are near us and colors that are far from us differently. For the most part we don't notice this difference

until our attention is drawn to it. Colors that are nearer to us are warmer, while colors that are far away are cooler. An example of this can be seen by having students stand on the grass in the schoolyard and look at the green color that they see. Looking across the street at a patch of grass, the students will notice that the green seems different. Upon close examination they will see that the grass by their feet has more yellow in it and is therefore warmer, while the grass that is farther away has less yellow in it and thus seems relatively cooler. If we were able to look far off in the distance at grassy hillsides students would again see a difference in the appearance of the green. When asked what the difference between near and far green actually is, many students will initially see it as a value difference, with one green being lighter or darker than the other. Given enough time to look very carefully someone will eventually see that the grass in the distance appears bluer in hue. This change is due to something called atmospheric effect or atmospheric perspective. **Atmospheric effect** occurs because when we look at things off in the distance we are looking through more "atmosphere" than we are with near objects. The effect is somewhat like looking through a cloud that cools off the distant hues.

When students are sufficiently adept at identifying cool and warm colors it is time to add the complication of **relative temperature**. Students who are first learning about color generally see things according to their **local** color. For example, oranges look orange, bananas look yellow, and apples look red. It takes some time for students to become aware of the nuances of shadows, reflected colors, and relative temperature. One of the easiest and most fun ways to teach about relative color temperature is by making comparisons in the classroom. Choosing two students with red shirts and then putting them next to each other allows students to see that some reds have more blue in them and are actually cool reds, while some reds have more yellow in them and are warm reds. We only see these differences when the colors are directly next to each other. As human beings we have a limited color memory that can be trained through awareness and practice.

Knowledge of relative temperature can be used as a tool by students in creating the illusion of three-dimensional space in their artwork. A heightened awareness of what actually happens in the physical world allows us to use this information to communicate ideas more clearly.

Color Diagram 2.10 A temperature divided color wheel

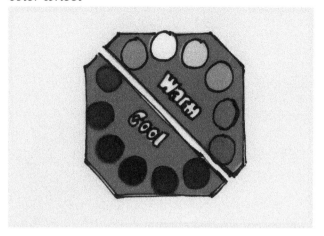

Colorama True or False-a-Thon

You earn credit for answering T or F correctly, or if your logic is written correctly even for a wrong answer. Use information from classroom work, the painting chapter and Color Vocabulary. If necessary use media such as watercolor, pastel or cut out examples of colors to solve the questions. These questions apply to paint and pigment mixing, not necessarily to light mixing. We will correct and collect this quiz in class at the class. You are invited to use classes to record responses. I will be using class time to review-demonstrate the quiz prior to turn-in. No "talse" or "frue"

1. _____ Black is a color.

2. _____ White is a color.

3. _____ Gray is the tint of black.

4. _____ Gray is the shade of white.

5. _____ "Sky blue," "corn flower blue" are not real hues; they are crayon names.

6. _____ Color "value" refers to the price of the pigments used in manufacture.

7. _____ The term "hue" refers to the name of a color.

8. _____ Color "saturation" means the intensity or the color purity.

9. _____ A synonym for "saturation of color" is "intensity of color."

10. _____ The shade of a color has the pigment black added to it.

11. _____ Tints are always perceived as "warm."

12. _____ Tints are always perceived as "cool."

13. _____ Colors in the family of red and orange are always seen as "warm" colors.

14. _____ Colors in the family of blue and green are always seen as "cool."

15. _____ Color complements exist only for the 12 colors of the color wheel.

16. _____ Yellow and Violet are compliments that have a great value difference.

17. _____ Green and Red colors of the same intensity and saturation have about the same value.

18. _____ Analogous color schemes create a "unity" in a composition because the group of analogous colors *contrast* with the rest of the picture.

19. _____ Complementary mixing produces a brownish gray version of the color.

20. _____ "Neutralizing" a color refers to color mixing that reduces the intensity of a hue.

21. _____ Mixing a hue with an analogous complementary can create either warmer or cooler neutralized colors.

22. _____ Hues in this list are analogous colors: blue green; green; yellow green; yellow.

23. _____ Analogous complements to the colors above (#22) would be: red orange; red; red violet; violet.

24. _____ The hues, red, blue and yellow are complementary colors to each other.

25. _____ Tertiary colors are mixed by combining secondary colors, e.g., green plus orange.

26. _____ Perform a color experiment-experience: if you stare at a color swatch for longer than you are comfortable, then look away from the color, you will see the complementary color.

27. _____ "Simultaneous contrast" means that adjacent colors (colors that touch) tend to appear as complements of each other. Another way to say this is that adjacent colors *force* each other's complement.

28. _____ The optical phenomenon described as *simultaneous contrast*, can be observed in the colors black, grey and white.

29. _____ By arranging color swatches it is possible to make the same mixed color appear to be different through the effect of simultaneous contrast.

30. _____ The effects of simultaneous contrast are limited to differences between color hues. Other characteristics of color are not involved.

31. _____ Teaching color is most effective through memorizing the colors on the color wheel.

32. _____ The gathering, arrangement and display of many colorful objects with specific hues provides an appropriate opportunity to discuss color without using paints or other media.

33. _____ A "color scheme" is a plot by colors groups used for political manipulation.

34. _____ An indication of an intentional "color scheme" may include a group of analogous colors or a triad of colors arranged in a harmonious design.

35. _____ The historical artistic movement of **Pointillism** relies upon **optical mixing** of color perceived through many small dots of color. The painter Georges Seurat's *Sunday Afternoon on the Grande Jatte* is a masterpiece that uses optical mixing.

36. _____ Individuals can explore personal color identities through mixing and evaluating color schemes in paint, gathering examples of colors they like, painting self-portraits, and reflective activities on color experiences.

37. _____ School age children from kindergarten through third grade are probably too young to learn about color terminology, since they are more concerned with learning how to manipulate pigments, rather than discuss their experiences in language.

38. _____ When working with paints, especially tempera pigments, children may need a larger sheet of paper to allow for exuberant movements.

39. _____ A comment such as: "Isn't Marina's painting great?" buttresses learning about painting and color *better* than complex comments such as: "Look how Marina used green right out of the pan, but has also added other colors to make several kinds of green."

40. Due with Quiz WRITTEN RESPONSE—due up to one week after: COLLAGE ARTWORK: **[15 points].** What are your favorite colors? Describe the colors. Where are these found in your life experiences? Are complements or analogous colors present? Are there colors you find difficult to be around? Describe an example of an extraordinary color you recall.

[15 Points Bonus—can be submitted with the quiz or up to one week after quiz due.]
Submit an artwork at least 11 x 14 that shows your significant colors mixed from paint or fabric samples, objects or media in a collage. Due as posting with the quiz, or artwork you can scan and post. Photographs that demonstrate these ideas, assuming they show your colors, will earn points too. Can you identify a palette of color choices that are uniquely yours? Make a visual to show your personal palette. Consider visual complements of your choices; are these colors part of the grouping? I have kept some postings from previous discussions to show possible responses.

Child Growth and the Visual Arts

"We must nurture our children with confidence. They can't make it if they are constantly told they won't."

—*George Clements*

"I want my children to understand the world, but not just because the world is fascinating and the human mind is curious. I want them to understand it so that they will be positioned to make it a better place."

—HOWARD GARDNER

www.infed.org/thinkers/gardner.htm

Children develop an aesthetic awareness even before the development of their cognitive responses. From the colorful mobile moving above their crib to the brightly colored building blocks they play with, a child's artistic growth begins when he is first able to see, hear, touch, and smell. At the age of one, most are expressing the need to make marks; often this occurs when a parent is sitting down writing bills or an older brother or sister is drawing or doing homework. Children want to emulate the actions of those around them. Offering a crayon or a large pencil and paper is a wonderful way of allowing an opportunity for the child to experience the joy of creating while also developing their eye/hand coordination. This ultimately validates the child's need to express himself visually and of course promotes a bonding experience with the adult. Most one-, and some two-year-olds, will become bored with drawing very quickly and go on to another experience; while two- and three-year-olds are more ready to sit down, spend some time, and discuss their ideas and feelings about what they are drawing.

At this age, many will verbally describe parts of their drawings, tell stories about what is being illustrated and share their thoughts and ideas with others sitting beside them. The adult should remember that the marks are not yet meant to be symbols for other things; they are the merely the result of the experience of drawing or painting. For example, a child might describe how they have a collection of "fast lines" while imagining that they are driving a race car or if they are working in clay making coils, they might call them *snakes*. By offering a child art materials at a young age, the parent or caregiver allows the

child the ability to express himself, as well as a wonderful and valuable lesson that will make them better prepared for school and life.

There are many different beliefs encompassing the visual arts and child development. These theories have evolved since education became a public entity. In the last half of the 20th century, educators and psychologists have become more and more interested in the cognitive theory, which was focused on perception, memory and creative problem solving. Jean Piaget, Swiss philosopher and natural scientist, believed that children went through a series of cognitive stages beginning with the sensorimotor stage. In this stage, a child experiences the world through movement and their senses and ends with the Formal Operational Stage where a child can think abstractly and logically. A variety of philosophies grew and evolved from which today's educators base many of their educational practices, three of which we will look into in the following pages.

Integrating the Visual Arts with Core Curriculum"

"Neither life nor art happens in a vacuum." Progressive art educators like Frank Wachowiak and Robert Clements, authors of *Emphasis Art,* set the national standard of integrated art lessons and art experiences for children in the United States for the last 63 years. As the traditional classroom continues to change, educators are constantly looking for new ways to effectively reach out and teach today's students. Other respected educators and their methodologies have long supported the use of integrated arts curriculum in the classroom. Benjamin Bloom and his theory of the three domains of learning naturally integrates the experiential nature of art making in the classroom with recognition of the three different types of experience for the child: cognitive, affective and psycho-motor. Art affects all learning domain areas. More recently and an ongoing support for the use of integrated visual arts lesson in the classroom is Howard Gardner's research on the multiple levels of intelligence. Gardner has identified 8 primary learning modalities/intelligences with which integrated arts curriculum will enhance the learning experience for your students. Utilizing the visual arts is an effortless way to become familiar with and recognize your student's learning modality/intelligence. Research is ongoing—see www.Harvard UniversityProjectZero.org for further information.

Integrated arts curriculum opens learning opportunities for all learners. Understanding the classroom instructional potential paves the way for all art lessons to be fully integrated with not only core curriculum, but life experiences as well. Explore the possibilities. Ask the questions, "So just how does my art lesson fit in with core curriculum areas?" and "How will I tie all this info together into a cohesive lesson?"

The following are guidelines that will help you narrow the information down and help you create original lesson plans that will make your lessons rich with core information that is artistically expanding and creatively meaningful for your students.

1. Remember—Visual Arts is also a core subject. California state teachers are required to teach an art lesson for 45 instructional minutes per week.

2. Know your grade level art curriculum requirements according to the State Standards. You'll be amazed by the range of creative experiences the standards state as well as suggestions for material exploration. If your school stock room does not have the necessary supplies, try the district warehouse. If they don't have it try

the county. If they don't have it, call the state. Keep trying. A good teacher should work tirelessly to get the materials necessary for his/her students.

3. Review all other curriculum standards areas. I look for logical application of the art skills and materials that I will be teaching for that grade level. I always review one grade below and one above. It's good to review and it's even better to introduce new ideas and concepts.

4. Know the resources in your area. For example, museums, zoos, libraries, historical sites, parks, arboretums/botanical gardens, art supply stores or retailers with art supplies all often offer support in a variety of ways. It can't hurt to ask.

In conclusion I often go through my classroom textbooks themselves; many of them include art extensions with images of historical and cultural artifacts, famous works of art and photographs of social events that celebrate the creation of art and its purpose within the cultural context. Simple Google searches often result in additional discovery of historical and contemporary works of art whose images are specific to the subject that I want to teach how to draw or paint. It's great when the students are learning and so am I. Look at historical artistic illustrations of bugs. Amazing and beautiful! Visit museums. All museums, not just art museums, and remember most of them have educator discounts on memberships, and special perks like expert advice and lending trucks come with those memberships. They also are very generous with your students and many have admissions reimbursement; don't be shy about asking. Museums are great resources; I've been struck by learning lightning more than once in a museum.

Give it a try; I'm sure you'll surprise yourself. There's a reason you went into education in the first place. Celebrate the joy and academic success that art and integrated art lessons will bring to your classroom.

Viktor Lowenfeld

Philosophy of Creative and Mental Growth

Viktor Lowenfeld, a renowned art education professor at Pennsylvania State University from 1950–1970s, described six stages of artistic development found in children which have become widely accepted. He felt that free expression through the use of art media was vital for the healthy growth of the child and went on to stress that at no time should the teacher place limitations or develop expectations on a child based on the characteristics of each stage. Children often skip stages or at times may even regress to an earlier stage both of which are normal and expected as each child develops. A child's earlier work may not show the structure or knowledge that later works show, but is no less valuable. A child's earlier work may portray a spontaneity and naiveté that will never again be produced. Lowenfeld felt that child art should not be considered the ultimate result, but rather the goal of art education. He states in his theory that the ultimate goal "is not the art itself, or the aesthetic product, or the aesthetic experience, but rather the child who grows up more creatively and sensitively and applies his experiences in the arts to whatever life situations may be applicable." (Michael, J. A., ed.. *The Lowenfeld Lectures.* University Park, PA: Pennsylvania State University Press, 1982: p. 16.)

Stage 1: Scribble—2 to 4 years

Lowenfeld's first stage is called the **Scribble** stage and usually occurs between 2 to 4 years of age. In its early stages, the children are merely making marks, demonstrating visual awareness, and enjoying the kinesthetic movement. Children at this age have little or no control over their drawings. This does not mean that there is no value in presenting children at this stage with the appropriate art materials; rather, a great many concepts and attitudes are being formed as the child draws. This stage goes on to include **Controlled Scribbling** which is the progression of Scribbling and shows more circular, complex forms and **Naming** which merely includes the child's stories and their first attempts at visualization through pictures.

Visual 3:1—Scribbling

The teacher's role at this stage is one of facilitator more than director. Preschool children normally have very little, if any experience with art materials. Bev Bos, an enthusiastic and knowledgeable author and preschool teacher, suggests "the most important thing is an exposure to those materials in a very basic, simple way—one that will provide for the repetition that children need. In order to learn, children must not only be actively involved but also do things over and over." Manipulation of scissors, pencils, crayons and hole punches are vital to the child's manual dexterity and ultimate success in school. Once the materials are presented, the teacher should step back and allow the child to create. Motivation may be suggested, but do not force the child to comply with preconceived ideas or models. Models, examples and dittos are merely telling the children that they are not able to create an acceptable image. These ultimately stifle a child's creativity and stunt the child's growth. Paint brushes, crayons, large paper and a lot of encouragement are all that a child needs at this time. Teachers, and parents, who allow a child freedom to explore and create are promoting school readiness as well as enhancing their social and cognitive development.

Stage 2: Preschematic—4 to 6 years

The second stage, **_Preschematic_**, occurs around the age of 4 to 6 years. This stage includes the appearance of circular images with lines protruding off, which are the child's first attempts at showing the human or animal figure. At this time the **_Schema_**, or visual idea, is beginning to be developed. Drawings at this stage include images that the child considers to be the most important in his or her world rather than concern with spatial organization or realistic representations of the world. Images may appear to be floating and are usually placed in a haphazard manner throughout the picture. Color is extremely important to a child of this age, yet it is more emotional than realistic. The details used within a child's concepts of his environment are very often an accurate measure of his awareness and conceptual development, and some feel may indicate intelligence.

Visuals 3:2a–c—Preschematic Stage
Visual 3:2a—John Devine—Age 3

40-61
Child Develop

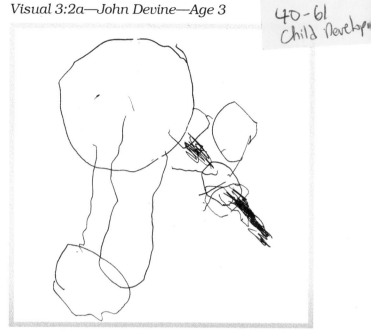

Visual 3:2b—John Devine—Age 4

Daddy and Nicholas
3 years

Stage 3: Schematic—7 to 9 years

The **Schematic Stage** is often recognized by the apparent awareness of the concept of space. This first attempt at showing spatial awareness is the **ground line**. Children may begin to have their objects that were "floating" previously drawn on the bottom of the page. Later a line will be drawn across the page and all of the objects will be placed on it. Some children even go so far as to draw multiple lines denoting objects in the foreground and background-while some draw a skyline illustrating their observation of the blue sky above. This concept of space is an excellent marker for teachers of a child's reading readiness since the concept of placing symbols in a spatial order is necessary for reading and writing. While these attempts at depicting space may seem simple and naïve to adults, they are actually a conceptual activity with little regard for realism and should be looked upon as a progression of a child's awareness of his environment. Color is used both emotionally and conceptually. When objects become repeatedly realistic in color, it most often represents a discovery of a definite color-object relationship, which is an indicator to the ability to categorize and make generalizations. The teacher should not force this awareness, but rather facilitate it through aesthetic perception exercises. Exaggeration between objects often shows the importance these items have for the child. The child himself may be larger than his house illustrating his self-importance. Flowers may be larger than the humans, family members both large and small, all demonstrating the child's strong feeling about a subject. It should be noted that children at this stage progress at different rates and may even vacillate back and forth in their use of symbols, space, or color.

Visuals 3:3a–i—Schematic Stage
Visual 3:3a—Jessica Devine—Kindergarten—"A Doggy"

Visual 3:3b—Jenna Smith—"Cat"

"Cat"

Visual 3:3c—Daniel Devine—Kindergarten—"The Pilgrim Didn't Want to Kill the Turkey Because it had a Baby on its Back."

rim was hunting for a turkey, didn't want to kill it since a little baby turkey on its

Visual 3:3d—Daniel Devine —"Two Caribous"—Kindergarten

My January Story

Visual 3:3e—Jessica Devine—"Bunkbeds"

Visual 3:3f—Jessica Devine Age 6—"Ground Line"

Visual 3:3g—Nick Devine—Age 7

Visual 3:3i—"Butterfly"—Emily Fischman—8 years

There are also several notable phenomenons that may be observed during the Schematic Stage. One of the most common of these is the **elevation of planes**. Children, in an attempt to show the viewer objects that may otherwise be invisible, will push up a plane. This is often observed on a sports field, tables, desks, and so on.

Visual 3:3h—Daniel Devine—"When I Grow Up I Want to be a Soccer Coach"

Visual 3:4a—Elevation of Planes—"Dinner Table"

Visual 3:4d—Elevation of Planes—A Soccer Field

Another phenomenon is the **x-ray vision** or **see through pictures**. When a child has a need to show the viewer what is on the inside of an object, they draw it as if it were transparent and with no regard for realism. For example, children whose mothers are pregnant may show the baby as if it could readily be seen. Others may want to show what is inside a present or a house and draw it as if one could see through the walls.

Visuals 3:5a–b—X-ray Vision
Visual 3:5a—"There's a Baby in Mommy's Tummy"

Visual 3:5b—See Through or X-ray Vision

A third phenomenon is **fold-over**. This is a child's attempt to show objects that are drawn facing each other. For example, a child's drawing depicts a person on one side of a street looking at a house on the other. Because the child is aware of the spatial input, the person may be drawn upside down denoting a logical representation of space if one were to fold the paper in the correct three-dimensional manner. This is often confusing to the viewer until they realize that the bottom of the house as well as the feet of the person are both next to the street. The child is becoming more and more cognizant of his surroundings.

Visuals 3:6a–g—Fold-over
Visual 3:6a

Visual 3:6b—The two boys are trying to sink the boy on the raft in the pool.

Visual 3:6c—Kelley Kepke—1st Grade

Once upon a time there was a little white bunny. She lived with two lazy friends a chick and a duck. One day she decided to gather some eggs.

Visual 3:6d—Jonathan Kepke—1st Grade

I've learned that God takes care of people when they get sick.

Visual 3:6e—Kelley Kepke—Age 8

I love birds because they are cute.

Page 1.

Visual 3:6f—Jonathan Kepke—"Bunnicula"

Visual 3:6g—Lindsey Kepke—2nd Grade

Dawning Realism—9 to 11 years

Dawning Realism is the child's first attempt at making an accurate depiction of an experience with a specific object; this may also be known as the **Gang Stage**. Children of this age group are becoming more and more self-aware and friendships are commonly of the same sex. Their artwork is not necessarily realistic, but rather is made from the child's point of view. Children at this stage begin to become aware of their inability to portray objects in a realistic manner and as a result they become increasingly self-critical. Linear perspective, shading, and the conscious effort to make objects smaller as they recede become characteristics that are first noted at this stage. Because of their inability to create realistic images, the child's artwork becomes rigid and less spontaneous. As a result, it is of great importance that teachers and parents guide a child in a direction that alleviates this frustration and refrain from adding to it by making critical and unthinking comments. There are a great number of exercises and techniques that may be taught at this stage that improves a child's ability to draw more realistically—some of which will be covered in the drawing lesson plans later.

Visuals 3:7a–h—Dawning Realism Child Art
Visual 3:7a—Going to the Beach

Going to the beach

4th grade Jonathan

Visual 3:7b—Kelly Hess—11 yrs old—"Cow"

Cow

Visual 3:7c—Kelley Kepke—3rd Grade

Visual 3:7d—Jessica Fischman—11 years old—"Cat"

Visual 3:7e—Jessica Devine—4th Grade —"Rabbits"

Visual 3:7f—Daniel Devine—4th Grade— "Aquarium and Tadpoles"

Visual 3:7g—Jessica Fischman—11 years old—"Sailing"

Visual 3:7h—Kelly Hess—11 years old— "My Family"

Education Through the Use of Visual Arts

Herbert Read, an English poet, historian, soldier and literary critic, became deeply interested in children's drawings and paintings. After the Second World War, an exhibition of British art was to be sent to tour the Allied and Neutral countries as an expression of good will. Deciding that it was too risky to send real works of art across the Atlantic, it was proposed that a selection of children's drawings and paintings be sent instead. Read was asked to aid in the collection of such works. During this time, Read became so moved by the expressive and emotional content of children's art that he became engaged in the study of their cultural background and creativity.

Read, having served in the British Army, formed strong convictions that another war was unacceptable, unthinkable. The ideal government was one that provided its people with the most equality while preserving individual rights and freedoms. He had been born to a tenant farmer who led a stable, comfortable life in rural Yorkshire. When his father died in 1903, his family was removed from their home and his mother was forced to enter the domestic service and placed Read in an orphanage. At the age of nineteen, Read encountered many works of art by artists such as Paul Gauguin, Vincent Van Gogh, Paul Klee and Wassily Kandinsky in the homes where his mother and her friends worked as housekeepers. The paintings of these artists were beyond shocking to the naïve, conservative young man. These childhood experiences ultimately lead Read to form strong political beliefs. He studied Communism, Socialism, and Marxism in an attempt to make sense of the world. In the end, Herbert Read felt that his main objective in social renewal was to raise the consciousness of the common man through education in the visual arts.

This concept was extremely revolutionary and went against the conventional educational philosophy in the mid 1930s. Read felt that a child's art expressed their experiences of the world around them rather than an idealized version. In his book, *Education through Art*, Read went on to discuss how all children were born artists of one type or another, but conventional education of the time repressed that creativity. He went on to say that childhood creativity should be encouraged and allowed to develop in a natural, undirected way. This is much like the view of today's preschool educators.

While working on the collection of children's art for the British Council, Read found a work of art entitled *Snake Around the World and a Boat*. He recognized this as a mandala—a universal symbol of psychic unity found as early as prehistoric art and throughout all the main cultures in history. Read was aware that the child did not knowingly produce this image, but his curiosity was peaked. He went on to discover that this symbol was created repeatedly in children's artwork throughout the world along with a variety of other accepted symbols. This creativity would later shrivel and fade away as children progressively became more and more involved in the formal education of that time. He went on to suggest that there were eight different types of child artists. Read did not develop a formal curriculum, but rather stressed the importance of visual arts education, placing it above all other subject matters. His belief was that the formal education of the day was systematically destroying the "individual creative fulfillment, mutual communication, and collective social health." (www.ibe.unesco.org/fileadmin/user_upload/archive/publications/ThinkersPdf/reade.pdf)

Stages of Graphic Representation

Note: This is a brief summary of the subject, for more information refer to *Children and Their Art*, by Al Hurwitz and Michael Day.

The Manipulative Stage (Ages 2–5 Early Childhood) (Ages are approximate)

- The *Manipulative Stage* is also known as the *Scribble Stage*. Scribbling implies an early phase of development and the term *manipulation* includes a broader period of exploring and trying new materials.

- By making a variety of marks and lines the normal child gains experience in making shapes and linear patters as they progress through the manipulative stage.

- During this time of exploring the child develops many linear and circular patterns. One such pattern is the *mandala*. The mandala is a universal symbol found in many cultures. It appears as a circle with crossed lines or often as a circle with lines radiating from it.

- During this stage an important development occurs that places the child realms ahead of other animals and points to the tremendous mental potential of human beings. This sub-stage occurrence is called *naming of a scribble*. Naming first appears when the child begins to tell stories about their scribbles. A second sub-stage involves the child describing what is about to be drawn. In both cases the scribble may not appear to be much to the observer. This occasion is important because it marks the point in time when the child begins to visualize. Each naming gives the child more experience and encouragement to develop more symbols and more stories.

The Symbol-Making Stage (Ages 6–9 Grades 1–4)

- When the child makes a connection between the image drawn and an idea, the shape of the image becomes a symbol for that idea. Sometimes the same shape will be used to express another idea totally different from the first.

- **It is important to realize that the early drawings of children are showing a concept or a specific idea.** From the child's point of view only basic symbols are needed to do this. A primitive symbol such as a circular shape with a few lines and marks means more than a head of a person—it could stand for the entire body.

- Children at this stage are aware of how humans look, they see the same things an adult sees. **The difference is that children draw what they know, not what they see.**

- As the child evolves through this stage **more details begin to appear** in their drawings. The human figure is shown with most of the details that distinguish it as to gender and social importance.

- **When two or more symbols are used** to relate a joined thought within the same composition, the child is demonstrating an advanced visual communication skill. It shows that the child is aware that objects in its environment are related.

- The **use of space** during this stage varies greatly from beginning to end. At first the child considers the picture plane (the sheet of paper) to be space for all objects and ideas. Symbols are placed all over the plane. Later on certain symbols (mother, dad, house, etc.) occupy major space though their size and placement in the picture plane. As the child's awareness develops the images begin to relate to the bottom of the edge of paper. This *baseline* is often shown as grass or a meaningful dark line. The baseline is followed by a *skyline* shown normally as a blue line on or near the top of the paper. Subject matter is placed between the two lines. This demonstrates the child's awareness of up and down and how the child relates to its environment Sometimes multiple baselines are drawn with various symbols placed on them to express a more complex concept.

- Color choices reflect an understanding of natural uses of color (sky is blue, grass green, etc.).

- It is not uncommon to see **X-ray views** during this stage. This is a method that allows the child to express the idea of something within another object. Other techniques common during this stage are: ***foldover***—showing a scene from both sides by drawing one side then turning the paper around to draw the other side (sidewalk with buildings on both sides). **Bird's-eye view**—the drawing appears to be seen from a high view looking down. **Multiple views**—within one drawing two or more views are used to express a complex idea.

The Preadolescent Stage   (Ages 10–14 Grades 5–8)

- This stage includes children from the fourth grade through the seventh and possibly the eighth grade.

- As the child progresses through this stage caution and self-criticism show in the child's artwork.

- This is a period of time where the child becomes more socially aware and sensitive to peer opinion.

- The preadolescent child is going through many social, physical, and mental changes. These changes are reflected in their artwork. This age needs additional help and art education guidance to progress through what is a difficult time.

- Interest in detail, perspective, subtle use of color, and art techniques makes the children in this stage exciting to work with.

Recalling-Reconstructing a Personal History of Artistic Development

The activity permits story telling about the self and prior arts experiences; it is also an opportunity to illustrate a handmade book.

Recalling that each of our personal experiences with the arts during childhood and adolescence may take some time. Even though many people say they have never done any art, once you begin to reconnect with your past through writing it down a fuller sequence emerges. The activity of thinking by the group will jog the memory, so encourage students to continue contributing insights after they leave the classroom for the day. The project can take several sessions to complete.

The idea is to collect your memories of art making, include media, subject, etc. Noteworthy are experiences that stand out, and a brief description of the reasons why they were significant then or now.

In addition to schools, other places where you may have experienced art making or art discussion include: museums, religious training, doctors' offices, homes of relatives and camps. Wilson and Wilson, researchers in children's artistic development observe that popular culture and entertainment are essential aspects of visual experience.

Do not leave out reflection on visual experiences from popular culture, such as theme parks, movies and television. How have the Internet and digital experiences, played a role in your artistic growth? What about the coloring books you may have enjoyed at one point? Was it important, or not, to color within the lines? When was the last time you drew a dinosaur?

It may be useful to collect ideas as a writing experience. Many students find, once they begin to frame a timeline recollections accumulate. Development need not be limited to visual art understandings, music and theater, sports and other educational experiences form vital contexts for this exercise.

Many preschool teachers such as Rhoda Kellogg feel that around the age of two a child discovers the joy of putting marks down on paper—art. She goes on to suggest that these marks may not appear to have any form or distinction, yet she goes on to present twenty basic scribbles and seventeen placement patterns.

At this stage, a child is learning to control his eye-hand coordination. This child will continue to scribble and all of the placement patterns will appear in his drawings by the age of three. Implied shapes may be observed by both the child and an adult, but around the age of three most children begin to outline shapes: circles, ovals, triangles, rectangles and even Xs. Adults must be aware that they may be able to give definitions to these shapes, but should not impose their personal ideas on children; nor should they rate a child's drawings as to how well they represent familiar objects. This is not the goal of the child and can inhibit the satisfaction that a child feels as he looks upon his own artwork.

Almost simultaneously, a child begins combining these outline shapes to form designs. A circle may be placed inside of a square or a cross inside both of them. This behavior allows a child to express new ideas that are repeated over and over until they become familiar, developing a confidence and style of their own. As was observed by Herbert Read,

Visual 3:8—Scribble Chart. Young Children begin to discover the world of art around two years of age when they begin to scribble. There are approximately 20 different types of scribbling ranging from dots to shapes in their early work. Seventeen scribble placement patterns have been identifies and these eventually will become shapes and compositional elemenst in later stages of artistic development.

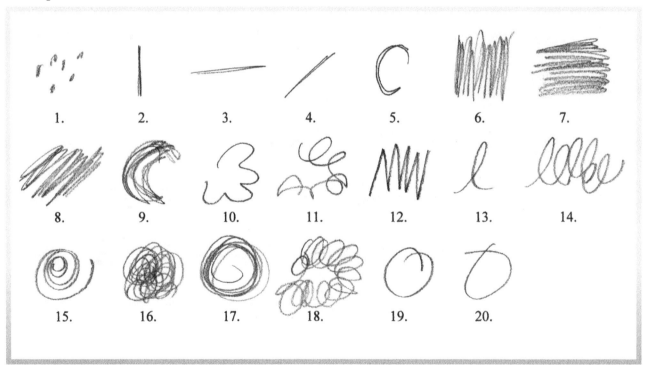

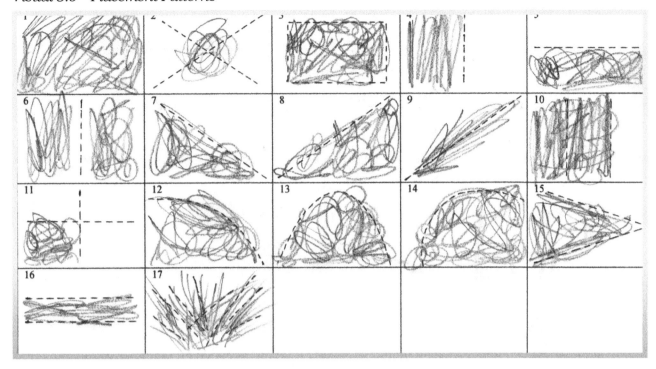

children at this age use universal images such as mandalas, suns, and radials. These concentric designs have spiritual significance in many religions such as Buddhism, Hinduism and Christianity. The American Indians used sand mandalas, as did the Aztecs in their time-keeping devices and religious expressions of circular calendars. Carl Jung, founder of analytical thinking, saw mandalas as a "representation of the unconscious self." He believed that careful observation could aid in identifying emotional disorders and guide toward a balanced and harmonious integration of a person's psyche. Today, mandalas are used to illustrate a representation of the cosmos, earth, sun, moon and circles of friends, family and communities. The basic structure of a mandala is the start of a child's progression toward drawing human figures, suns, animals, wheels and infinitely more.

At the age of four, children begin to draw the human figure. Many of their first representations of man resemble a sun and can be easily misidentified. A human often becomes a large circle with the arms and legs radiating out from it. There is no need for a body which often does not appear until a child is being toilet trained or merely needs a place to put his "tummy button." These figures are very often balanced with little concern for realism. Hair may be added to offset the legs; a circle with ten lines radiating out may be a hand. At this point a child should feel free to explore and draw with no guidance or help from an adult. Expressing pleasure and asking about the child's art will be all that is necessary.

Around the age of five, a child begins the pictorial stage. Their drawings start to include images that adults are able to recognize. Children use squares with circles under them to depict cars, triangles over squares to depict boats, and circles with lines depicting people. The bottom of the page becomes a ground line. Later, a green line may be drawn across the page with brown underneath depicting grass over the dirt. The children have a need

Visual 3:10—Examples of Mandalas and Radials. Mandalas are balanced design and appear in children's art around age three. They consist of circles, squares and crosses. From these mandalas children add lines to create suns, radials, and eventually, human figures.

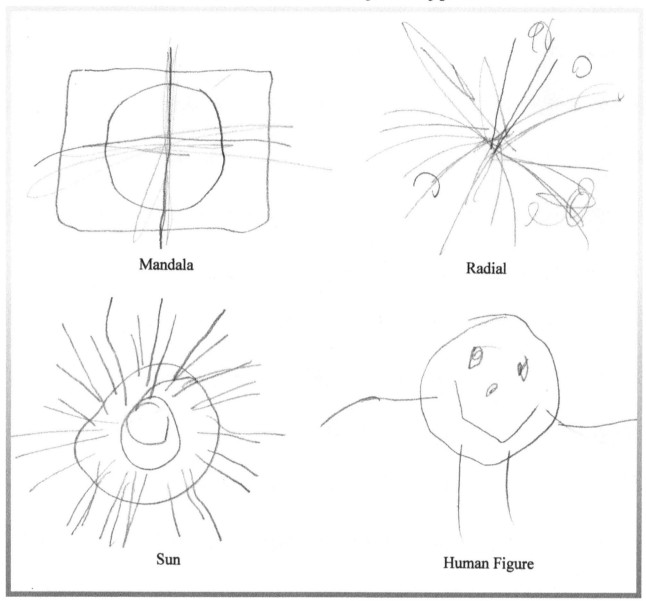

Mandala

Radial

Sun

Human Figure

to show what they know—not what they see. No matter where in the world a child lives, these images are often the same and are meant to be representational not realistic. In another year or so, children's drawings begin to tell a story; they no longer are thinking in terms of individual objects. Manual dexterity is increasing and control of a variety of tools is developed. Children are still spontaneous and have a tremendous desire to create. At this age, adults may start to "critique" a child's art, pointing out that trees are not blue and people are not as large as houses. Educators should recognize this in no way is helping the child; rather this is the beginning of a child losing interest in art because of adult criti-

Visuals 3:11a–g—Examples of Human Figures
Visual 3:11a—Peyton Ruy—Age 3—"Mommy"

Visual 3:11c—John Devine—Age 3½—"Daddy"

Daddy
Jan. 21, 19??

Visual 3:11b—Peyton Ruy—Age 3½—"Daddy"

"Daddy"

Visual 3:11d—Nicholas Devine—3 years old

My mom is happy when...
I tickle her feet

I LOVE YOU, MOM!
HAPPY MOTHER'S DAY!!

Visual 3:11e—John Devine—Age 4½—"Daddy"   *Visual 3:11g—Mason Smith—4 years old*

Visual 3:11f—Jenna Smith—3½ "years old—"Mason, Me, Mommy, Daddy"

cism. In an attempt to please the adult, children often resort to stereotypical images or ideas such as hearts, smiley faces, rainbows and flowers. This stifles creativity and is not in anyway desirable. By directing children to look closely at objects that they wish to draw, the adult will be improving their artistic perception and ultimately aid in the child's artistic growth.

Regardless of the age of a child, one of the best things an adult can do to promote healthy development is to offer a variety of art activities and experiences on a daily basis and share the child's excitement as they experiment and play. As a child grows, so does his ability to stay on task. Efforts should be made to keep activities open-ended with a variety of materials that may be as simple as paper towel tubes, ribbons, glue sticks, and recyclables. If possible, an adult can listen attentively, become involved with their own project and ultimately provide positive feedback and enthusiasm.

In conclusion, all educators become aware that children progress at a different rate in art, just as they do in every other subject. James C. Mills explained that art growth, like any other aspect of a child's growth, occurs in spurts. An effective teacher therefore must observe and document a child's growth over a period of time. Collecting and reviewing individual children's art should be a vital and necessary practice. This can be done in a variety of fun and practical ways. An entire class' work could be collected, bound and presented as a book. These books could be made throughout the year and presented at parent's night affording the parents the opportunity to observe not only their child's progression, but also the artwork of other children. Another way might be to create a portfolio for each child and add a variety of their work throughout the year ultimately creating documentation of a child's progress, but also an effective tool for conferences with parents, administrators or other school personnel.

Visuals 3:12a–e—Children's art from age 5–7
Visual 3:12a—Nicholas Devine—6 years old—"Snowmobiling"

Visual 3:12b—Daniel Devine—2nd grade

This is a picture of my family. Some of the things we like to do together are:

Visual 3:12c—Jessica Devine—"Friends"

Visual 3:12d—Daniel Devine and Molly

My May Story

I am taking my dog Molly
walk. We went around the

Visual 3:12e—Emily Fischman—8 years old—"Surfing"

1. What are the six stages of artistic development that Viktor Lowenfeld suggests that all children go through?

	Name Stage	*Draw an Example*	*Briefly Describe*
a.	_____	_____	_____
b.	_____	_____	_____
c.	_____	_____	_____
d.	_____	_____	_____
e.	_____	_____	_____
f.	_____	_____	_____

2. What is a schema?

3. At what level does a child use images such as a ground line, elevation of planes, and X-ray vision?

4. Draw an example of the following phenomenon.

   a. X-ray or see through vision

   b. Elevation of planes

   c. Fold-over

5. What did Herbert Read feel was his main objective? What do you think this means?

Effective Teaching Methods

"It is the supreme art of the
teacher to awaken a joy in creative
expression and knowledge."
—*Albert Einstein*

"We have inadvertently designed a system in which being good at what you do as a teacher is not formally rewarded, while being poor at what you do is seldom corrected nor penalized."

—ELLIOT EISNER

What makes an effective teacher? Everyone has a teacher that made an impact on their lives. What set that teacher apart from the rest? What did they do that made them different? More effective? In this chapter, we will explore the characteristics that make an exemplary teacher as well as an exemplary art teacher. Not all great teachers are the same— and they shouldn't be! But what can you do to make your classroom the one that the students want to have? The classroom that the parents request? What can you do to make learning exciting and worthwhile not just to one or two students, but to your whole class? What type of teacher will you be?

The Characteristics of an Effective Teacher

Although there are a vast number of differing opinions on what makes an effective teacher, there are a number of characteristics that are prevalent in most cases. Although they may seem simplistic in nature, these characteristics are readily agreed upon by administrators, students, parents, and fellow teachers alike. Not all great teachers have every characteristic, but it does pay off to keep these ideals in mind as one ventures into the classroom.

One of the most noted characteristics is *enthusiasm*. If a teacher comes into a classroom excited and motivated, it is most likely that the children will be enthusiastic also. Meeting them at the door and knowing their names seems a minor detail, but it can set the tone for the rest of the day. A sense of humor and a confident nature also provides for a safe, fun environment in which to learn. If the teacher seems to enjoy the subject and has attempted to present the material in an interesting manner, the children will respond in kind.

Organization and a competency of the material are excellent characteristics for a teacher as well. Having the lectures thought out ahead of time and differing slightly from the textbook reading ensures that the vital information is presented in a variety of methods. Trying to relate the information presented in real life, practical ways also helps the students grasp how these facts are relevant in their lives. Adequate preparation of materials and supplies makes for a more cohesive and efficient lesson.

An effective teacher is constantly in command of their classroom and aware of the subtle nuances. Interaction with the students is encouraged and valued with immediate feedback when possible. Praise is given for correct answers as well as those presented with thought and reasoning. Adequate explanation of why the answer was correct or incorrect will aid in the learning process. When discipline is needed, it is delivered fairly and calmly allowing the child an opportunity to redirect his or her behavior to the task at hand. This chapter will address all of these concerns and more.

Assessment

Can you think of other characteristics of an effective teacher? List them below.

Who was your most effective teacher? What characteristics of theirs would you like to emulate?

What do you think the most challenging characteristic will be for you personally? How will you combat this?

Art Lesson Planning and Curriculum

Melanie Vogel

The art curriculum and lesson planning process takes into consideration the nature of art and art concepts, the developmental age as well as the learning abilities of the child, and the values and needs of society and culture. Curriculum planning also addresses the standards and goals found in the National and State Visual Art Frameworks as well as guidelines proposed by individual school districts. The teacher will draw from all of these sources and develop art lessons to meet the individual needs and interests of students.

Art is taught at the elementary level three ways: first as a subject unto itself, second, connected to the other arts disciplines (music, dance, and theater) and third, integrated with other core academic subjects as will be discussed further in Chapter 5. National and State Frameworks provide an organized, progressive approach to art instruction with content defined in the areas of Artistic Perception, Creative Expression, Historical/Cultural Context, Aesthetic Valuing, and Connections/

Relationships/Applications. Each of these broader areas contains specific standards for each grade level. These standards build on one another, allowing teachers to apply concepts and experiences learned from the previous year to be expanded upon and infused with new ideas and skills in the present. Lesson planning must take into account the learning capabilities and multiple intelligences of the child. Children learn at different rates in different ways. Values and societal issues of the local community and school system influence how and why art is taught. Technology expands the arts into new arenas of thought and creativity and is an important part of the arts curriculum. The knowledge and understanding of the larger visual culture is just as important as the learning of traditional fine arts. All of these ideas must be considered when lesson planning.

The National Standards for the Visual Arts list six broad content areas:

1. Understanding and applying media, techniques, and processes

2. Using knowledge of structures and functions

3. Choosing and evaluating a range of subject matter, symbols, and ideas

4. Understanding the visual arts in relation to history and cultures

5. Reflecting upon and assessing characteristics and merits of their work and the work of others

6. Making connections between the visual arts and other disciplines

The California State Framework lists five standards:

1. *Artistic perception* refers to processing, analyzing, and responding to sensory information through the language and skills unique to the visual arts. The children will be involved with looking at objects in nature and their environment as well as artwork and learning to express their thoughts about each through the use of art vocabulary.

2. *Creative expression* involves creating, performing, and participating in the visual arts by applying a variety of processes and skills and using a variety of media to communicate meaning and intent in original works of art.

3. *Historical and cultural context* concerns the work students do toward understanding the historical contributions and cultural dimensions of the visual arts, noting human diversity as it relates to art and artists.

4. *Aesthetic valuing* deals with responding to, analyzing, and making judgments about works in the visual arts; assessment and meaning found in one's own work as well as others. This standard will be different from Aesthetic Perception due to the higher level thinking skills used.

5. *Connections, relationships, applications* involves connecting and applying what is learned in the visual arts to other art forms, subject areas, and to careers.

Development of competencies and skills in creative problem solving, communication, and time management that contribute to lifelong learning and career skills is included here.

The Educational Process

There are a great number of philosophies and theories surrounding the educational process and how teachers can best serve the students in their classroom. Some of these philosophies will be discussed in this chapter, but one must keep in mind that these beliefs are constantly being challenged and changed. No one practice or belief is suggested; rather, it is hoped that by creating an awareness of these beliefs and philosophies more effective, compassionate, and erudite teachers will result.

Howard Gardner—Multiple Intelligences

One of the most respected educators of our times is Howard Gardner. Born in Scranton, Pennsylvania, in 1943, Howard learned at an early age that his childhood was vastly different from that of his peers. His parents were of Jewish descent and had fled from Nurnberg, Germany, in 1938. They had brought with them a son, Eric, who unfortunately died in a sleighing accident just before Howard was born. His parents, fearful of losing another child, severely limited the risky physical activities and instead encouraged more creative and intellectual activities. This was to set the tone for Howard's career.

Although Dr. Gardner initially entered Harvard hoping to receive a degree in law, he soon realized that his true calling was that of a scholar. It was at this time that Howard began studying the human mind and how individuals think and reason. After completing his doctorate in 1971, Gardner remained at Harvard working on *Project Zero*, lecturing, and authoring over fifteen books delving into topics such as the Multiple Intelligences and the educational practices of today.

In Gardner's work, the main premise presented was that the educational ideal should be *teaching for learning.* In other words, today's teachers must not limit their work to sharing the information supplied by the textbooks alone. Rather, the informed educator must present the information in a variety of manners, ensuring that their students not only memorize the given information, but understand the information and are in turn able to use it in new, original situations. For example, if a child learns in a science class that vinegar is an acid and other foods like milk and baking soda are bases, they are hopefully able to memorize and recite that information back when tested. Then the teacher may incorporate that learning in an art lesson the following day using "magic cabbage." By boiling red cabbage for one minute, the class will see that the resulting water is purple. Painting on paper with that same water will result in a transparent purplish wash much like watercolor. But if the students brush a little vinegar on the dry paper, the magic begins. Cabbage juice is an acid/base indicator. When vinegar—an acid—touches the cabbage painting, the purple will markedly change to pink. The teacher was able to impart the same knowledge through an alternate path of an art lesson and ultimately has ensured that more of the students will remember the science lesson as well as having made learning fun.

In his book, *Frameworks of the Mind,* Gardner discusses the first seven intelligences: linguistic intelligence, logical-mathematical intelligence, musical intelligence, bodily-kinesthetic intelligence, spatial intelligence, interpersonal intelligence, and intrapersonal intelligence. The first two are the most widely acknowledged in today's schools. He goes on to discuss how the human mind rarely uses one of these intelligences at a time; rather, these intelligences are used to complement each other as a person becomes involved in creative problem solving situations as well as in the development of skills. The most challenging issue in today's educational system is how incorporate this knowledge and provide a competent and constructive course of study for our children. The Theory of Multiple Intelligences was developed by Howard Gardner and his colleagues suggest that each person's knowledge is made up of a variety of seven different intelligences:

- **Linguistic intelligence** involves an understanding and enthusiasm to spoken and written language. The ability to learn languages and effectively use language to express oneself is paramount in their quest for knowledge. These people will in turn make wonderful writers, poets, lawyers, and speakers.

- **Logical-mathematical intelligence** involves the ability to analyze problems logically, carry out mathematical operations, and investigate issues scientifically. Detecting patterns, reasoning deductively, and thinking logically all come naturally to a person with this intelligence.

- **Musical intelligence** involves aptitude in the performance, composition, and appreciation of musical patterns. The ability to recognize and compose musical pitches, tones, and rhythms is apparent in these individuals which seems to correspond to a large extent with the linguistic intelligence.

- **Bodily-kinesthetic intelligence** involves the use of one's whole body or parts of the body to solve problems and coordinate bodily movements.

- **Spatial intelligence** incorporates the ability to recognize and use the patterns of wide space and more confined areas.

- **Interpersonal intelligence** is related with the ability to understand the intentions, motivations, and desires of other people allowing people to work effectively with others. Gardner feels that this intelligence is seen in effective educators, salespeople, religious and political leaders, and counselors.

- **Intrapersonal intelligence** involves the ability to understand oneself, to appreciate one's feelings, fears, and motivations.

Many teachers feel that it seems impossible to meet the needs of all of these learning styles, but by using a variety of media and approaches, one quickly sees that all of the children benefit from such a teaching style.

Visual 4:1

Visual 4:2

Visual 4:4

Visual 4:3

Visual 4:5

Bloom's Taxonomy of Learning: The Three Domains of Learning

As all educators know, there is more than one type of learning. A committee of colleges lead by Benjamin Bloom identified three distinct levels: cognitive, affective, and psychomotor. This philosophy is known today as Bloom's Taxonomy. Benjamin Bloom was continually trying to demystify the complexities of the thinking process, what would be the best method of teaching our children how to think, and the educational goals that would best aid in this endeavor. His life's work has been focused on helping educators become more effective. As a result of these studies, Benjamin Bloom and his colleagues determined that there were three domains, or categories, of intellectual behavior which are vital in learning, and which ultimately could be further divided into subdivisions. These are not considered absolutes, but are widely accepted in today's educational circles.

The **cognitive domain**, also known as knowledge, consists of six levels: knowledge, understanding, application, analysis, synthesis, and evaluation. Knowledge is the lowest of these levels and includes activities such as defining, memorizing, repeating, relating, and placing in order. Comprehension is the next, including such actions as classifying, discussing, explaining, locating, and restating. Illustrating, interpreting, and solving are included in Application, while analysis, comparison, criticism, and discrimination are activities in Analysis. Finally, the higher level of learning is done with Synthesis including composing, creating, designing, formulating, preparation, writing and evaluation which includes appraising, judging, evaluating, supporting, and arguing. As you can see, the study of the visual arts is directly involved with the higher level of learning of this domain.

Affective domain, or attitude, is the area that encompasses the growth in feelings and emotions. This domain includes the behaviors involved in managing our feelings, values, appreciations, enthusiasms, and attitudes. It is further divided into five major categories: receiving phenomena, responding to phenomena, valuing, organization, and internalizing values.

Finally, the **psychomotor domain**, or manual and physical skills, did not initially involve a compilation of skills; the explanation was that since this work was centered on higher education (college level) that little training was involved in the manual skills. One wonders why the sports department, the theater department, or the visual art departments were not consulted. Today, most accept that this domain includes the physical movement, coordination, and use of motor-skill areas. It is further divided into seven categories: perception, set, guided response, mechanism, complex overt response, adaptation, and origination. **Perception** is the ability to guide motor activity such as adjusting the heat on a stove to ensure proper cooking or the detection of nonverbal communication while watching a demonstration of art or dance. Second is **set** which is the response to different situations, recognizing one's limitations, and the desire to learn a new process. **Guided response** is shown when a person has the ability to follow instructions or perform a mathematical equation that had just been explained. Copying, tracing, and sketching are all techniques used in the visual arts that indicates mastery in this level. **Mechanism** is the stage where a person has become proficient in an activity such as using a computer or measuring ingredients for a scientific experiment. **Complex overt response** is involving complex movement patterns and displaying a competence. Assembling, manipulating, and sketching are all activities used in this level. When a level of expertise is achieved and a person is able to respond effectively to an experience or use knowledge to perform a task that was not previously demonstrated, the level of **adaptation** is achieved. Alterations, changes, and revising are all actions denoting this level. Finally, **origination** occurs when a new theory arises, a new routine is developed, or an original piece of art is created. Composition, construction, initiation, and creating are all actions involved in origination.

Bloom also went on to explore how children learn and what educational practices were the most successful. Most educators had believed that intelligence was based on the ability to learn basic facts and use that knowledge. In an attempt at measuring this ability, Alfred Binet designed a test that was to become known as The Intelligence Quotient Test, or IQ test. This test was primarily used in the beginning to identify a student's weaknesses and ultimately provide them with additional support and guidance. Another test of this nature is the SAT, or the Scholastic Aptitude Test, which is used to determine a student's abilities and readiness to enter colleges and universities. Although these measurements and guides are useful and serve a valuable purpose, today's schools tend to place a great

deal of importance on these tests failing to address many educators' reservations that it is not an accurate portrayal of a student's abilities. These tests do not take into account test anxiety, creative problem solving, and individual student's personal issues. Today's educational system is taking a serious look at this process and reconsidering their present pedagogical methods.

One of the most widely used forms of assessment is the multiple choice and fill-in-the-blank tests. This method merely ensures that a student is overloaded with facts and statistics; the student's ability to understand the information or ability to use this knowledge in their own lives is not assessed. This method of assessment has now been even further promoted by the standardized testing that is used in our schools today. While this is assuredly a simple manner of assessment, does it truly measure a student's total understanding of a subject? And is the student who does well on a test of this nature actually have the ability and drive to make a difference in our community? Will they be able to solve the problems facing our country? Will they be able to find a cure for cancer? Overcome diversity? Become successful and productive citizens? Or is there perhaps a better alternative to this simplistic manner of teaching and assessment?

John Dewey and Constructivism

Education is life itself.
—JOHN DEWEY

John Dewey was one of the first educational philosophers and advocates of school reform in America and was infuential in the creation of today's educational policies. His belief that school was "unnecessarily long and restrictive" made him a controversial personality, but ultimately he was able to promote the "progressive education movement" and the development of experiential education. (*http://wilderdom.com/experiential/JohnDewey PhilosophyEducation.html*). His hope was that American children would gain an education that enabled them to make a truly viable contribution to society and felt that the best way to achieve this was to involve the children in real-life tasks. For example, he felt that children could learn proportions better by using measurements in cooking projects to rather than reading a chapter in a book and was ultimately influential in promoting art education in the late 19th and 20th century in the United States.

Dewey was best known for rejecting the premise that schools should focus on repetitive, rote memorization and suggested that a real-world approach might be more beneficial. Through these real-world approaches involving workshops and experimentation, it was hoped that children would be able to demonstrate their competence and knowledge through creative activities and collaboration. Children would be taught how to think for themselves and ultimately be able to express and share their knowledge and beliefs.

In the 1980s, Dewey's philosophy was combined with Piaget's work in developmental psychology resulting in what became known as **Constructivism**. The main focus of this approach was that children should learn by doing, rather than observing. For example, if a child wanted to learn how to swim, he would need to get into the water rather than check out a book describing the process of swimming. Through their trials and errors, children would ultimately attain a better understanding of a process. Through interpretation, articulation, and re-evaluation, the comprehension of a subject would be more thorough and in depth. Constructivism often uses group collaboration and peer criticism as well

as active and involved practice of the material to incite a more complete grasp of the subject matter.

This approach is often found in alternative classrooms and the time necessary to implement this process tends to limit its use in today's public school classrooms. In an attempt to promote this manner of learning, a teacher might keep in mind several suggestions that aid in the augmentation of this approach. Encouragement of student initiative and dialogue is invaluable and can only be achieved with an open-minded teacher. Asking thoughtful and open-ended questions will encourage this pursuit of dialogue and further the children's growth and understanding of the concepts presented. Ensuring that the students would be able to shift focus from the original topic to another when instructionally appropriate shows the teacher's open-minded pursuit of true knowledge and using this shift to meet the needs of all of the students. Ultimately, constructivism's main goal is to have the children generate information and knowledge from their individual and group experiences.

How can this information be used in today's classroom? Each teacher must be aware that children learn and process information in a variety of ways. Information must not be merely presented through assigning chapters in a textbook and then measuring that knowledge through a test. Knowledge must be attained and use of that knowledge must be promoted.

Today's educational systems tend to focus on the lower level of learning. Why is this so? Why is this not considered detrimental not only to our children, but to society as a whole? Bloom went on to discover "that over 95% of the test questions students encounter require them to think only at the lowest possible level . . . the recall of information" (www.officeport.com/edu/blooms.htm). How can today's educators improve our children's thinking processes? One would hope that the leaders in education would recognize that teaching merely the basics is not the answer. Rather, today's educators must strive to engage our children in activities that excite, stimulate, and even challenge their thought processes as well as their desire to learn.

Assessment

Write down one or two thoughts that you found valuable in your future classrooms for each of the educators discussed in this chapter. What are the pros and cons of these practices?

Howard Gardner

Benjamin Bloom

John Dewey

http://www.edwebproject.org/edref.mi.th3.html

Visual 4:7

Visual 4:9

Visual 4:8

Visual 4:10

Visual 4:11

Visual 4:13

Visual 4:12

Visual 4:14

Visual 4:15

Visual 4:16

Visual 4:17

Visual 4:18

Assessment

Did you have a learning experience where the teacher included psychomotor and multisensory objectives in the lesson? Did it leave a lasting impression?

Have you ever created a work of art where feeling or emotion was the motivating force in the process? How did this experience differ from one where the grade was the main motivation?

Go to the internet and find the seven intelligences described by Gardner. List them, write a brief profile of what each type of learner would be like, and then explain which one best describes you and why.

Objectives and Effective Goals

Art is often associated with words and ideas that say *imagination*, *spontaneous*, *personal*, *experimental*, and *wonder*. Standards, objectives, rubrics, and assessment don't seem to fit the same description. And how do you grade creative expression? There are effective ways to teach art that allow for freedom of expression and creativity along with assessment in learning. Teachers can allow for individual interpretation, exploration, and discovery within the framework of instructional goals. Teachers need to model and value creative thought, wonder, imaginative thinking, and sometimes uncertainty. The wise teacher will remind students there are many ways to make art as well as express meaning. The enlightened teacher will remove personal bias and encourage students to appreciate diversity and variations in artistic style. After all, art is generated from personal thought, feelings, and experiences, but can also be dove-tailed with specific goals to enhance both learning and development of a well-rounded individual.

Objectives or goals are what you want the student to learn and know. Assessment is evaluating the outcome of the objectives. Assessment questions address clearly defined goals. Did the student accomplish what he or she was asked to do? Thus, objectives and assessing student performance work hand in hand. Teachers should provide a variety of stimulating, motivational experiences and emphasize objectives which meet the needs of individual students, especially those with different learning styles, ability levels, and disabilities.

National and state art goals and standards contain broad guidelines which can be tailored to a variety of lessons and easily integrated with other curriculum areas of study. For example, a national standard states "students will understand there are various purposes for creating works of visual art." A specific goal might say, "Students will learn how Australian aboriginal art is a visual record of the stories and traditions in a culture where there was no written language."

Evaluation and Assessment

There are not only many ways to teach art, but there are also many ways to evaluate art. First, the student can evaluate his or her art in relationship to the learning objectives. This can be done through individual or class discussion following the completion of an art project. Art "critiques" at the elementary level should address objectives as well as the aesthetic ideas inherent in art. They should not be used as a forum to criticize or compare student work. Questionnaires or quizzes can assess student listening, learning, and process skills. Writing about art in a journal dedicated to the topic is a valuable way to process experiences and extend ideas and applications. Displaying artwork shows what students have learned and accomplished and boosts esteem and pride. It can also foster a sense of belonging to a group and, at the same time, honoring individuality. Displaying art in community settings such as the city hall, library, or department of education office can proclaim the breadth of learning and creativity taking place in the schools. Teachers can use art games or a PowerPoint presentation and have students identify artists or art as it relates to the lesson objectives. Keeping art work in a portfolio can help students evaluate progress and skill development over a period of time.

Rubrics, which are scoring guides, can help students meet expectations and evaluate performance both during and after art production. Rubrics can help teachers assess student work more accurately and give parents a picture of how and why their child was given a specific grade on a project. Art progress reports are another way to evaluate work

and cover broader concepts such as perception, initiative, creativity, cooperation, etc.

A simple rubric is shown below, but teachers may wish to design more complex rubrics and use a similar format for progress reports as well.

How should we grade presentations about looking at and discussing works of art? To ask "how to assess" leads us back to the question "What are we hoping to teach the student with this method." In essence we are trying to deepen the process of looking by providing a structure for students to engage in looking longer, and arriving at a judgment after careful consideration. A rubric describes a progression of learning indicators. A rubric usually draws upon teacher experience with a learning activity, and reflection upon what students reveal during a given process. Notice the rubric assesses both teacher *and* student participation.

Below is an example of an assessment rubric. Obviously this could be expanded upon with an understanding of what your students are studying, their previous experiences with looking at art, and degrees of comfort with the work itself. Familiarity with works should be encouraged through multiple looking opportunities. If students know what is expected of them their performance will improve accordingly. Teachers also learn from students and thus may improve the quality of preparation by sharing qualities defined by the rubric. Rubrics open up the possibility of students articulating their own grading if students relate the rubric to their own performance. Another feature of these rubrics is that the criteria become more complex moving to the right.

Rubric for Looking at and Discussing the Experience of Artworks

Evaluative Content	Beginning	Proficient	Intermediate	Advanced
Formal Elements of Art	Identifies areas of interest in work. Suggests contents without naming.	Uses terms from elements of art.	Also, connects terms to parts of how it is present in the work (usually with pointing or gesture).	Also relates formal elements and principles, e.g., composition, to meaning of work.
Content and narrative	Suggests a story about the work.	Narrative connected to many elements found in the picture.	Focusing on relative importance of narratives in relation to work.	Meaning of work related to style, and forms described, and knowledge of context (historical info) about work.
Presentation by *teacher or student*	Speaks clearly, identifies areas of interest and personal discovery.	Plus, clear indication of relationships within the work.	Listens to questions, relating these to study of picture. Shares knowledge without necessarily dialoguing with students.	Allows students to discover the picture after intro; encourages and focuses question and answers by students that lead to dialogues in the classroom.

Rubric for Assessment of Vases and Faces

Evaluative Content	Beginners	Proficient	Intermediate	Advanced
Formal elements and Principles of Art.	Notices shape of profile and cuts it out or draws it in paper; some correspondence between sides.	Precisely notices shapes; neatly places design on page; greater accuracy and correspondence.	Plus placement of two sides in relation to ground space created (negative space).	Plus greater refinement in accuracy of details seen; more visual tension/ambiguity in the negative space relation to faces.
Content and narrative	Follows directions for completion.	Describes motions of cutting or drawing while observing. ("I am cutting left, my pencil is moving to the right.")	Describes the relation of negative space as a figure ground relationship.	Plus articulate statement of how negative space or positive space can be seen at the same time.
Critiques/ Discussion *teacher or student*	Sees that "done is good."	Notices and compares differences within group.	Plus, evaluates based on understanding of terms in the lesson vocabulary and objective.	Plus, shares across the evaluation a connection of figure ground; uses vocabulary to discern differences; sensitivity to listening for responses.
Additions: Craft, etc.	Pasted down to page.	Careful placement of design alignment of base.	+	

Whole Class Assessment and Judgment Practice

Where students have a hand in making decisions about how work is valued, a greater sense of ownership of the critique process occurs, and greater participation results. If students know how to engage in discussions of artworks that they make, and have the opportunity and structure to practice sharing ideas, they will. Here is an idea for a critique which does not involve the often painful, possibly boring process of teacher lead discussion. This distributed criteria rubric approach demonstrates the California Visual Art Standards of 1.0 Artistic Perception and 4.0 Aesthetic Valuing.

Students are reluctant to engage in the process of valuing work for many reasons. These include: desire not to offend; sense of incomplete understanding of what's being evaluated; general reticence to be critical; other reasons particular to developmental stages of the students.

The example which follows is based upon a project called the Oaxacan Animal Sculpture. Over multiple sessions, students have created colorful sculptures using wood, papier mâché and paint. The works are arrayed on each student's desk work area, and all distracting materials put away.

The comment sheet is prepared in relation to the project. A teacher can create such a sheet based upon comments shared during the previous days of the project. (Notice the comments are particular to the Oaxacan Sculpture.) Each student has their own sheet of comments.

As each student distributes their own card comments to members of the class, a potential group discussion emerges. Notice that students exercise their evaluations as they move through the classroom depositing the comments on desks as they view each other's artworks. The discussion follows based upon the groups, which form as students share common categories. For example, everyone with a "good use of analogous color" can describe how their work meets the criteria. Or a teacher might poll class members on **why** they made their judgments.

A group discussion, which might begin with a tally of comments, should accompany this activity.

This collection of comments resulted from a papier mâché, Oaxacan animal sculpture completed in an actual classroom.

You will need to develop your own comment sheets related to your own lesson, but they should clearly connect with criteria students know (or are learning) about through the lesson activity.

Other possible categories include: Good work habits, cooperative maker. **Keep the commentary about the artwork or the cooperative behavior—not about the person.** This is not an effort to run a popularity contest, nor to lower self-esteem.

The time for this activity might be short, as little as 10 minutes, until student practice allows for extended time. A good rule of thumb is to let the students do most of the discussing. The teacher's role is to facilitate and guide conversation, not to necessarily correct all of the students' perceptions and judgments. If the teacher is talking all the time, or the discussion strays too far from the work, then it is probably time to move on. With practice students will get better at staying on track. Ditto for teachers.

Oaxacan Animal Sculpture Class Comments for Student Distribution and Subsequent Discussion

Most colorful	Strong contrasting colors	Best representation of live animal theme	Analogous colors used effectively	Significant attention to detail: Write detail _____
Animated appearing form	Scariest animal	Most natural appearing	Strong use of implied textures	Best looked at from a distance
Excellent craft of layering papier mâché	Attention to detail of painting	Action pose convincingly presented	Most humorous sculpture	Poetic interpretation of theme: Write the theme _____
Imitation of historic example	Most imaginative animal	Most likely to become a commercial toy	Strong use of contrasting values	Personal favorite: Why? _____

Writing a Lesson Plan

Art lesson plans can be gleaned from a variety of sources or designed to correlate to curriculum. One strategy for designing an art lesson plan is to become familiar with visual art content standards at the national and state levels. If the lesson is to be integrated with a core subject such as math, science, or social studies, the teacher needs to become familiar with the standards for that subject as well.

Art lessons must take into consideration the child's developmental readiness, motor skills, abilities, ages, and interests. A lesson designed for kindergarten may not be challenging enough for third grade students and a lesson for sixth graders might assume interest, knowledge, and skill development far too advanced for second grade.

As motivation or a "lead-in" to creative expression, teachers should provide related experiences through visual presentations, museum field trips, artifacts, guest artists, research, and discussion. Reproductions, prints, video, and the internet provide visual stimulation. The use of models for subjects and artifacts along with still life arrangements can help students develop their observation skills and "inner eye." Students can be primed with knowledge of artists and their place in history in advance of the art-making process. Clear objectives can be discussed and discovery through exploration and experiment allow for building confidence and problem solving skills before developing a finished product. The teacher is motivator and guide and lesson plans set the stage for a creative, educational and exciting experience.

There are different varieties of lesson plan outlines or formats and teachers may have personal preferences for putting one together. The most important factor in writing a plan is being clear in objectives and procedures so there is no confusion or lack of information. Diagrams, visual illustrations, or photographs accompanying procedural steps greatly aid in supporting a successful outcome.

Shown below are examples of lesson outlines and respective lesson plans utilizing these formats.

Lesson Plan Format

(Your lesson should be written clearly and concisely so anyone could teach from this plan.)

1. **LESSON TITLE:** The name of the lesson (also list for what ages and/or grade levels).

2. **OVERVIEW:** A brief description (2 or 3 sentences) that addresses the content, media, and curriculum connection.

3. **MATERIALS:** List everything you will need to teach the lesson including items to keep areas clean and manageable.

4. **OBJECTIVES (Goals and Visual Art Standards):** *Artistic Perception.* Write out what students will learn and accomplish in this lesson. In addition to art concepts, such as "students will understand contrast, and the use of positive and negative space in their composition," you might list what developmental characteristic(s) would be addressed. For example: "improves eye-hand coordination or encourages interaction and cooperation in a group setting." Framework standards for the grade level are to be included in the objectives (Cognitive Domain objectives).

5. **VOCABULARY:** *Artistic Perception.* List and define key words students may not be familiar with.

6. **BACKGROUND/MOTIVATION:** *Artistic Perception, Historical, and Cultural Context:* What artist, art movement, historical connection, culture, art elements, and principles etc., will you introduce and discuss? What are you going to do, show, or say to get children excited about learning and doing this project? You might include literature, writing, visuals *(boards, prints, posters, slides, videos, etc.)*, music, dance, or skit) Psychomotor Domain

objectives and learning can take place in this part of the lesson plan. Connections to other core subjects can be made at this time. *Connections, Relationships, Applications:* Inviting an artist speaker or a trip to an art museum might precede the art making experience.

7. **PROCEDURE:** *Creative Expression.* Describe, in detail, step-by-step, the instructions for the art project. Ask yourself if there is enough information so that the instructions are easily understood and complete. *Affective Domain* objectives of feelings, drives, and emotions are expressed through the art making process.

8. **ASSESSMENT:** *Aesthetic Valuing.* Assessment needs to address each objective (*rubric*). This can be in the form of questions children ask themselves or discuss as a group. Basically, this is where the students express what they have experienced and learned in the lesson. Affective Domain feelings, emotions, and ideas can be expressed verbally through assessment.

9. **INTEGRATION:** *Connections*Relationships*Applications.* How might this lesson tie into other areas of the curriculum such as language arts, social science, math, and science? How could you connect this lesson to the performing arts disciplines (Music, dance, theater)? How would you modify the lesson for different grade levels? What other media or materials could you use in place of the ones in the lesson? Explain how you might adapt the lesson for gifted or special needs students. How might you connect the lesson to careers in the arts?

10. **REFERENCE:** List source if this lesson was not your own!

Aesthetic Scanning, Creative Writing and the Arts

"Conversation is the legs on which
thoughts walk; and writing, the
wings by which it flies."
                    —*Countess of Blessington*

Aesthetic Scanning

"I was walking along a path with two friends—the sun was setting—suddenly the sky turned blood red—I paused, feeling exhausted, and leaned on the fence—there was blood and tongues of fire above the blue-black fjord and the city—my friends walked on, and I stood trembling with anxiety—and I sensed an infinite scream passing through nature."

—Edward Munch

This quote was found in the diary of Edward Munch about his painting, *The Scream*. No one looking at this painting would say that it is beautiful or that it makes them feel good; yet, it is viewed as one of the masterpieces of the world. When looking up the term **aesthetics** in the dictionary, one often finds something to the effect of *"the study of the beautiful."* But we also realize that not all art is beautiful and is not created to be so. Edward Munch's *The Scream* is a depiction of an agonized man at the base of a diagonal walkway surrounded by an acid red-orange sky. In this chapter, we will look upon aesthetics as anything "that evokes an emotional response in the viewer." The artwork may be beautiful and serene or angry and frightening such as *The Scream*; it might not even be a piece of artwork, but the process of looking at that object must affect a person eliciting an emotional response. A person can have an aesthetic response to a sunset, a flower, or a rock found alongside the ocean.

Aesthetic scanning is then the process of looking at and studying a piece of art, an object in nature, or just about anything that the viewer is visually interested in. Very often when a child is asked to look at something, he or she does so in a cursory manner. In this chapter, we will endeavor to challenge the teachers to make their students actually spend time, look closely, think about what they see, and then respond. These activities should not be solely directed at historical pieces of art, but should include looking at the children's own artwork and that of their peers.

Reviewing their own artwork not only gives value and meaning to it, but it also very effectively enables the child to think, respond to, and hopefully grow artistically. This activity is actually documented and seen as being an integral part in state and national requirements for a quality educational program. In the California Content Standards, the fourth standard is called *Aesthetic Valuing.*

Aesthetic Valuing

The California State Standards state that the children will be involved in responding to, analyzing, and making judgments about works in the visual arts

Students analyze, assess, and derive meaning from works of art, including their own, according to the elements of art, the principles of design, and aesthetic qualities.

It goes on to make specific suggestions for each grade level. For example, the tasks that would be appropriate for a second grader to participate in would fulfill the following:

Derive Meaning

4.1 Compare ideas expressed through their own works of art with ideas expressed in the work of others.

4.2 Compare different responses to the same work of art.

Make Informed Judgments

4.3 Use the vocabulary of art to talk about what they wanted to do in their own works of art and how they succeeded.

4.4 Use appropriate vocabulary of art to describe the successful use of an element of art in a work of art.

http://www.cde.ca.gov/BE/ST/SS/vamain.asp

The National Educational Standards are very close in nature and state:

NA-VA.K-4.5 Reflecting upon and assessing the characteristic and merit of their work and the work of others.

- Students understand there are various purposes for creating works of visual art
- Students describe how people's experiences influence the development of specific artworks
- Students understand there are different responses to specific artworks

(The above standard is for Kindergarten through 4th and below is the same standard for 5th through 8th. How do the compare? Contrast?)

NA-VA.5-8.5

- Students compare multiple purposes for creating works of art
- Students analyze contemporary and historic meanings in specific artworks through cultural and aesthetic inquiry
- Students describe and compare a variety of individual responses to their own artworks and to artworks from various eras and cultures

"Developed by the Consortium of National Arts Education Associations (under the guidance of the National Committee for Standards in the Arts), the National Standards for Arts Education is a document which outlines basic arts learning outcomes integral to the comprehensive K–12 education of every American student."
—CONSORTIUM OF NATIONAL ARTS EDUCATION ASSOCIATIONS

http://www.education-world.com/standards/national/arts/index.shtml

In an attempt at developing a child's thinking critical skills, a teacher must first provide a positive learning environment where a child feels safe to offer his or her thoughts and ideas. An open discussion is not only permitted, but mandatory, and a teacher's role should be that of a mediator and facilitator. Children will learn that theirs is not the only correct opinion and will ultimately learn to listen and understand other's viewpoints. The fresh, open, thoughtful comments that char-

acterize a child's viewpoint can not only aid in the personal growth of their peers, but [also] afford a tremendous opportunity for the teacher to learn about these children [and] their thoughts.

When we ask the children to verbalize about an object, we are not only requiring them to look closely at an object, we are asking them to use linguistic as well as visual expressions. These activities will not only improve their artistic abilities, but will further their language growth. Furthermore, the children will be analyzing, critiquing, and responding to which are the higher levels of thinking as discussed earlier in the text.

These skills will also develop their artistic skills, giving them new ways to approach a variety of problem solving skills. When creating their own artwork, a child may remember a color combination that they found effective and try it out themselves. The process of expression is constantly involving the critical thinking skills—allowing for production of more relevant and thoughtful art pieces.

The Four Stages to Looking at Art

Most visual arts educators agree that there are a variety of stages that a child can go through when looking at art. Four stages that are readily accepted are:

1. Descriptive Phase—List the objects that you see, or describe what you see.
2. Formal Analysis—This is often centered around the art vocabulary terms such as the Elements of Art and the Principles of Art. Is this piece unified? Does it show balance? Where was the artist standing when he created this piece?
3. Interpretive Stage—What was the artist trying to say? What mood is portrayed?
4. Informed Response—Do you like this piece? Why or Why not?

In the ***descriptive phase***, a child may merely list the objects that he sees in a piece.

The teacher will then become a facilitator as ask what type of objects. For example, if a child says that he sees a horse, a train, two people, and a road, the teacher might ask what color is the horse? What are the people doing? From what direction is the train coming from? What do you think is going to happen? This will further encourage the child to look closer, be more descriptive, and become more involved. A list of the Elements of Art may be a wonderful addition to help with the child's involvement. Words such as texture and form may provide another aspect of discussion that would normally not be included.

During *formal analysis*, a child is directed to think about the formal composition of a piece. Is this piece unified? Is there anything that does not feel as if it belongs? Is the artwork balanced? If so, is it symmetrically or asymmetrically balanced? How did the artist create the rough, textual area of the road? Are there a variety of colors? Do they contrast? Are they warm or cool? Reminding the students of the Principles of Art would be very beneficial here, while keeping in mind not all of the terms will be used in every piece of art.

Next, in the *interpretive stage*, the children will become involved in a discussion of what they felt the artist was trying to say. Remind them that not every person will feel the same. In fact, an individual may have a very different response to a piece on different days. Mood, experiences, and growth all can alter the response that is evoked when looking at an artwork.

Finally, in the *informed response* stage, the children are asked to decide how they feel about a piece. No longer are they able to say, "I like it" or "I don't like it." They must give reasons—thoughtful and insightful reasons. The questions that a teacher might lead with could be: What mood did the artist try to evoke? What color schemes were used to make you feel this way? What do you like best about this piece? Why?

Now let's put this into practice. In a classroom, the teacher should place a piece of art, a still-life, or an object where everyone has a clear view. Allow the children to take out a piece of paper to jot down ideas. First, have them list all the objects that they see. After this is done, encourage them to write down descriptive terms next to the objects (adjectives next to the corresponding nouns—we really are using language arts!) Then ask the children to decide if the piece is unified. Remind them that unified means that everything in the piece feels as if it belongs. If not, what feels out of place? Then go on to ask them to write down a mood or feeling that this piece evokes. Finally, do they like it? Make sure to have them jot down a reason or two for this. Now it is time to draw them into a discussion. Make sure that their comments are directed toward the piece and not each other. Remind them also that not everyone will respond in the same way—and this is good! The discussion portion is at times difficult to start. Many children are uncomfortable to express their thoughts in front of a class in fear of being put down or laughed at. The teacher must at all times be aware of this and keep a tight control over the direction of the discussion. After the class has experienced this process enough times, it will become second nature. Heated discussions are not bad and may allow the children the freedom to express their ideas openly in time. This sharing of ideas allows the children to grow not only artistically, but in their response to and understanding of the diverse populations in our classrooms today.

Creative Writing

After exploring the aesthetic scanning process a number of times with the class, it is now time for an individual exploration. Many teachers today have a specific time for writing in a journal or diary. The objective for this is not to focus on the rules of language or grammar, but rather to focus on creative expression. While some children are able to set down and compose unbelievable stories, others need direction or a prompt. Having an artwork or an object to direct their thoughts is an excellent way to promote both the expressive language and artistic expression at the same time. Many children are not adept at this and several states have found a lacking in this course of study. While creative writing has become more desired and expected at the university level, some children have never experienced this type of activity at the elementary stage. Needless to say, if a child has not experienced the creative thought process or creative problem solving at an early age, it is increasingly difficult for them to learn as they progress. It would be even more beneficial for the children to be aware that the main objective in this activity is not grammar, but on the creative expression.

ACTIVITY: Select a piece of art that you have little or no experience with. You must be able to look at this piece during the entire activity. Go through the following stages. Have a copy of the Elements of Art and Principles of Art available.

Descriptive phase—List the objects that you see.

Formal Analysis—Is this piece unified? Does it show balance?

Interpretive Stage—What was the artist trying to say?

Informed Response—Why do you like this piece? or Why do you not like this piece?

Name: _____

Name and Address of the Museum or Gallery: _____

Title of Artwork: _____

Artist: _____

Medium used: _____

Aesthetic Scanning for Third Grade and Above:

Elements of Art: line, shape, color, value, texture, form or mass, and space

Principles of Art: balance, unity, emphasis, contrast, variety, repetition, pattern, and rhythm

Describe what you see.

What are the principles of art that the artist has made use of and how did the artist achieve this effect? For example, if contrast is a primary force, describe what is contrasting.

What do you think the artist was saying? Why?

How does this artwork make you feel? Give several reasons why.

A handout that may be used for younger children who are experiencing the Aesthetic Scanning process for the first time:

Aesthetic Scanning

What do you see?

LINES

What kinds of lines do you see?

straight	curvy	wavy	thick	thin
horizontal	vertical	diagonal	elegant	jagged

SHAPES

What kind of shapes do you see?

circles	squares	rectangles	triangles	ovals
organic	geometric	positive	negative	imaginary

COLORS

What colors do you see?

Primary colors: red   blue   yellow

Secondary colors: green   orange   violet

Intermediate colors: blue-green, blue-violet, red-orange, red-violet, yellow-green, yellow orange

warm colors   cool colors   complementary colors

analogous colors   monochromatic colors   tints   shades

VALUES

What values do you see?

whites or light values   darks or dark values neutrals

high contrast   low contrast   medium contrast

TEXTURES

What type of textures do you see?

rough	smooth	bumpy	soft	slick	hard

FORMS OR MASSES

Do you see any three-dimensional shapes?

spheres   cubes   cones   cylinders   pyramids

SPACE

What type of space do you see?

positive   negative

foreground   middle ground   background

overlapping forms   atmospheric space

Analyzing Art

STEP 2: Looking at Composition ("I notice. . . .")

The following six terms are referred to as the "principles of design." They describe how the "elements of art" were organized (arranged) by the artist.

1. EMPHASIS—FOCAL POINT

What is the first thing that you see when you look at the painting? Why does it attract your attention? What kind of contrast has the artist used to guide your eye (big among small, dark among light, etc.)?

2. BALANCE

What kind of balance is used?

SYMMETRICAL (each side of the painting is similar)

ASYMMETRICAL (each side of the painting is different)

RADIAL (branching out in all directions from a common center, as a wheel)

A BIT ASYMMETRICAL (each side of the artwork is a little different)

3. CONTRAST

What contrasting things do you see?

various shapes

opposite colors

different textures   sizes

types of lines

different values   color intensities   ideas

4. PATTERN—RHYTHM

What do you see repeated in the artwork? Describe.

lines

textures

values

shapes

colors

Which are repeated the most?

5. MOVEMENT

Where are your eyes encouraged to move in the artwork? What has the artist done to create this feeling of movement?

strong lines

particular shapes: triangles, thin rectangles, thin ovals

recognizable objects: cars moving, people looking or walking, etc.

What direction is the movement?

6. UNITY

How has the artist made every part of the artwork seem to belong?

By repeating: colors, shapes, textures, etc.

By using a consistent style (method of working with the art materials)

Do any parts seem not to belong?

Additional sources for Aesthetic Scanning and Art Criticism:

A program of the *John F. Kennedy Center for the Performing Arts*, ArtsEdge is also a partner of *Thinkfinity*, a consortium of national education organizations, state education agencies, and the Verizon Foundation. Thinkfinity Content Partners develop free, standards-based, discipline-specific educational Web sites for K–12 teachers and students.

http://artsedge.kennedy-center.org/aboutus/

Building Community Through the Arts

"We cannot always build the future for our youth, but we can build our youth for the future."
—Franklin D. Roosevelt

by Dru Maurer

Ralph Waldo Emerson said: "A *creative economy is the fuel of magnificence.*"

Creative people, commerce, institutions, local arts groups, and community patrons play an important role in cultivating a creative and vital community. According to Richard Florida, "Creative thinking is the currency of the 21st century, flash points for artistic, technological, economic or social innovation, where there is a concentration of creative people and institutions, there is also a creative synergy in business and technology."

Engaging community members in cultural activities, local government, education, and local nonprofit groups can facilitate opportunities for people to connect and build strong creative programs. A good analogy would be the Great Depression and the joy and fellowship that the arts and music brought to the forefront in the midst of the doom and gloom, featuring the genius of Louis Armstrong, Benny Goodman, and Duke Ellington. These legendary talents formed a creative alliance that still sustains the magic of the "Swing Era."

Some research indicates that three of the top four places where people attend arts and cultural events are community venues rather than conventional locations. People enjoy the gathering in open air spaces, churches, and public buildings. Reasons include volunteer opportunities, community service hours for youth, and meeting grounds for friends and families.

One of the assignments for the Art 380 students is to volunteer for a cultural arts program. The goal is for the student to gain insight and experience a hands on dynamic in working with the public.

The City of Mission Viejo offers an annual festival every spring called "Arts Alive," and students are invited to participate and earn extra credit points. The vision of the festival is to celebrate the importance of local government's investment in the arts and the environment: to the economy, the education and job preparation of its citizens, and to the health of civic life.

The festival emerged into a new decade of community spirit, education, and volunteerism and began in April of 2007. Each year, the festival focuses on a decade of art history. The city hires professional artists and educators to facilitate outdoor studios, and performances to showcase the arts featured during that timeline. The program engages all ages, student participation, community service hours, local talent, and fosters a creative process for all.

Mission Viejo provides a community opportunity for the public to be an integral part of a public art project. The city has completed several pieces, such as mosaic tile, planting along the Oso Creek Trail, and working on projects which will become permanent installations on roadways. The program has been extremely successful in raising public awareness, ownership, and pride in one's community. The completed projects continue to foster interest and unity within the community. Many of the Cal State Fullerton Art 380 students have played a vital role in the completion of these projects for extra credit. The program is an annual occurrence and statistics show many of the students (whom have graduated) come back with their families to participate in the festival. The arts have proven to be a huge part of community building for the City of Mission Viejo.

Recommended actions for advocacy in the arts and audience development are fostered through local partnerships which include:

- Municipal Membership in Arts Orange County
- Local Businesses and Chambers of Commerce
- Key Clubs and Volunteer Organizations
- Local School Districts—Arts Educators and Administrators
- Local 501(c)(3) Groups

- Pacific Symphony
- Orange County Philharmonic
- South Coast Symphony
- Saddleback Community College
- Students from Cal State Fullerton University
- Publications on Spark OC
- Participation in the Imagination Celebration of Orange County
- Membership in the California Arts Education Association (CAEA)
- California Alliance for Arts Education (CAAE)
- Sustaining a presence with local government—attending council meetings and civic programs.

There are specific steps communities can take to create a healthy cultural ecology. Every successful municipality has specific policy levers they can use to create systemic change. According to a 2005 Rand Corporation report, *"The arts won't flourish unless more art lovers are minted through sustained exposure during childhood . . . this means (a shift) towards the grass-roots cultivation of youngsters and parents through public schools and community arts programs."*

Data compiled by Arts Orange County and the Orange County Community Foundation reveal the following:

1. Orange County residents agree on the importance of a vibrant cultural sector in Orange County and recognize the social and personal benefits of the arts.

2. The need to deepen relationships with the arts leads to increased patron attendance and financial investment.

3. Orange County residents place a high priority on the importance of the arts in the development and education of children. However, there are differences in the quality and quantity of arts instruction between the county's 27 school districts.

4. The next step is to develop a collective understanding of how arts, culture, creative people, and creative businesses can play a key role in building a vibrant community and develop local policies for strengthening and developing them.

5. Leadership at all levels will be required to make Orange County a more creative community.

Websites listed below give students opportunity to research lesson plan ideas and virtual contact with museums throughout California. This information was provided by the California Arts Education Association Website (the CAEA offers an inexpensive membership to students. Their contact information is California Arts Education Association, 28447, Anaheim, CA 92807, Phone (714) 637-1816). The CAEA offers an arts education conference every year, either in Northern or Southern California. This conference features vendors, arts educators, and a networking opportunity for teachers.

"A teacher affects eternity; he can never tell where his influence stops."
—HENRY BROOKS ADAMS

Art Resources

Art Education Resources

Artlex
Art Education Timeline from Penn State
Art Materials Guidelines
Art Teacher Connection
Arts and Activities
ArtsEdge
Arts Education Partnership
Americans for the Arts
ArtsEdNet (Getty)
California Alliance for Arts Education
California Approved Textbook List (pdf)
California State Dept. of Ed.
Ceramics and Pottery
Chicana and Chicano Space
College Art Association (CAA)
Digital Art Resource in Education (DARE)

Eyes on Art2
K-6 Arts Lessons
Lowenfeld's Stages of Artistic Development
NAEP—Developing an Arts Assessment
National Art Education Association (NAEA)
Orange County Museum of Art Lesson Plans
Stages of Graphic
    Representation—Hurwitz-Day
Teachers Count
Teacher Resources—National Gallery of Art
Foundations in Art Teaching Education
    (FATE)

Art Advocacy

State Legislators
Federal Legislators
2004 California State Visual Arts Standards
UC/CSU a-g requirements
A National Quick-Reference Resource Guide
    on NCLB and Art Education for Secondary
    Principals
CA Arts license plates
California Alliance for Arts Education (CAAE)
    They have put together an advocacy
    packet called *Taking Charge: Becoming an
    Effective Advocate for Arts Education*
Kennedy Center Alliance for Arts Education
    Network
Advocacy Publications from NAEA
Americans for the Arts
Arts Education Partnership Critical Links

California Art Museums

Asian Art Museum of San Francisco
American Museum of Ceramic Art
Bakersfield Museum of Art
Bowers Museum

CA African American Art Museum
California Museum of Photography, Riverside
Cartoon Art Museum
Center for Contemporary Art, Sacramento
Claremont Museum of Art
Craft and Folk Art Museum, Los Angeles
Crocker Art Museum
de Young Museum
Exploratotium
Fresno Art Museum
Fresno Metropolitan Museum
The Getty
Hammer Museum
Hearst Art Gallery
The Huntington Library
The Irvine Museum
Laguna Art Museum
Long Beach Museum of Art
Los Angeles County Museum of Art
Museum of Contemporary Art—LA
Norton Simon Museum
The Museum of Craft and Folk Art, San
    Francisco
Museum of Contemporary Art, San Diego
Museum of Latin American Art
Oakland Museum of California
Orange County Museum of Art
Museum of Photographic Arts
Pacific Asia Museum
Palace Legion of Honor CA
Palm Springs Desert Museum
Pasadena Museum of California Art
San Francisco Museum of Modern Art
San Diego Museum of Art
San Jose Museum of Art
Santa Barbara Museum of Art
Triton Museum of Art
Yerba Buena Center for the Arts

Art and Its Historical Implications

"No man knows what he can
do until he tries."
—*Publilius Syrus*

Creating a love of learning is a vital and significant goal of a teacher, but creating a love of history as well as other cultures and civilizations may be equally essential. Thankfully, one does not have to be an art historian to accomplish this. With the desire to grow and share your knowledge with your students, you have opened up an exciting new dimension to your curriculum. In this chapter, we will give a rudimentary time-line of the history of art, share ideas on how to incorporate art into the social studies program, and share a number of fun and exciting ways that a teacher can get started.

How to Get Started . . .

After realizing that you don't have to be an expert in art history and that it is perfectly acceptable—and even desired—for you to grow in your knowledge with your class, it is time to get started. A simple way to begin is to hang up posters and photos of artwork in your classroom. This in itself will begin a discussion and often lead to a more in-depth study of the subject. Having the children keep a portfolio of their own artwork and pictures that they have found in old magazines, from online sites and even from an old calendar is another excellent way to begin your study. Even the youngest children can find joy in arranging a selection of magazine pictures into common subject matter such as landscapes, still-lifes, animals, portraits or even color. Planning a field trip to a museum or gallery would be extremely valuable, but often is not feasible due to cost or distance. Instead, see if a local artist could visit your classroom and show their artwork while explaining the process. There are also a number of virtual tours online which may allow your class the opportunity to "travel"! Try making a big deal out of this—ask parents to pack a sack lunch, give out tickets and have a questionnaire ready for the children to fill out.

Some virtual tours that may get you started . . .

National Gallery of Art in Washington, DC
http://www.nga./gov/onlinetours/index

These are free tours; all are outstanding visual overviews of some of the greatest works of American art and indigenous arts and crafts in the world. The feature on this site is organized by genre, galleries, and periods in art history. Be sure to also look at their open access images for free downloads with permission.

The Smithsonian American Art Museum & Renwick Gallery in Washington, DC http://americanart/si.edu/

Start with looking up collections and research; within this department they will arrange free 15-minute video conferences for your students. You must join the Center for Interactive Learning and Collaboration. Videos and lesson plan extensions are fully integrated throughout National and State Standards and Content in the following areas: Visual Arts, Social Science, and Language Arts. All the collections are well organized and easy to search.

Los Angeles County Museum of Art in Los Angeles, CA http://www.lacma.org

Please preview their videos for current exhibitions and special ticketed events free of charge; insightful curator talks, collection secrets, and restoration of works in process are few of the videos available to your class. Furthermore, delight in their beautiful 20,000+ open access high-quality free download library that is well organized and user friendly.

The J. Paul Getty Museum in Los Angeles, CA http://www.getty.edu/art

Check out the short videos for an insightful and well produced walk through art history that features the works in their collection and the galleries. And, while you are at this site, peek at the Getty's Google Art Project; ambitious in nature, it is a work in progress. Be forewarned: there's graphic nudity in the Contemporary collection, so it is not appropriate for the classroom. Keep scrolling for the specific period you are looking for in art history, and turn the pages of these in-depth looks at the specific periods without ever leaving the classroom.

The Nelson Atkins Museum of Art in Kansas City, MO http://www.nelsonatkins.org Search the permanent collections, using the collections toolbar, for an inside look at large diverse collections, with images available that are perfect for putting together your own or student-created PowerPoints.

The Metropolitan Museum of Art in New York City, NY http://www.metmuseum.org/toah

Use the amazing Heilbrunn timeline of art history as your new and favorite classroom tool to make art history come alive and put it in its correct historical and social context. This site feature is easy to navigate, with famous classroom images and great lesson plan extensions.

Also check your public library for videos on artists. You will want to preview all of these options first, but there are several excellent children's videos such as "Linnea in Monet's Garden," a cartoon version that shows the actual garden that Monet had created and his paintings that correspond to each scene. *YouTube* also has some lovely videos including several on Van Gogh with Don McLean's *Starry Night* playing. Keeping your eyes and mind open will prove that there are unlimited resources available at this time. Following, you will find a basic Art History Timeline. Not all genres are included and a space for additional styles that you come across and would like to include is provided.

Art History Timeline

32,000–1500 B.C. Prehistoric Art

Prehistoric art is most often thought of as the era that came before the invention of writing.

This art includes cave paintings, small stone sculptures, petroglyphs, geoglyphs and megaliths such as Stonehenge. Art during this time was made to aid in mankind's struggle for survival. Although the exact reason for their creation is unknown, many feel that cave paintings symbolized the desire for a successful hunt or may have had religious or ceremonial purposes. Small stone sculptures have been found and are often of the female figure. There are many beliefs ranging from a form of a mother/goddess to the belief that these early people may have been primarily matriarchal. Beads, blades and tools were also found. Petroglyphs were found throughout the [history] and are images drawn into a rock by chipping, carving or pecking away at the rock. Geoglyphs are large drawings made on the ground that are produced by arranging stones, gravel or earth. The Nazca Lines in Peru are one of the most famous along with many others found in Australia, Iceland and the Soviet Union. Megaliths such as Stonehenge prove that ancient man was capable of amazing constructions and had a strong interest in the stars and sun and their effects on the earth.

Visual 7:1

Flip through a magazine and find an example of Prehistoric art. Cut it out and glue it in the above square.

Or, consider a trip to the *Museum of Man* at Balboa Park in San Diego. View world famous prehistoric artifacts (www.museumofman.org). Another outstanding field trip for close examination of ancient artifacts is at the Natural

History Museum of Los Angeles County (http://www.nhm.org). This is just one of the museums in Exposition Park.

3500–332 B.C. Egyptian Art

Children and adults alike are enthralled with the Egyptian culture. From the Great Pyramids to the hieroglyphics found on their walls, the knowledge gained is limitless. All activity from the creation of art to the daily activities of the common man revolved around the Pharaoh, or king. The Pharaoh was considered to be a god on earth and it was believed that they had control over the earth, sun, and the water—specifically the Nile River. The pyramids were huge tombs that were built as a home for the Pharaoh after his death; these tombs were filled with everything that the Pharaoh might need in the afterlife such as slaves, artwork, boats, furniture and even toiletry items. The walls of the tombs were covered with reliefs and paintings depicting the life of the Pharaoh and reminding him of the way to the netherworld.

Visual 7:2

Outstanding images and video tours can be found in the Metropolitan Museum of Art in New York, NY. Search http://www.met museum.org/collectionandgalleries, Egyptian,

Greek, and Roman for rarely seen images of art and artifacts from these ancient cultures.

1100–30 B.C. Greek Art

The ancient Greeks were in a constant search for perfection and believed in a "perfect order" for society, government and the arts. The ancient city of Athens was dedicated to Athena, the goddess of wisdom, war, hunting and even weaving and other crafts. The Parthenon was the center of the Acropolis and was an attempt at building the perfect temple with a fifty-foot statue of Athena in the central corridor. The ancient Greeks had four main art forms: architecture, sculpture, painting and painted pottery. The sculpture was realistic and stressed the perfect human form. Painting was found on the walls of homes and government buildings depicting everyday life and sadly very little remains today. The painted pottery, on the other hand, is often found in relatively good repair and images of battles, gods and goddesses and everyday life are painted on the sides of these vessels.

Visual 7:3

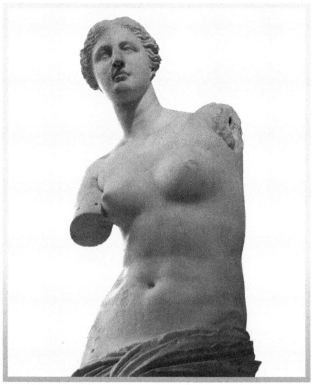

© 2009 by Galina Barskaya. Used under license from Shutterstock, Inc.

510 B.C.–476 A.D. Roman Art

The Roman civilization was created through armed conquest and shows the influence of many civilizations. The architecture of this era includes such remarkable features as the arch, a diverse system of highways and aqueducts and vast temples and government buildings. The sculptures of this era showed an appreciation of the classical Greek artifacts, yet lent toward a more accurate portrayal than the perfect ideal. Murals were again painted on walls and were found in residences as well as public buildings. Some of the most preserved examples are found in the city of Pompeii that was covered and preserved by a volcanic eruption of Mount Vesuvius in 79 A.D.

Visual 7:4

© 2009 by Laurelie. Used under license from Shutterstock, Inc.

476 A.D–1400 A.D. Middle Ages

The Middle Ages include such periods such as Byzantine, Christian and Gothic Art. It was previously known as the "Dark Ages"; this term was used to denote the period of decline in the arts and society as a whole from the fall of the Roman Empire to the Renaissance. This cultural decline took place in Western Europe and was later avoided when scholars pointed out many accomplishments made at this time. The artwork of this time had a religious theme and included such monuments as St. Mark's in Venice and Notre Dame. Stained glass emerged to help tell the biblical stories to the illiterate and provided an overwhelming atmosphere within these structures. Frescos, painting on wet plaster, and reliefs also decorated the interiors of these massive structures.

Extensive catalogues of tapestries, manuscripts, prints, metalwork, and paintings are available at the Metropolitan Museum's website. Search http://www.metmuseum.org/toah.

Visual 7:5

© Cory Langly/Corbis

1400–1600 A.D. Renaissance

Renaissance means rebirth and was marked by the renewed interest in scholarly pursuits as well as art. Life was much easier which allowed for growth in the arts: literature, philosophy, art, politics, science and religion. Italy was a center of great growth and families like the Medicis were able to be patrons to some of the greatest artists of all time: Leonardo da Vinci, Raphael, Titan and Michelangelo. As Italy's power began to fail, the focus gradually shifted to other parts of Europe. Such masterpieces as *The Last Supper*, *The Sistine Chapel*, *David*, *The Pieta*, and *Assunta* are still available today. Great advances were made in art including the development of linear perspective.

From early to late Renaissance, the Norton Simon Library of Art in Pasadena, CA has remarkable examples of this period's work. Their well-organized and user-friendly website makes visits possible when Italy is too far: http://www.nortonsimon.org/collections. Be sure to check out the multimedia section on the toolbar for videos of historical and technical lectures and tours.

Visual 7:6

© 2009 by Ken Durden. Used under license from Shutterstock, Inc.

Visual 7:7

1600–1800 A.D. Baroque Art

The artists during the Baroque period were concerned with technical knowledge and the theatrical devices such as chiaroscuro and high emotional impact. The Italian artists were still supported primarily by the Catholic Church and most artwork was of a religious nature. In Spain and France, the artists focused on recording the lifestyle of the kings and their courts portraying elaborate and extravagant scenes and excessive decorations.

Visual 7:8

1750–1850 A.D. Romanticism

Following in the Baroque love of emotion, the Romantic period portrayed great emotion, but restrained from the excess and decorative nature. Scenes were of a mix of classes—no longer limited to the wealthy. There was a renewed interest in the medieval civilization and past cultures and themes ranged from historical events to dreams.

Visual 7:9

1850–1900 A.D. Impressionism

The Impressionists were looked upon as rebels and focused on light and its changing qualities, visible brush strokes and pure, unmixed color. The subject matter was of everyday people doing ordinary things and included a great deal more movement than the previous realists. These artists even rebelled from the norm of painting in studios and would paint en plein air, or in the open air. Their love for nature was not originally recognized by the salon as great art. But art collectors such as Duncan Phillips had seen the visual value, and visual poetry of this movement and in honor of his father and brother opened a heartfelt collection which houses some of the most world famous Impressionist paintings. *The Phillips Collection* in Washington, DC is set in a Victorian mansion.

Check out the collection and video app featured on the multimedia section on the toolbar at http://www.phillipscollection.org.

Visual 7:10

Visual 7:11

1875–1900 A.D. Post Impressionism

Falling closely on the footsteps of the Impressionists, the Post Impressionists worked loosely, applying paint in a thick, textural manner with distinct brush strokes; yet they were not as concerned with the light and were more inclined to distort form for expressive effects. One of the artists from this period was George Seurat who developed his style known as pointillism—painting dots of color side by side to give the illusion of a third color.

Outstanding images and biographical information about specific artists from this period can be found at the National Gallery of Art in Washington, DC: http://www.nga.gov. Another website to look specifically for Van Gogh is http://www.vangoghgallery.com/museum/list.html. Scroll the list and choose a museum of your choice; the links work every time.

Visual 7:12

© Corbis

Visual 7:13

1907–1920 A.D. Cubism

The Cubist movement refused to record images as seen in nature; rather, the images would be broken up, analyzed and reassembled. Faces would be shown from a variety of viewpoints with a profile view having two eyes. The surfaces appeared to intersect and had a flat, ambiguous feel. This movement was extremely shocking and confusing which lead several critics to believing that this reflected the post-war society in Europe.

The progress of the Cubist can be viewed at the Norton Simon Museum of Art in Pasadena, CA or http://www.nortonsimon.org/collections.

Visual 7:14

© Burstein Collection/Corbis

Visual 7:15

1910–1945 A.D. Surrealism

Imagery and dream-like subjects were a focal point of the period known as fantasy art or Surrealism. Supernatural images ranged from gently floating figures to harsh, grotesque beings. The illogical subject matter and symbolism gave a sense of mystery and power to these pieces. Perhaps one of Marc Chagall's quotes best describes this type of art, "My art is an extravagant art, a flaming vermilion, a blue soul flooding over my paintings"

The impact of Surrealism is apparent today in contemporary animation. Its imaginative dreamscapes are fertile ground for today's creators of reality. The museum that had its focus on surrealism is the Dali Museum in St. Petersburg, FL. The museum and its website are modest in size but there is nothing small about their educational resources: http://www.thedali.org. Click on "Education" at the Dali, then on the left go down to "Educational Resources" for some thought-provoking insights and lesson plans.

Visual 7:16

Visual 7:17

the art world, but with the chaos of World War II, many artists came to the United States fearing censorship and prejudice. In an attempt at communicating ideas and emotions without the use of recognizable symbols, these artists subconsciously applied the paint in an abstract manner using color combinations that had explicit emotional associations derived from studies earlier in the century. Jackson Pollack's drip paintings, de Kooning's grotesque images of woman and the rectangular fields of color in Rothko's paintings seem vastly different, but all were considered expressionists.

No one understood and respected the rebellion, defiance, and creative fervor of the new generation of artists like Peggy Guggenheim. The dedication and passion of her interest in the Abstract Expressionists and subsequent art movements are part of the reason this "1st American Art Movement" took the world by storm and has opened the door for absolute creative freedom in all subsequent art movements, removing all creative restrictions and boundaries. Check out this huge collection: Solomon R. Guggenheim Museum, http://www.guggenheim.org. Go to "Collections." then enter the relative search, sit back and enjoy the access to free images and don't forget their mobile museum app; the download is free.

1945–1960 A.D. Abstract Expressionism

Abstract Expressionism was the first art movement that originated in New York. At this time, Paris was considered to be the center of

1960–1970 A.D. Pop Art

In direct contrast to the intellectual and aloof movement of abstract expressionism, Pop Art celebrated everyday object and saw humor and delight at the traditional concepts of what was art. Pop Art dealt with popular images in an irreverent, almost comical manner. Giant boxes of Brillo Pads, enlarged copies of cartoon squares, and popular figures were all subject matters that the Pop artist incorporated.

Visual 7:19

1964–1970 A.D. Op Art

Op Art is a style of painting that is abstract and makes use of optical illusions. When a person looks at an example of Op Art, there is

a great deal of movement, hidden images or a sense of warping, twisting patterns. Many of these illusions depended upon the precise repetition of shapes and a highly contrasting interaction of color.

As this was primarily a British and European movement, we find the most extensive collection in the world at The Tate Museum in London, England. You can enjoy the experience of, and learning about, modern art in an interactive way. Spend some time in their webquest videos. These thought-provoking, aesthetic-inspiring art experiences are a must for any student viewing modern art for the first time. For images and information about artists or for movements, search using the artist's name or style name. Type "Find Art and Artist" and enjoy your students' responses.

Visual 7:20

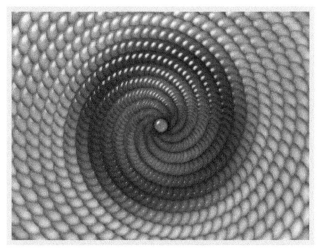

© 2009 by Dan Tataru. Used under license from Shutterstock, Inc.

1970–1980 A.D. Conceptual Art

Conceptual Art is more concerned with the idea or concept that a piece presents than the traditional aesthetic concerns. Some are called installations and may range from a set of written instructions to the ready-mades that may merely be a commonplace object presented in a nontraditional way.

In conceptual art, the idea or concept is the most important aspect of the work.

When an artist uses a conceptual form of art, it means that all of the planning and decisions are made beforehand and the execution is a perfunctory affair. The idea becomes a machine that makes the art.
SOL LEWITT

Visual 7:21

1970–1980 A.D. Performance Art

Performance Art began in the 1960s in the United States and was used to label any live, artistic event including films, poetry readings, musical presentations as well as "Happenings," "Events," and "Fluxes." Performance Art has to be live and is considered to "have no rules." This type of art could range from a film entitled "Sleep" which portrayed a man sleeping for eight hours to an artist painting a model's body in a store front.

Visual 7:22

1980–1990 A.D. Neo-Expressionism

As a reaction against Conceptual Art and minimalism, the Neo-expressionism paintings were characterized by rough, almost violent approaches to applying paint and a return to more conventional formats such as easel painting. Often these paintings were large and constructed quickly; at times, found objects would be incorporated. Strong color, slashing brush strokes and distorted images proved that these artists were more concerned with the action of creation than following the conventional traditions.

Visual 7:23

1980–1990 A.D. Post-Modern Art

The style of Post-modern Art is difficult to describe in a simplistic manner; it involves the use of various art forms used throughout history in a new, unique approach. Blandness and monotony of modern art is rejected and often has a tongue-in-cheek type of humor. Promotion of irony and parody are paramount, a diverse use of a variety of mediums is found and the attempt to blur the distinction between high art and low is obvious.

Visual 7:24

1980–1990 A.D. Computer Art

Computer Art is any art where the use of computers plays a large part of the production or display such as videogames, gallery installations, animation and other digital techniques.

Keeping in mind that there are a great many more styles of art, you may wish to add your own favorites.

ADDITIONAL ART STYLES

Art and Social Studies

Although there are a great number of time restraints placed on teachers today, a great teacher is always looking for ways to supplement their coursework and make the learning more meaningful and enjoyable for their students. Art and social studies can make a truly remarkable match. An understanding of other times and cultures can be more readily developed when the artistic records are shared. Studying about the totem poles found in the Pacific Northwest would be enhanced greatly if a teacher included a virtual tour of this culture and then had the children create a totem pole for the classroom. The same could be said while studying the American Revolution and having the children create a quilling project using paper that had been placed through a shredder. Not only would the children be learning of a past art technique, but they would be recycling paper for a virtually free art project. In the following chapter, you will find a selection of lesson plans that could be a valuable addition to your social studies curriculum.

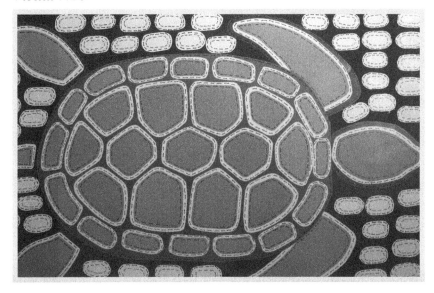

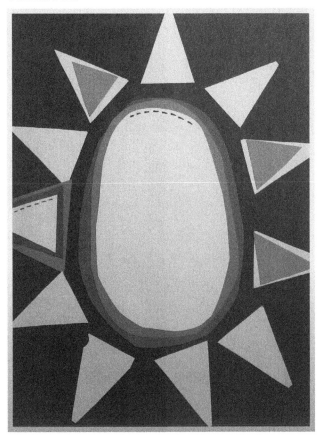

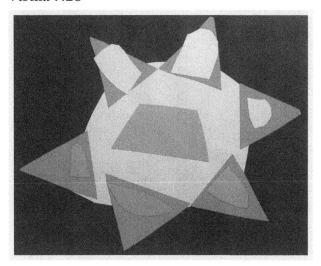

Molas, Art of the Kuna People

by Rosio Holguin

Cultural Re~
115-116, 12
127, 138

I will be teaching my students the culture, history, technical or visual information of Molas, an art form created by the **Kuna** Indians of Panama. **Molas** means clothing in Dulegaya, the native language of the Kuna. A Mola consists of a handmade blouse which is an important part of the traditional dress of Kuna women. Kuna women's entire costume traditionally includes a patterned wrapped skirt (saburet), a red and yellow headscarf (musue), arm and leg beads (wini), and a gold nose ring (olasu). Mola blouses have intricate designs which originate from the art of body painting which the Kuna practiced until colonization by the Spanish in 1502 and subsequent introduction to Christianity. Kuna women then began applying the intricate patterns used in body painting to the front and back of blouses, by using **reverse appliqué technique**. The technique is achieved by using several layers of cut cloth and sewing them together. Each piece of cloth varies in color such as black, bright red, orange, green, etc. The variety of color then allows the image to appear through elaborate cutwork. Molas art is inspired by the cosmic **geometric patterns** of body painting. Additionally Kuna women like to depict realistic and abstract designs of flowers, birds, and sea animals which are inspired by the geographic location. Molas also depict traditional themes from Kuna legend and culture. Kuna women typically begin crafting and wearing Molas after they reach puberty and in some cases even younger.

The Kuna Indians live (mainly) in 3 autonomous territories in **Panama**. These territories were granted by the government to the Kuna people in 1925. Among these territories the most populated is Kuna Yala meaning "Kuna Mountain" in **Dulegaya**. Kuna Yala is located in the San Blas Islands on the north east coast of Panama. The Mola is partly cited as being responsible for the granting of these coastal territories. This occurred when the Panamanian government attempted to suppress the traditional Mola costume and subsequently led to what is now known as the Kuna rebellion. Today the Kuna Indians remain a strong knit, largely self sufficient, tribal society. They also continue to practice rich traditions, passing them on to future generations. Kuna women are now very well known for their intricate Molas which have become a respected art form. The sale of Molas has become an important source of income and Kuna Yala a popular site for tourists interested in experiencing the rich Kuna culture and their bright, vivid Molas.

Objectives

Artistic Perception—I will be providing students with examples of Molas Art. Students will become aware of the traditional use of Molas as a functional piece of art by the Kuna women. Students will also become aware of the origin of Molas and the methods employed in their design, i.e., the use of fabric, color, pattern, etc.

Creative Expression—Students will create their own artistic interpretation of Mola Art on black construction paper. Students will represent a traditional Mola using methods of layering, color, geometric patterns and design (i.e., fish, flowers, birds).

Historical and Cultural Context—Students will become aware of the importance of Molas as part of the Kuna cultures traditional identity and the materials used to create them, and how Molas have adapted to social changes (i.e., body painting, colonization, independence). Students will also walk away with a basic understanding of how tradition can often shape historical events.

Aesthetic Valuing—Students will also be able to discuss their use of colors, layers, geometry and style of pattern. Students will discuss how their aesthetic decisions like that of the Kuna people, relates to the importance of personal identity.

Integration—Students will become aware of the geography of the Kuna territory in Panama. Students will also understand how the regions' landscape influences the Mola designs created there (i.e., floras/fauna).

Materials

- 8 x 10 sheets of assorted construction paper (at least 4 sheets per student). Must have 1 black and 3 brights.
- Glue sticks
- Scissors
- Sharpies or black crayons

Procedure

1. With a bright paper, draw a main image i.e., bird, fish or crab and carefully cut out with scissors.

2. Paste the cut out image onto black construction paper. With two remaining papers, cut a variety of geometric shapes (squares, circles, triangles, etc.) and layer on top of the main shape and surrounding it as well. Note: leave gaps to ensure the black background is visible. Once finished with design use sharpie or crayon to simulate stitch marks.

Evaluation

1. Did the student create a central design using traditional imagery employed by the Kuna? i.e., birds, sea life, etc. Y/N

2. Did the student use a variety of colors and geometric shapes surrounding a central image? Y/N

3. Did the student represent a simplified version of the layering technique (reverse appliqué) used by Kuna women? Y/N

4. Can the student explain what a Mola is? What the traditional crafting methods and origins are? Can they name the tribe and geographic region in which they live? Y/N

Art and Its Cultural Implications

"The beautiful thing about learning is that no one can take it away from you."

—*B.B. King*

Art and the Cultures of the World

by John L. Devine

Culture is defined by the Webster's Dictionary as the integrated pattern of human knowledge, belief, and behavior that depends upon the capacity for learning and transmitting knowledge to succeeding generations. In the twenty-first century, culture has become a concept central to anthropology that covers all human actions that are not the results of genetics. Examples of this modern idea of culture include the variety of ways that people live in different parts of the world and the ability to represent and record experiences both orally and with symbols, such as in a written language, as well as to express the human imagination through various forms. This expression of the human imagination has come to be known as art. Art is the product or process of engaging senses, emotions, and intellect through creations and modes of expression which includes paintings, sculpture, music, film, literature to name a few.

In the past the term "melting pot" has been used to describe a multi-cultured society uniting to become uniform. The idea is that the cultures melt together to create one large common culture. The term has particularly been used to describe the United States. The United States is a nation of immigrants from all around the world. It started with the first humans coming across the Bering Strait some fourteen hundred thousand to forty hundred thousand years ago. After these peoples migrated south across the Americas, the first Europeans began migrating to the Americas after Spanish Conquistador Juan Ponce de León became the first documented European to arrive on the United States mainland on April 2, 1513 when he landed in Florida. In 1607 the first English settlements were established in the Virginia Colony in Jamestown, and the Pilgrims arrived in the Plymouth Colony in 1620 and in 1614 the Dutch settled along the lower Hudson River and founded New Amsterdam on Manhattan Island (now New York City).

As the Spanish were exploring and expanding in Florida and the Southwest of the United States, the French began coming to the United States in 1682 where they founded New France that included modern day New Orleans and land that stretched from the Gulf of Mexico across the United States all the way up to the Great Lakes. During the sixteenth century when European countries were colonizing the Americas all the way up to the nineteenth century, the transatlantic slave trade saw an estimated twelve million Africans from all over the continent of Africa being shipped across the Atlantic to be enslaved in the Americas. Other groups that came to the United States include the Irish starting in the 1600s, Chinese immigrants starting in the early nineteenth century, Italian immigrants starting in 1640, Mexicans, Japanese, Filipinos, Germans, Polish, Russian, and so many other groups throughout the history of the United States.

With all of these groups and cultures coming to the United States and living together to form one nation, a new "American" culture was seemingly established. Many people came to pursue the idea of the American dream and while they pursued this common goal, their cultures began to mix. You see the mix of cultures today in art, food, music, literature, television and many other mediums. An example is the very American music style called Jazz. Jazz is the combination of African melodies with European harmonies and has been enjoyed around the world and continues to influence other musical styles today. However, despite this great mix of cultures, the idea of a cultural melting has been challenged since total assimilation does not truly take place in the United States.

If you travel to any major city like Los Angeles, San Francisco, and New York, you will often times find the city divided into districts and areas of different cultures and groups of people. An example is in New York City where you have areas like Chinatown and Little Italy. The fact is that many times groups of people from similar backgrounds tend to stick together and congregate close to each other in order to achieve a sense of comfort. This can be seen anywhere around the United States and has led many to question if the term "Melting Pot" is accurate. Recently, the ideas of a "salad bowl" or "cultural mosaic" have been used rather than the term "melting pot."

The idea of the "salad bowl" refers to the idea that various cultures are mixed together—like ingredients in a salad—but do not merge together to form a homogeneous culture. In Canada, this idea is referred to as a "cultural mosaic," a mosaic being a piece of art that is created with small pieces to create a larger image. Both the "salad bowl" and the "cultural mosaic" concepts describe a situation where each culture keeps its own distinct qualities while at the same time contributing to a larger society or culture. With these ideas in mind, the study of different cultures becomes exceedingly relevant in a world that seems to be constantly shrinking.

Today's economy is connected on an international level. In the average American household you can find items that are from all around the world. An example is that most electronics have components that are manufactured in Japan. China is one of the top manufacturers of goods and most of our oil comes from countries in the Middle East. Luxury goods like coffee and tropical fruits come from South America. With the international economies becoming more intertwined, more and more people are relocating because of jobs and better opportunities for living. Studying various cultures that live together will help promote tolerance and build a sense of community. Countless groups have been discriminated against in the United States throughout the country's history. An example that is studied in most classrooms is the Civil Rights Movement.

While there is still a great deal of discrimination taking place in the United States, most will not argue that the Civil Rights Movement has had a monumental impact on our country by lessening discrimination. The Civil Rights Movement lives on today in classrooms around the United States. Names like Rosa Parks, Martin Luther King, and Malcolm X have become household in due part because every classroom in the United States has the Civil Rights Movement built into their curriculum. While great strides have been made for ending racial discrimination against African Americans, many lesser known groups continue to be targeted and racial discrimination is far from being ended in the United States.

Teachers today need to take the initiative and teach about different cultures from around the world. Discrimination is created from fear, ignorance, and unawareness about other cultures and groups of people. One great tool that teachers can use in the battle against discrimination in the classroom is art. Art is the expression of the human imagination and is capable of engaging all of the human senses. Art is not just limited to paintings and sculptures; there is also music, photography, literature, film and more. Art can also be used to make the average lesson plan more exciting and help put more energy into the classroom. It allows students to use their imaginations and be creative in ways that is often missing in the modern lifestyle.

There are plenty of other opportunities for multicultural education in the classroom for other subjects as well. This can be done from items in the news or even by expanding on a question from a student in the classroom. If you don't know the answer, take some time to do research on the topic or ask a friend in order to better educate yourself and ultimately your classroom. Examples are in math a teacher can explain how the modern day numeric system was developed by Indian mathematicians, adopted by Persian mathematicians in India who then passed the numeric system on to the Arab traders who brought it west all the way to Europe. Social Science teachers can expand on curriculum by giving opportunities for students to educate the class about their cultural backgrounds. Literature teachers can encourage students to read works from around the world and can be as simple as talking about a children's story from a different part of the world. Educators have a great opportunity to do a great deal of good in the classroom that will ultimately transfer to the community. This may even mean ending stereotypes by taking instances of discrimination and using them as educational opportunities and incorporating different cultures in the classroom. The first step is educating yourself on the different cultures in your community.

As you identify the variety of cultures that exist in your community and your classroom, consider the ways in which you can incorporate the historical and contemporary aspects of those cultures through the use of the National and California Department of Education Social Science Content Standards. All cultures have rich visual histories. Each culture has uniquely used arts and crafts to tell the story of its life at that specific point in time. These cultural works of art and the artifacts that were left behind tell us much about that culture and the quality of life that they had.

Through the use of historical and cultural arts and crafts assignments, students gain a greater understanding of mankind as a whole, and a greater understanding of the contributions that all cultures past and present have made, and can make, to the growth of humanity.

The following is a list of cultures listed as curriculum in the Social Science State Standards and Content:

My Community; California history and all the cultures involved in settling California; European immigration and colonization of the Americas; prehistoric man and Native Americans, Greeks, Romans, Egyptians, ancient Japanese, ancient Chinese, ancient Africans, the Aztecs, the Mayans, the Incas, and the ancient Indians. Who said education lacked

content? The integration of the visual arts and cultural arts makes history come to life. Trips to museums and cultural sites help students more fully understand the importance of art and culture to advance mankind, and to provide a greater sense of understanding of the importance of diversity as our world becomes increasingly more global. Art is the timeless and universal language.

The following is a list of Southern California museums and sites that feature impressive collections of cultural arts, crafts, and artifacts, as well as sites of historical and cultural significance.

Local Cultural and Historical Museums and Sites

Bowers Museum An outstanding museum filled with art and artifacts for Native American, Mezo-American, and the early Spanish California rancho period; they also house "Kidseum," a hands-on museum filled with cultural arts, crafts, and artifacts for children. Excellent educators programs.

2002 N. Main St., Santa Ana, CA 92706 (714) 567-3600, http://www.bowers.org
Open: Sun., Tue., Wed., Thu., Fri, and Sat., 10 a.m.–4 p.m.

Cost (weekday/weekend): Adults: $13/15 Seniors (62+) and Students (12+): $10/12, Children under 12: FREE.
*FREE the 1st Sunday of every month.

The Irvine Museum This small private museum has focused their collection on early California and plein-air painting. Excellent docent-lead tours are included by request for classes. This is a must for My Community and California history. If you ever wondered what rural Orange County looked like, this is the museum to visit. Always check their current exhibitions, as they do thematic shows in addition to having incredible archives of historical photographs.

18881 Von Karman Ave., Suite 100, Irvine, CA 92612

(949) 476-0294, http://www.irvinemuseum.org

Open: Tue., Wed., Thu., Fri., and Sat., 11 a.m.–5 p.m.

Cost: Adults: $5, Children, Students, and Seniors (60+): FREE.
FREE the 2nd Wednesday of every month.

The Muzeo An insightful look at how ancient cultures lived and worked. Artifacts and installations make everyday ancient life breathe. Excellent traveling exhibitions that make the ancient world come to life.

241 S. Anaheim Blvd., Anaheim, CA 92805 (714) 956-8936, http://www.muzeo.org

Open: Every day, 10 a.m.–5 p.m. *Cost:* Adults: $13, Children: $9.

The Muckenthaler Cultural Center focuses on local N. Orange County history. Exhibitions are set in a turn of the century mansion and the park-like grounds. The center will provide docent-lead tours and hands-on art experiences for students with advance arrangements.

1201 W. Malvern Ave., Fullerton, CA 92833 (714) 738-6595, http://themuck.org

Open: Wed., Thu., Fri., Sat., and Sun., 12 p.m.–4 p.m. Extended hours: Thu. 5 p.m.–9 p.m. *Cost:* Adults: $5, Students, and Seniors: $2, Children: FREE.

The Gene Autry Museum is a museum that has it all for lovers of the history of the West and Southwest, Native American cultures, and the influences and impact of Spain and Mexico on the Western United States. They also have contemporary Los Angeles artists' exhibitions. Excellent tours, support for teachers, and free bus reimbursement for Title I schools.

4700 Western Heritage Way, Los Angeles, CA 90027
(323) 667-2000, http://www.theautry.org/

Open: Tue.–Fri., 10 a.m.–4 p.m. Sat. and Sun., 11 a.m.–5 p.m.

Cost: Adults: $10, Students and Seniors: $6, Children (3–12): $4, under 3, FREE.

The Natural History Museum has an amazing collection of prehistoric to contemporary artifacts from a multitude of periods of time. All galleries have social and scientific accompanied displays. Think of this as the west coast Smithsonian. 900 Exposition Blvd., Los Angeles, CA 90007 (213) 763-3466, www.nhm.org *Open daily:* 9:30 a.m.–5 p.m.

Cost: Adults: $12, Youth (13–17): $9, Children (3+): $5, under 2: FREE.

Mission San Juan Capistrano is part of the Spanish mission system in California. This beautifully preserved and restored mission houses one of the most impressive collections of mission art, artifacts, architecture, and a living museum of mission life. A must trip for any 4th grade class; or check out their website if a visit isn't possible, and remember the other California missions in your local area. 26801 Ortega Highway, San Juan Capistrano, CA 92675

(949) 234-1300, http://www.missionsjc.com Check for hours, as they vary for celebrations and special events. *Cost:* Adults: $9, Seniors: $8, Children (4–11): $6, Children 3 and under, FREE.
*Admission includes free audio tours for all ages.

The Japanese Pavilion at Los Angeles County Museum of Art is part of the LACMA complex. The Japanese Pavilion, along with the ancient art collection, is a trip your students will remember the rest of their lives. Much of the collection and educational support is available on their website, but they do everything they can to help you and your class come for a visit.

5905 Wilshire Blvd., Los Angeles, CA 90036. Education Department: (323) 857-6108. Free admission and tours with advance arrangements. LAUSD title I schools receive limited free bus transportation by request. If you are planning a trip to the LACMA, utilize their extensive and supportive Education Department. You and your students will have an incredible museum experience.

Open: Mon.–Thu., 11 a.m.–5 p.m. Thu., 11 a.m.–8 p.m. Fri., 11 a.m.–8 p.m. Sat. and Sun., 10 a.m.–7 p.m.

Cost: General admission prices: Adults: $15, Seniors and Students: $10. Groups of 10+: $12. General admission does not include entrance to special ticketed exhibitions. Be sure to check with ticketing in advance for correct exhibition admission.

The lesson plans following are meant to spark your imagination. Make sure to do some background research. For example, there is a wonderful legend of a small carp who was told to keep preserving and his greatest wish would come true. Lots of exciting images and even a dragon or two will be in the conclusion.

A Brief History of Japan

by John L. Devine

When many people think about Japan as a country, they often think about electronics, video games, and sushi. While Japan is a leading developer of electronic goods, it is a country with a very long and rich history. Much of this history is shaped by the fact that Japan is an Island nation that is positioned off the Asian mainland with the first human inhabitants arriving around 35,000 B.C. This island nation is situated near the Asian mainland; there is still a large body of water that separates the two pieces of land that has acted as a barrier and isolated Japan for much of its history. Japan has relished this solidarity and even enacted such policies as the sakoku policy in 1633 that prevented foreigners from entering Japan on penalty of death.

In the past Japan was ruled by a divine figure known as an Emperor. According to the Constitution of Japan the Emperor is, "the symbol of the state and of the unity of the people." Japanese myth says that Emperor

Jimmu was the first emperor according to the order of succession of a royal line that is still in place today. Shintoism is the indigenous spirituality of Japan and the Japanese people and these followers feel Emperor Jimmu is a direct descendant of the sun goddess, Amaterasu.

The first centralized capital city of Japan was the city of Nara and this time is referred to as the Nara period—the years 710 to 784 AD. Nara derived its name from the Japanese word narashita which is translated to "made flat." It is important to note that many of Japan's large cities are located on relatively flat planes. Japan is made up of many islands; the main ones are often times referred to as the Home Islands and are Hokkaido, Honshu (the mainland) Skikoku and Kyushu. All together, the country of Japan is comprised of 2,456 islands that create a total area that makes Japan slightly smaller than the state of Montana and slightly bigger than Germany.

During the Nara Period, the Emperor held the majority of the political power and Japan's economy revolved around agriculture and was centered on villages. Most of Japan's population believed in a religion that was based on the worship of natural and ancestral spirits. The Nara period is also the time when the first works of Japanese literature were created which was the result of the imperial court concentrating efforts on recording and documenting its history. The first of these works were political in nature and used to record and justify the supremacy of the rule of the emperors within Japan. The end result was the spread of written language across the land.

The Nara Period also saw the creation of roads and an increase in economic and administrative activity. Nara also became a center of Buddhist art, religion, and culture. All of Japan's economic activity was centered in Nara and outside of the capital there was little commercial activity.

Around 1185 AD, Japan entered a feudal period. Feudalism is a system for ordering society around relationships that were derived from the holding of land in exchange for service and/or labor. Those who were put in power ruled over areas of land and everyone on it. This period in Japan was dominated by powerful regional families, the daimyo, and the military rule of warlords known as shogun. The emperor was still around and in power, but mainly acted as a figurehead and held minimal political power. Most of the people in Japan worked on farmland and paid the daimyo to live on the land and for protection. During Feudalistic Japan, Christian missionaries led by Francis Xavier arrived in 1649 and were initially welcomed. However, their aggressive attempts to convert the Japanese led to the present ruling daimyo, Toyotomi Hideyoshi, who decided that the Christian presence was divisive and might present the Europeans an opportunity to divide Japan. This persecution would lead to the destruction of the Christian community in Japan around 1620. Feudalism lasted all the way until 1868 in Japan throughout the Edo or Tokugawa era.

The Edo or Tokugawa era was marked by the centralization of power into the hands of hereditary shogunate that took control of the religion and regulated the entire Japanese economy, and the Japanese nobility. The shogunate also set up uniform systems of taxation and avoided international involvement and wars. It became an era of relative peace and prosperity in a nation that numbered around 31 million people. It was also during this period that the ruling shogunate began to suspect that foreign traders and missionaries were actually forerunners of military conquest by the European powers. It is for this reason that the shogunate began trying to dispel Christianity as they felt the Japanese Christians would be susceptible to joining any European invaders. Their fears came to fruition in 1637 in a revolt known as the Shimabara Rebellion. During the rebellion, around 30,000 persecuted peasants and

Christians fought against the ruling class. They were ultimately defeated by a samurai army of more than 100,000. After the eradication of the rebels, the shogunate placed foreigners under tighter and tighter restrictions. The government monopolized foreign policy and expelled traders, missionaries, and foreigners with the exception of Dutch and Chinese traders who were restricted to the man-made island of Dejima in Nagasaki Bay.

The policy of isolationism lasted for more than two hundred years in Japan. There were numerous attempts to open Japan's doors to trade; one excellent example was in 1844 when William II of the Netherlands sent a message urging Japan to open its doors that was ultimately rejected. Japan's borders would ultimately be opened by a show of force when on July 8, 1853; Commodore Mathew Perry of the United States Navy came with four modern warships. These modern steel hulled warships—The Mississippi, Plymouth, Saratoga, and Susquehanna—steamed into the Yokohama bay and displayed the power of a modern western power with their modern cannons. Commodore Matthew Perry displayed the power of his cannons during a Christian burial that the Japanese happened to notice. Perry then requested that Japan open its borders to trade with the west. These ships would become known by the Japanese as the kurofune, or the black ships.

The following year at the Convention of Kanawaga, Perry returned with seven warships and demanded that the shogun sign the Treaty of Peace and Amity which would establish formal diplomatic relations between Japan and the United States. Within five years after this, Japan would sign treaties with other Western countries. These treaties were unequal and Japan felt it was threatened through a policy of gunboat diplomacy.

The Japanese people saw the signing of these one-sided treaties humiliating and a source of national shame. As a result, the current shogun was forced to resign and the emperor was restored to power. This began a period of fierce nationalism and intense socio-economic restructuring known as the Meiji Restoration. The military was modernized and many Western institutions were adopted including a Western legal system and a parliamentary constitutional government created under the Meiji Constitution. The Japanese modeled their constitution after the constitution of the German Empire. This also ended the rule of the shogunate. Perry's intervention would come to be seen as a pivotal turning point in Japanese history. This new united Japan would come to be known as the Empire of Japan and would last from 1868 all the way to 1945.

The newly formed Empire of Japan had one monumental flaw that held it back from being one of the prominent powers in the world, a lack of raw materials needed to industrialize. Other nations that had been industrializing prior to this period—the United States, France, Great Britain, Germany, and Russia—all had sources of raw materials needed to industrialize. These resources included iron, coal, gold, silver, copper, and other metals and minerals. The islands of Japan contained few of these resources, but did have forests, farm land, and the ocean. The ocean has always been a great source of income for the Japanese people. From it they received food and protection. The ocean was the greatest contributor to the Japanese seclusion and would continue to offer Japan protection for years to come, especially after it constructed a large and modern navy.

During the Meiji Restoration and in the coming years, Japan set out to become independent of all foreign powers and walk in the footsteps of the then current international powers and attempt to conquer and claim lesser developed areas abundant in raw materials. Great Britain, France, Germany, and the Dutch all have overseas holdings that provided them with raw materials. Many of these colonies existed in Africa which at this time had almost been completely divided by European powers. Japan decided to focus its efforts in Asia and began conquering pieces of China and South East Asia.

Japan became involved with the first Sino-Japanese war with China in 1894 when it took hold of the Korean peninsula and the Chinese province of Manchuria. Japan came out victorious in the Sino-Japanese war and became the first modern imperial power in Asia. This led to tensions with Western power Russia that led to the Russo-Japanese War in 1904. The results of this war shocked the world. Japan proved that a Western power could be defeated by an Eastern power, something that the West thought was impossible. The outcomes of these wars left Japan the dominant power in the Far East and it controlled an area extending over southern Manchuria and Korea. Despite Japan's growing power, it did manage to stay peaceful with the West and even joined the Allies in World War I. However, Japan's pursuit of land and power would ultimately lead to its defeat and the downfall of the Empire of Japan.

The Great Depression hit Japan in the 1930's and created political tensions. It was believed that multiparty politics was divisive to the nation and promoted self-interest when unity was needed. This resulted in the creation of a large single party, the Imperial Rule Assistance Association, which absorbed the major political parties and many prefectural organizations such as women's clubs and neighborhood associations. However, despite all of the acquisitions made by the IRAA, it did not have a cohesive political agenda and there was a lot of in-fighting. They did however agree on many things including ongoing wars in China and the Pacific. The ongoing violence in China would ultimately lead to conflicts with the West and lead to World War II.

Japan wanted to continue expanding in Asia and the Pacific in order to remain a global power. While some countries such as Great Britain, France, and the United States resented Japan's continued aggression in the pacific, Germany and Italy supported Japan and also wished to expand their own borders. The common goals of expanding and establishing global powers led Japan, Germany, and Italy to form the Axis Pact on September 27, 1940. After the Axis Pact was formed, Japan continued expanding its empire. It was defeated by the Soviet Union in 1938 and signed a Soviet-Japanese Neutrality Pact that would allow Japan to continue its expansion in South East Asia and China and allow the Soviet Union to tend to matters in Europe. Japan's expansions were brutal and bloody and led to many atrocities including the infamous Nanjing Massacre. The Nanjing Massacre was a mass murder that occurred during a six-week period following Japan's capture of the former capital of the Republic of China Nanjing.

The United States was an ally of China and supported China with money, airmen, supplies, and even threatened to interfere if Japan continued its aggression. When Japan invaded French Indochina, the United States placed an embargo on petroleum products and scrap iron that it was trading with Japan. This was devastating to the Japanese Empire which was heavily reliant on foreign oil to continue its expansion and to run its economy. It is estimated that imported oil made up about eighty percent of Japanese domestic consumption and without it Japan's economy would have come to a halt. These actions by the west left Japan with two options: the first was to withdraw from its recent conquests, admit defeat, and live in shame as the Western powers were able to easily defeat this growing empire with a strike of a pen, or attempt to go to war with the formidable United States.

Japan's ultimate decision was to go to war with the United States. The reason for this was the Japanese leaders believed one quick and decisive attack could knock the United States out of a war quickly and allow Japan to continue expansion in the Pacific. Europe was involved in a War with Nazi Germany which left the United States alone in the Pacific. The

U.S. had expressed a desire to remain out of a war and was still recovering from the Great Depression. If Japan was to be successful in a war with the United States, it would have to win the war within six months or risk defeat. The United States was preparing for an attack, but thought Japan would attack the Philippines since they were closer to Japan. Japanese Admiral Yamamoto organized a surprise attack at the American naval base at Pearl Harbor where the U.S. stationed most of its Pacific naval fleet. Yamamoto would use a relatively new weapon, the aircraft carrier, to attempt to wipe out all of the U.S. battleships and aircraft carriers and hopefully convince the U.S. to sign a treaty and allow Japan to continue expansion in Asia. On December 7, 1941, Japan launched its attack and surprised the world. The attack was extremely successful and knocked out all of the U.S. battleships in the Pacific. However, there were a few flaws in the attack. Japan had failed to take out the U.S. aircraft carriers which gave the U.S. weapons with which it could retaliate. After the attack the U.S. immediately entered into World War II and allied itself with France, Great Britain, and the Soviet Union. This would become a turning point in World War II.

During World War II, the United States transformed itself into an economic juggernaut and was able to supply materials to Europe while fighting the Japanese in the Pacific. The U.S. was able to achieve a huge victory at the Battle of Midway which halted the Japanese offensive in the Pacific. The U.S. was able to quickly build a much more powerful navy than Japan and quickly island hopped its way across the Pacific Ocean to the Japanese home islands. The Japanese quickly began preparing for a U.S. invasion of their Home Islands. This invasion would have been the largest in human history with estimated casualties estimated in the millions. However, the U.S. had been secretly developing a weapon with a devastating power to end the war. These were the nuclear bombs Fat Man and Little Boy. On August 6, 1945, the U.S.

dropped the atomic bomb, "Little Boy," on the Japanese city of Hiroshima. The attack was devastating and resulted in over 70,000 people, thirty percent of Hiroshima's population, being killed instantly. When Japan did not surrender immediately, a second atomic bomb, "Fat Man," was dropped on the city of Nagasaki on August 9, 1945. The bombing of Nagasaki resulted in the immediate death of around 75,000 Japanese citizens. Countless more Japanese would die from the attack from radiation poisoning and cancers caused by the radiation. The nuclear bombings of Hiroshima and Nagasaki were so devastating, that their use is still debated to this day. No nuclear weapon has been used in war since.

Prior to the second atomic bombing, the Soviet Union broke off its Neutrality Act and invaded Manchuria on August 8, 1945. Even after the atomic bombing of Nagasaki on August 9th, 1945, Japan's officials were divided on whether it should surrender. However, on August 15, 1945, Japanese Emperor Hirohito announced Japan's unconditional surrender. The formal and official surrender took place aboard the U.S. battleship Missouri in Tokyo Bay on September 2, 1945. The U.S. was prepared to drop a third atomic bomb on August 19 and a fourth in September of 1945. It is estimated that the third bomb would have probably been dropped on the Japanese capital of Tokyo.

After World War II the Japanese Empire was dissolved and Japan lost all of its overseas possessions and only retained the Home Islands. The Allies held an International Military Tribunal for the Far East in which seven politicians were executed. Emperor Hirohito was not convicted and was stripped of all political powers and, in order to keep the peace, allowed to be a head of state and a religious figure. After the war, Japan was placed under the international control of the American-led Allied power. The Allies decided that it would be beneficial to quickly forgive Japan for war crimes and rebuild Japan as a democratic state. In 1952 the United States and forty five other Allied nations signed the Treaty of Peace with Japan and the country regained full sovereignty. Under the terms of the peace treaty, the United States is allowed to maintain naval bases at Sasebo, Okinawa, and Yokosuka. Under the treaty, Japan is not allowed to maintain an army but is allowed to have a restricted Self-Defense Force. The purpose of the U.S. naval bases is to provide defense for Japan and give the U.S. a strategic foothold in the Pacific.

Throughout the postwar period, Japan's economy boomed. This is due to the increase in manufacturing. It is a top producer in economic spheres that include; steel working, car manufacturing, the manufacturing of electronic goods, and other goods. This was largely due to the fact that Japan had a very educated population. Japan caught up with the West in foreign trade, GDP, and general quality of life. While Japan has experienced recession and economic speed bumps, it remains an economic power and key player in many international issues.

Children's Day Koi Flag

Jordan Brazelton

Time: Approximately three hours, or two one hour and a half sessions.

Goals

General Goals

- Children will learn the history of Boy's Day (now Children's Day) in Japan and the significance of the koi fish in Japanese culture (Historical/Cultural).

- Children will look at various examples of authentic koi flags as well as fish to observe colors, patterns, and unique characteristics, as well as be able to identify the basic parts of a fish: fins, scales, and gills (Artistic Perception, Connections, Relationships & Applications).

- Children will look at how patterns can create an appealing design (Artistic Perception).

Specific Goals

- Children will apply their knowledge of the fish anatomy (fins, scales and gills) to create their own koi flag out of two pieces of white construction paper (Creative Expression).

- Children will use pattern in their designs, using crayons, color pencils or markers to depict fins, scales and gills (Creative Expression).

- Children will attach strings and ribbons/crepe paper tails to form kite tails (Creative Expression).

Motivation

Children will be introduced to the Japanese culture using photographs of children in Japan on Children's Day with their koi flags. Small koi fish may also be brought into the class to be put on display while the students work on the project to show them real-life examples of colors to use on their own fish.

Vocabulary

Fin	Gills	Koi
Children's Day	Pattern	Scales

Materials

- Two equal sized pieces of white construction paper*
- Scissors*
- Glue sticks*
- Choice of media: crayons, color pencils, or markers*
- Yarn/string*
- Ribbon/crepe paper*
- Pencil

*Materials may be provided by the teacher, or as a class set.

Procedure

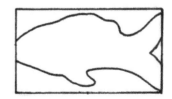

Step One: Make sure you have two equal pieces of construction paper. Take one piece and lightly sketch out the shape of the fish. The mouth should start along one edge of the paper, and the tail end at the other to make sure the fish will not be too small.

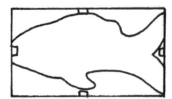

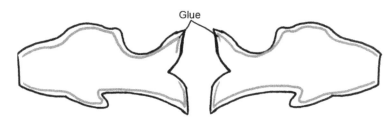

Step Two: Once you have the shape of your fish, place the other piece of construction paper lined up with the one you've drawn on. Children may want to tape the pieces in place to keep them from slipping and becoming misaligned.

Step Five: Now glue along the insides of the fish, leaving the tail area and mouth open and not glued. Place the two sides together so they line up and let the glue dry.

Step Six: Attach a string or piece of yarn to the mouth of the fish, so that they can be hung on display or be used as kites.

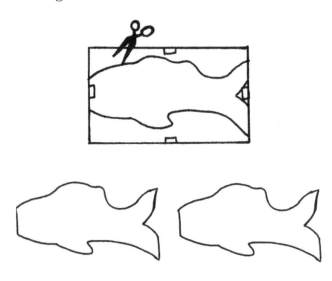

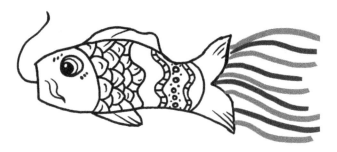

Step Three: Cut along the outline you have drawn with scissors. When you are done, you should have two fish shapes that are exactly the same.

Step Seven: Attach crepe paper strips or ribbons to the tail of the fish for decoration. You now have a finished koi flag for display or play!

Evaluation

Children will be evaluated on the following criteria:

Step Four: Time to decorate! Children may choose to do both sides the same or two different designs on either side of the fish. Make sure the use of repeating pattern is a theme. (Note: Check to make sure the children are coloring on the correct sides on each of their fish, so that they will line up again when placed together.)

- Did the children create a two-sided koi flag/kite?
- Did they utilize the use of patterning in their choice of media?
- Did they include important parts of fish, such as fins and gills?
- Did they attach strings and ribbons to create tails?
- Did they have good craftsmanship?

Australian Aboriginal Rain Stick

Rebecca Lipnisky

Grade Level: 4th Grade

Time: Approx. 3 Hours (three 1-hour periods)

Goals

General Goals

Students will learn about:

- musical instruments used by the Australian Aboriginals (3.0 Historical/Cultural Context)
- how Australian Aboriginals translated information from generation to generation through works of art and storytelling (3.0 Historical/Cultural Context)
- contrasting colors (1.0 Artistic Perception)
- balance (1.0 Artistic Perception)
- symbolism (1.0 Artistic Perception)

Specific Goals

Students will:

- create a rain stick using a mailing tube, nails, beans, and the papier mache method (2.0 Creative Expression)
- create their own sheet of original symbols to use on their rain stick (2.0 Creative Expression)
- create an original design on their rain stick (2.0 Creative Expression)
- paint their rain stick with acrylic paint to make a balanced design using contrasting colors and their symbols to tell their story (2.0 Creative Expression)

Motivation

Preparation

Create a colorful poster of various Australian Aboriginal symbols and their meanings with examples of a few stories that have been told by using these symbols. Come up with your own story about a fond memory or important time in your life using symbols from Australian Aboriginal art as well as symbols we use today (i.e., a heart means "love," a moon means "night time," and a paw print can mean "a family pet"). Make up some of your own. Remember to keep it simple. Collect images of rain sticks used by tribes and recordings of Australian music that includes the use of rain sticks.

How to Start

Hang up the poster showing various Aboriginal art symbols and a story from aboriginal art. Discuss with the students how the Aborigines used symbolism to tell stories and pass information from generation to generation (3.0 Historical/Cultural). Present your own story via symbols to the class.

Ask students what symbols we use today that represent things or have specific meanings (3.0 Historical/Cultural). Next, ask students to come up with original symbols of their own on a sheet of blank paper—5 is the minimum number. They will use these along with the Aboriginal symbols to tell a story about a fond memory or important time in their life (2.0 Creative Expression). This could be about their first pet, a birthday, a trip somewhere special, a tradition, or a favorite activity. The possibilities are endless!

After the Project

Each student will have a chance to present their rain stick to the class. The class will analyze the use of symbols and attempt to tell the story that is depicted on the student's rain stick (4.0 Aesthetic Valuing). The student will then tell their story, explaining their symbols and how they represent an experience from their life (5.0 Connections/Relationships/Applications).

Vocabulary Words

aboriginal	culture	translate
symbolism	balance	contrast

Materials

Per Student

1 of Each:

- 1 small paintbrush (#4)
- 1 medium paintbrush (#12)
- 1 paper or plastic cup for rinsing brushes
- 1 paper or plastic plate for carrying/mixing paint
- 1 paper or plastic bowl for starch
- 5" x 5" pieces of foil (2)
- 1 newspaper, torn up into squares the size of cookies or coasters (reserve 1 piece to cover desk with)
- 1 sheet of plain printer paper for original symbols
- school glue

Teacher

- Laminated poster of Australian Aboriginal symbols
- Laminated photos of rain sticks used by Australian Aboriginals
- Half gallon buckets of acrylic paints in the following colors: Red, Orange, Yellow, Green, Blue, Purple, White, Black

- Cardboard mailing tubes—1 for each student
- Box of nails—12 nails for each student. Nails need to be shorter than the width of the mailing tube (approx. 1")
- 3 rolls of masking tape
- Source of Australian music containing the rain stick instrument (optional)
- Feathers, beads, and/or twine for students to decorate sticks with
- 1 lb of dried pinto beans for every 4 students—each student will get a ½ cup of beans
- 1–2 gallons of liquid starch

Procedure

1. Take the mailing tube and push nails through, spacing them out from one end to the other.

   Tip: Push nails through the seam that spirals the tube.

2. Take one piece of foil and cover 1 end of the tub.

   Take a strip of masking tape and secure the foil to the tube.

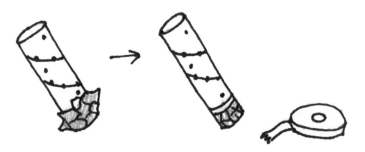

3. Carefully pour a half cup of dried beans into the rub.

   Hear the rain!

4. Repeat Step 2 on the opposite end.

   The beans are now enclosed in the tube.

5. Time to papier mache!

   Dip strips of newspaper into the bowl of starch, dragging the excess starch off on the edge of the bowl.

6. Piece by piece, place the starched paper on the tube. It's best to start from one end and build a single layer to the other. Have the edges of the starched paper overlapping. This adds support to the stick.

7. Once the first layer of papier mache is on, repeat steps 5 & 6 two more times so that there are 3 layers of papier mache on the stick.

   Note: It is okay to work wet-on-wet and you will find the second and third layers absorb some of the starch already on the stick. This saves starch! Excess starch left in the bowl can be poured back into the jug for future papier mache use.

   **Student Safety: Be sure that students smooth out any rough points, edges, and big creases while newsprint is still wet. These areas become hard and sharp once the papier mache has dried and can injure the student or others.

8. Write your name with a dark marker on a piece of newsprint and stick it on the rain stick. Let rain sticks dry completely.

9. Now it's time to paint! Pour a few table-spoons of paint colors onto the plate. A little goes a long way.

10. Take the No. 12 and No. 6 brushes and begin painting the rain stick with contrasting colors and a balanced design. Reference the symbols you have come up with on your piece of paper and any from the Australian Aboriginals. Tell your story by painting the symbols that depict your story around or across the rain stick.

    Tip: It's best to first start with the "background" color and larger shapes, then working on symbols and detail once the first layer of paint is dry.

11. Once the paint is dry, you have the option to add twine, feathers, and/or beads to decorate your rain stick!

Evaluation

- Was a sheet of at least 5 original symbols produced?
- Is the rain stick painted with acrylic paint?
- Was the papier mache method used to create a rain stick?
- Are their original symbols used to tell a story on the rain stick?
- Is the painted rain stick balanced?
- Are there contrasting colors?
- Was good craftsmanship used?

Masks of the Pacific Northwest

Coast Native People
by Melanie Vogel

Overview

The students will learn about the characteristics of tribal art, specifically masks and totem poles, from the Pacific Northwest coastal tribes. Using some of the design elements found in the masks, they will construct a two-dimensional animal face mask of their own, using four colors of construction paper.

Materials

black 9 × 12 construction paper (1 for each student) plus extra half sheets

red, yellow, turquoise (green or blue can be substituted) construction paper cut in 6 × 12 (half) pieces (1 ea. for every student)

scissors

glue sticks

Objectives

Students will investigate the art of the Pacific Northwest coastal tribes, learning about the significance and symbolism, the use of masks in storytelling and ritual and how masks and totem poles are made. Using the four basic colors the native peoples use in painting their art and arranging layered colored shapes symmetrically, the students will create a two-dimensional paper animal face mask.

Procedure

Show photographic or three-dimensional examples of masks, totem poles, clothing design and paintings on shelters of various tribes including the Kwakiutl, Haida, Bella Coola and Tlingit. The Southwest Museum in Los Angeles is a good resource as well as Knott's Berry Farm's Mystery Lodge store. Bower's Museum and the library have a good selection of books too. Point out the symmetry, the ovoid shapes (curved corner rectangles), the shapes within shapes and the use of design to fill the interior of a given area. Talk about the mythology, animal symbolism and various rituals related to the tribe. Talk about wood carving and the use of predominately black paint (made from carbon based material), red as a secondary color (made originally from ochre, later from vermillion imported from China), blue-green as the tertiary color (made from copper based elements) and the use of yellow or white sparingly in the design. Ask students to think of an animal face that they would like to make. Perhaps it is a favorite animal or pet, or you might ask them to think of an animal that might symbolize them or their personality. Some students may need to look at a photo of their animal first to see the defining facial features.

Begin mask design by folding the black 9 x 12 sheet in half. From the fold, have students cut a half circular shape, contouring the edges if desired (Fig. 1). Next, unfold the paper and lay flat. The shape should be largely oval and symmetrical (Fig. 2). Have students fold, in half, the remaining colored sheets so that when cutting shapes for eyes, cheeks or anything requiring two symmetrical shapes, they will then be the same. Layer shapes in alternating colors by cutting pieces one size smaller to fit within the previous shape (Fig. 3). Fill in all areas of the face with shapes to create the surface filling characteristic of the tribal art (Fig. 4). Glue down all pieces well with the glue stick. Encourage students to extend their design beyond the edges of the mask if desired. Remember, this is a creative variation or extension of this art form, not a direct copy of a particular mask. They can be displayed in a vertical column with a contrasting color background to give a "totem" look.

Assessment

Ask the students the following questions: What could you add to your mask design to fill in areas of negative or open space? Does your mask seem complete to you? In what ways does the animal, you chose to make, symbolize you? What have you learned about the Pacific Northwest Coast tribal art?

Integration/Extension

Have students make three-dimensional masks using paper mache, feathers and raffia using some of the same design elements from the Pacific Northwest Coast tribal art. Decorate a wooden flute with animal designs or make a totem from wrapping paper rolls and adding cardboard extensions. Finish by painting. Investigate, in nature, various forms of symmetry. Research various ways symmetry is found in mathematics. Research and write about a particular tribe and their way of life. Read some of the mythology stories from these tribes. Write your own story using these as inspiration. Find out what instruments are used by these tribes. Students might try making one.

Written for *All the Arts for all the Kids*

Fullerton School District

This lesson can be adapted for use with other indigenous tribe's masks, as viewed in visuals 8-1–8-4.

Further Reading:

http://witcombe.sbc.edu/ARTHLinks.html

http://www.metmuseum.org/toah/

http://www.artfaces.com/artkids/postmod. htm

Visual 8:1

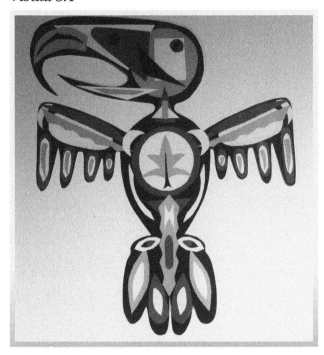

Visual 8:2

Visual 8:3

Visual 8:4

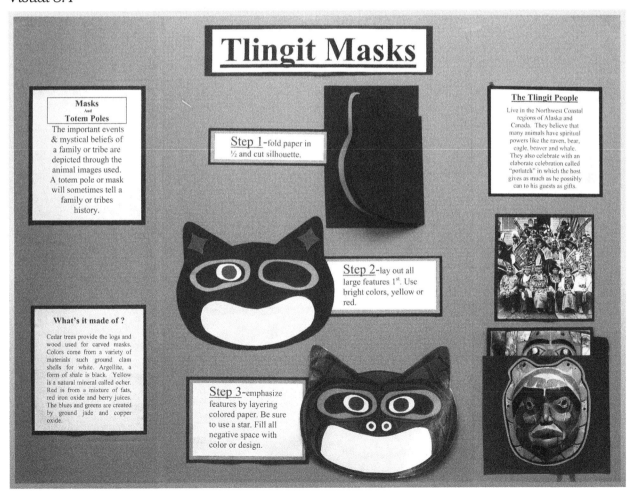

Chinese Dragon Lesson Plan

by Brandon Wong

Introduction of the Chinese Dragon

I will be teaching my students the history, culture, and visual information about the Chinese Dragon, which is used quite often in the Chinese culture. This dragon first appeared in the Chinese culture during the Yin and Shang Dynasties; and it later was placed o.n the national flag during the Qing dynasty, which was between 1644-1911 AD. The Chinese culture is filled with mythological stories and creatures, and the dragon is one that is depicted in various artworks and tales. The legend of these dragons is that they are thought to give life, and because of this ability, their breath has come to be called "sheng chi," or divine energy. They are also said to symbolize royalty, nobility, prosperity, good luck, and good fortune. Some of the general characteristics that are given to the dragons include helpfulness, wisdom, and generosity. During the Han Dynasty there was a scholar by the name of Wang Fu who recorded the anatomy of the Chinese dragons in great detail. Each dragon is said to always have nine characteristics: a camel's head, a snake's neck, an eagle's claws, a tiger's paws, a demon's eyes, a cow's ears, a deer's horns, a clam's belly, and 117 carp scales. The 117 scales consist of 81 scales of the positive yang essence, and 36 scales of the negative yin essence. The Chinese Dragon has characteristics taken from various tribes that were dispersed throughout China, and the dragon was a symbol of the unity of the country. The bones of the dragons are also believed to posses healing powers. Another element of the dragon's physical appearance is the various colors that can be seen. There are seven different colors, and each repre-sents different qualities that these dragons will specifically posses. Yellow represents royalty, and a yellow dragon robe was reserved to be worn by the emperor. Gold dragons symbolized wealth, wisdom, kindness, and the ability to face challenges head on.

Blues and green colorizations would represent good fortune, good health, or good luck; and similarly, the red would represent good fortune, as well as passion. The last two colors are white, which represents purity; and black, which represents vengeance and worry.

The physical characteristics are not the only things that separate the various types of dragons. There are nine different species, or types, of dragons that are shown in the Chinese culture, and they include the Celestial Dragon, the Spiritual Dragon, the Earth Dragon, the Underworld Dragon, the Horned Dragon, the Winged Dragon, the Coiling Dragon, the Yellow Dragon, and the Dragon King. Each dragon has different powers has different characteristics. The Celestial Dragon is the most important, because it is the ruler of all the other dragons and it is in charge of protecting the heavens and homes of the deities. The Spiritual Dragon controls the weather, while the Earth Dragon controls the rivers. The Underworld Dragon is the guardian of precious metals and jewels buried in the earth, while the Yellow Dragon is known for its great knowledge. The characteristic of the Horned Dragon is that it is the mightiest; however, the Winged Dragon is the only one that has the ability to fly. The last two dragons are the Coiling dragon, which dwells in the ocean; and the Dragon King, which rules the seas.

Chinese dragons are important to the Chinese culture, because they play a large role in many of the ceremonies that take place throughout the year. During both the Moon Festival and Chinese New Year celebrations, people dress like the dragons and do a traditional dance. This Dragon dance is also done during traditional Chinese weddings.

Objectives

Artistic Perception—Students will view depictions of the Chinese Dragon. The students will be aware of the colors used to depict the Chinese Dragon. Students will become aware of the various elements used in the Chinese Dragon depictions.

Creative Expression—Students will draw a personal interpretation of the Chinese Dragon. Students will utilize one of the watercolor painting techniques. Students will use colors that are used to represent the Chinese Dragon.

Historical and Cultural Context—Students will become aware of the dragon's significance to the Chinese ceremonies. Students will learn as to how the Chinese Dragon first began in the Chinese culture.

Aesthetic Value—Students will discuss why they chose to add certain elements to their dragons.

Integration—Students will gain a better understanding of a part of the Chinese culture. Students will understand the importance of the Chinese Dragon in their various ceremonies.

Materials

- Pencil
- Black, Blue, Green, Red, White, and Yellow Crayons
- Watercolor
- Brush
- 9 × 12 Construction Paper

Procedure

1. Sketch the body of a dragon.
2. Outline the body with a red oil pastel.
3. Outline features with black, blue, green, white, and yellow oil pastel.
4. Create a pattern on the body with black oil pastel. (Be sure to leave the head white.)
5. Fill in the body with watercolor.

Evaluation

1. Did the student represent a Chinese Dragon using traditional colors and characteristics? Y/N
2. Did the student follow the directions and use the waxing watercolor technique? Y/N
3. Can the student answer a question about the history of the Chinese Dragon, its relation to various Chinese ceremonies, and some of the characteristics of a Chinese Dragon? Y/N

9

"Tell me and I will forget; show
me and I may remember;
involve me and I understand."
—*Chinese Proverb*

Radial Symmetry in Design

Using the Elements and Principles of Art
by Melanie Vogel

Overview

In this lesson, students will discover radial symmetry found in nature and interpreted in design by artists through the centuries. Employing the elements and principles of art, students will create a radial design using marker and oil pastel.

Materials

- newsprint to cover work surface
- 12" × 12" construction paper (red, orange, or magenta) precut to size
- 10" Styrofoam plate
- pencil/eraser
- Sharpie permanent marker
- oil pastel set
- 12" × 12" black, white, or colored construction paper for mounting artwork
- glue stick

Objectives

In this lesson, students will explore radial symmetry found in the natural world. Students will be exposed to a variety of historical works of art using radial symmetry as the basis for design. Students will understand and use elements and principles of art including line, shape, color, contrast, pattern, balance, emphasis, movement, rhythm, value, variety, and unity.

Content Standards for Grade 3

1. Identify and describe elements in a work of art, emphasizing line, color, shape/form, texture, space, and value. (Artistic Perception)

2. Create a work of art based on observation of objects and scenes in daily life, emphasizing value changes. (Creative Expression)

3. Compare and describe various works of art that have a similar theme and were created at different time periods. (Historical and Cultural Context)

4. Identify successful and less successful compositional and expressive qualities of their own works of art and describe what might improve them. (Aesthetic Valuing)

5. Write a story or poem inspired by their own works of art. (Connections, Relationships, Applications)

Vocabulary

Radial: having parts arranged like rays coming from a central point

Symmetry: Regularity or balance in the arrangement of parts

(Elements of Art: Line, Shape, Color, Space, Form, Texture, Value)

Principles of Art:

Balance: A visual feeling of equal weight in a work of art

Contrast: Opposites to add interest such as light and dark, thick and thin, large and small

Emphasis: Visual center of attention or focal point

Movement: Motion conveyed through line shape or color. Eye moves around the art.

Pattern: Repeated elements such as shape or line

Rhythm: A visual repetition to create continuity

Variety: More than one element for interest

Unity: Combining line, shape, form, space, value, etc., to create a visually pleasing work of art

Motivation

Show students examples of radial symmetry found in the natural world (actual objects and/or slides, prints of flowers, snowflakes, orb spider web, citrus fruit crossection, tree growth rings, starfish, sea urchin, peacock tail feathers, etc.). Discuss or have students take a nature walk to find objects with radial symmetry. *(artistic perception)*. Have students join hands in concentric circles and move or dance in opposite directions (Psychomotor Domain). Show examples of artwork through the centuries, where artists have incorporated radial symmetry in the design. Discuss the context, media, and meaning. Examples might include stained glass "rose" windows from 16th century European gothic cathedrals, floral design in the woven rugs of middle eastern countries, the Aztec calendar, Wheel of Life from Hindu Sun Temples, Hopi and Navajo basketry and pottery (aerial view), quilt design, and contemporary graphic design. Point out the elements of art used in these designs, focusing on line, shapes used (geometric/organic), and color. Demonstrate different ways of starting a radial design: concentric circles, crosses and x's as in a divided pie, or building a series of shapes and lines from the center outward. *If this lesson is to be integrated with math or technology, demonstrate the use of a protractor, measuring device, or computer program to be used to create the artwork.* Invite the students to begin thinking about and sketching some ideas for their own radial design.

Procedure

1. Place Styrofoam plate faces down on construction paper. Trace circumference using a Sharpie marker.
2. Find center of circle (eyeball it) and place a dot for reference:
3. Start design, **in pencil**, using radial lines, concentric circles, or shapes from the center point. Create a continuous, repeated, balanced pattern that radiates from the center of the circle and flows (visually) all the way around within that circular space. Use a variety of shapes and sizes within the design.
4. Trace design in black Sharpie marker.
5. Color all areas of design with oil pastels. Color firmly for intensity and encourage students to blend areas to create interesting colors or blend light to dark to create value gradations. *Suggest a color scheme, such as complimentary or analogous, which allows for a clear pattern to be established.*
6. Cut out design and mount, using glue stick, on a contrasting color, black, or white construction paper mat or poster board.

Assessment

Students can assess their work individually or as a discussion group. Refer back to the objectives. Questions to ask: How is my design like radial design in nature? How is it different? What inspired my design? Why did I choose the colors that I did? How do I feel when I look at my design? (Affective Domain) What elements and principles of art did I use in my composition? What gives my design balance? Did I use variety and contrast? What would I do differently if I could change my design? What do I like about my composition?

Extension/Integration

1. Incorporate this design with a math lesson on fractions using measurement (protrac-

tor and rulers) to create a geometric pattern

2. Talk about patterns and symmetry in the history of quilt making.

3. Use a radial design to write a poem by placing the words as radial design elements or as a spiral within a circle format.

4. For science, have students research various flora and compare radial symmetry in leaves, flowers, branches, and stems.

5. Gifted students could use thematic images to create their design (e.g., draw animals, plants, and a geographical feature from a habitat such as the ocean or desert to create a radial symmetric design).

6. Developmentally challenged students could paint or draw colors and designs in predrawn and cut circles, naming them as they work. Invite a basket maker, potter, or quilter to your classroom to demonstrate radial symmetry in their art. Take a field trip to an art museum and explore radial symmetry found in the art from different time periods and cultural groups.

Art Lesson Websites

Arts Edge
http://artsedge.kennedy-center.org/teach/les.cfm

Crayola
http://www.crayola.com

Getty Education
http://www.getty.edu

Kinderart
http://www.kinderart.com

Princeton Online
http://www.princetonol.com

The Smithonian Institution
http://smithonianeducation.org

For definitions of art and visual culture terms: http://www.artlex.com

To find a specific artwork, type the artist's name and artwork title into a search engine such as Google.

Classroom Management

Experienced teachers know it is vitally important to be organized and prepared in advance of the school year. A visually stimulating, spacious, and organized classroom creates a welcome environment for a successful art making experience. Attractive bulletin boards and visual art "galleries" of student work and prints of famous works of art brighten the walls and provide inspiration. Some preparation tips include having work areas, storage areas, and lecture areas separate from one another. Work areas could include color coded identifying numbers, signs, or mobiles hanging above the tables. Labeling storage and supply areas enables students to take responsibility for locating needed materials and for efficient clean-up procedures. Seating charts and nametags help the teacher learn student names quickly and promote respectful behavior. Teachers should discuss classroom expectations and behavior the first day of class. Mutual respect between teacher and student is reinforced through a structured, caring approach. Teach safety procedures at the beginning of the year and assign classroom jobs on a rotating basis. Allow ample time for clean-up at the end of each lesson so students take responsibility for keeping the classroom neat and organized. Following are some additional suggestions to keep in mind:

Show your enthusiasm for art through positive, cheerful introductions each day.

1. If possible, it would be ideal to alternate lecture areas occasionally.

2. Have students sit close-up on the rug so they become focused on the lesson. This also provides a nice change from sitting in chairs all day.

3. Get student's attention by waiting silently at the front of the class and making eye contact with all.

4. Try to vary lesson structure by playing music or introducing a guest speaker.

5. Bring in works of art, reproductions, and artifacts.

6. Show a video or dress up as a famous artist and have students guess who you are.

7. Create opportunities for discovery whenever possible.

8. To address positive behavior, give students reward slips or incentives to earn a set of new markers or pens from a classroom "art store." Redirection and positive reinforcement work more effectively than shouting to quiet a class.

9. If a student misbehaves or breaks class rules, have structured consequences in place such as making eye contact, physically moving to the area where the student is sitting, saying their name in a statement, and reminding them of the class rule. If these actions do not work, a time-out away from the art activity may be in order. Never act hastily unless there is danger to you or other students. Remain calm and controlled and follow through with loss of privileges.

10. Strive to introduce the lesson objectives without lengthy explanations. Many students lose interest after five minutes.

11. Be aware of distractions such as talking, loss of eye contact, or shifting in chairs. These are signs that students want to begin the art activity. They need the information, but also want to feel that they have enough time for the activity.

12. Demonstrations help clarify procedure and reinforce visual learning.

13. Encourage students to ask questions and experiment rather than copy the teacher's example. Remember, the national and state standards ask for *original* artwork to be produced.

14. Students who are off task can be brought back to the present moment by asking them a question, giving a warning, or simply directing their attention to the project at hand.

Most students are able to self-start a lesson, but others may feel overwhelmed, anxious, or perplexed. Often they will say they don't know where to start or they don't have any ideas. Remember, some students may feel inadequate or may be distracted with thoughts of life circumstances outside the classroom setting. Give them a starting task or simple direction such as "start with a circle for a head in the top quarter of your paper." Use genuine praise and encouragement. The effective teacher moves around the classroom while students are working and interacts in a patient, positive manner. Students are more likely to feel successful when teachers show interest and are willing to help. Never correct student work by drawing on their art. If need be, demonstrate or sketch an idea on a separate sheet of paper. Remind students that their art is unique, just as they are individually, and that they don't need to compare with one another. They are all artists in their own right. Ask permission to show a student's project to the class when it demonstrates original thought or creative inventiveness in order to inspire creativity, not copying. Do not embarrass any one student by constantly showing their work as the expected model. Another excellent way to keep students on task is to provide nonverbal cues by writing the rubric and objectives on the board. If students finish a project early, have them evaluate their work in an art journal which can also be used for sketching new ideas. Keep these organized in a file system so they are available in the classroom and not taken home. Early finishers can also help the instructor by preparing art materials, mounting art, or collecting and cleaning tools.

Projects can be extended over several days. Encourage interest by providing some new objectives for students to incorporate in their work. Perseverance, thoughtfulness in execution, and craftsmanship bring satisfaction and a sense of accomplishment.

Carefully plan clean-up procedures so the class doesn't erupt in uncontrolled chaos minutes before the final bell. Clean up can be as simple as providing buckets of water and sponges outside the classroom for removal of extra paint and clay from hands and allowing two or three students out at a time. Another solution may be assigned monitors who could wash brushes and paint cups, eliminating lines at the sink. Provide baby wipes or damp paper towels for each student to wipe their hands and to clean desk surfaces. Have one or two students collect the artwork and others to be responsible for collecting and putting away supplies. Provide areas for drying wet materials in advance. Ideally, a drying rack provides a condensed area to lay work flat and separated, but this may not be available in each classroom. Keep unfinished work in art portfolios. These can be made from folded poster board, stapled on the edges into a "pocket" and organized in a large box or placed upright on a shelf and should be easily accessible to the students. Success in the classroom is achieved through planning, organization, empathetic rapport, and exciting motivation.

For further exploration:

http://www.education-world.com/standards/national/arts/visual_arts/k_4.shtml

http://www.thomasarmstrong.com/multiple_intelligences.htm

http://www.teach-nology.com/teachers/lesson_plans/language_arts/writing/

http://www.uwstout.edu/soe/profdev/rubrics.shtml

http://www.theteachersguide.com/Class Management.htm

http://www.honorlevel.com/x47.xml

http://www.proteacher.com/070037.shtml

Glue Line Drawing

Katrina Ruzics

Suggested Age: 2–4th grade

General Goal

The children will be able to identify at least four different types of birds, including the blue-jay, robin, seagull and owl, and talk about what types of habitat the birds would live in (Connections, Relationships and Applications). They will also be able to distinguish warm and cool colors, tint and shade (Artistic Perception).

Specific Goal

The students will create their own original artwork of a bird. On a black piece of paper, they will draw the picture going off between 2–3 sides of the paper to ensure the drawing is more interesting by not being in the center of the page. Then the children will trace over their drawing with glue to make black outlines. After the glue has dried, they will color it with pastels using warm and cool colors, tints and shades (Creative Expression).

Motivation

Show photos of birds to the children and discuss those different types of birds and how their characteristics make them different from each other. Talk about what type of habitat each bird lives in. Then plan a field trip to a bird aviary where the children can have a bird scavenger hunt.

Vocabulary

Contrast	Blue-jay	Beak
Line	Robin	Habitat
Tint/Shade	Seagull	Talons
Warm/Cool colors	Owl	Feathers

Materials

Student:

- at least one photo reference of a type of bird covered in the lesson
- #2 pencil
- 1 black piece of drawing paper
- Elmer's Glue

Teacher:

- pastels to distribute
- butcher paper (optional)

Procedure

1. While using the reference photo, draw the bird on a black piece of paper using a #2 pencil. Make sure the bird is drawn large enough that it takes up most of the paper and goes off at least 2–3 sides of the page.

2. After the bird is drawn, trace over all the pencil lines with Elmer's Glue.
3. Once the bird is traced, place the paper in a safe place to dry overnight.

4. When the glue has dried the lines will look clear. This will give the bird a black outline.

5. Next, color the bird and the entire background with pastels. If the bird has warm colors in it, use cool colors for the background. For a bird with cool colors, have a warm background. This will help the bird stand out more.

6. Use white and black while coloring to give the bird tints and shades.

Note: If the teacher wishes, butcher paper may be placed on the table tops before using the pastels. This will help keep the tables clean.

Evaluation

Did the child use good craftsmanship?

Did the child draw a type of bird covered in the lesson?

Does the drawing go off the page on 2–3 sides?

Were all the lines traced with glue?

Did the child color the entire page with pastel up to the glue line?

Did the child use warm and cool colors?

Did the child make tints and shades on the bird?

Suggested Time: 3–4 hours over a 2 day period. About 1 hour for the line work and 2–3 hours for coloring on the second day.

THE DAILY NEWS ----- November 4, 1954

The Life of a Wild Beast!

Henri Emile-Benoit Matisse was born December 31, 1869 in northern France. His Father's strong knowledge as a business entrepreneur provided Henri with a fondness towards business. Henri dabbled in a number of different interests such as law and business before his passion for art emerged at the age of 19. He began to nurture his love for painting after recovering from appendicitis, and declared in painting he discovered "a kind of paradise". In the years to follow he studied art in various locations. Matisse was inspired by a number of different teachers with whom he studied. He married Amelie Parayre in 1898. Together they had two children, and she played an influential role in his work. His experimentation with bright colors lead to the signature Fauvist style, or the wild beasts, he is known for today. During the rest of his life Matisse continued to perfect his artistic vision despite a devastating illness that challenged him and threatened an end to his career. He was able to overcome his hardship by innovating a new medium, cut-outs, that remained true to his original style. He continued to stay dedicated to art until cancer took his life November 3, 1954.

Henri Matisse (1869-1954)

Style of Art

Matisse is commonly referred to as the most important painter of the 20th century. He was a master of supreme decoration and expressive use of color, he created impressionistic domestic and figurative subjects all the way to abstract cut-outs. His unique style is said to have reshaped the world of art! Cooper stated, "his innate knowledge of how colors and shapes could come to life are just spectacular".

Matisse used a variety of artistic media. Not only was he a painter, he was a book illustrator, printmaker, stage and costume designer as well as a master of cut-out collages.

Japanese cultural inspirations are evident in his work as well. He took the primitive style of their art and molded it into a style of his own using line, color and composition. From this came a unique form emphasizing expression over detail.

The Woman with the Hat (Paris, 1905)

The Green Line (1905)

An Interesting Life

Although Henri lived through several events such as wars, slaughters and political uprisings, his style of art was unaffected. Despite how it may have personally affected him, his works went unchanged and stood fast with his style. His work portrayed images of comfort, refuge, and satisfaction.

Fauvism is an early - 20th century movement begun by a group of French artists, lead by Matisse, which is identifiable with the use of bold distorted forms, vivid colors and vigorous brushstrokes, and it literally means "wild beasts". Fauves emphasized the importance of a paintings color equally with the paintings subject matter, which was used to communicate meaning. Detail fell to a lesser importance in lieu of bright color and strong lines, which created a sense of movement. This new form of art that had never been seen before shocked artist worldwide and was the beginning of a new artistic movement.

Polynesia, The Sea (1946)
Gouache on paper cut-out. 77" by 123"

" There is nothing more difficult for a truly creative painter than to paint a rose, because before he can do so he has first to forget all the roses that were ever painted"   ~Henri Matisse

Cut-it-out!

In 1941, Matisse was diagnosed with abdominal cancer and had surgery which resulted with a devastating effect on his health and ability to paint. Since most of his time was spent in a wheel chair, he decided to turn to another form of artistic expression; paper cut-outs. Matisse continued with his same style as before; vivid and strong colors, and daring compositions. As old people do, especially old immobile famous artists do, Matisse had an assistant who would help him with his work. His cut-outs form extremely large collages, filling entire walls. He claims that these were his greatest works of art! Some of his collages that are well known today are *Polynesia*, *The Sea* and *The Snail*. Towards the end of his life while living in the French Riveiera, his work took on more of an abstract form and a sense of selfless experimentation. He continued his work all the way to his death, November 3, 1954.

References

http://www.artelino.com/articles/henri_matisse.asp

http://www.fortunecity.com/victorian/parkwood/249/five.html

Cooper, James.
     http://www.artst.org/matisse/bio/

Herrera, Hayden. *Matisse, a Portrait.* New York; Harcourt Brace & Co. 1993.

Spurling. Hillary. *The Unknown Matisse; a Life of Henri Matisse: the early years 1869-1908.* New York; Alfred A. Knopf. 1998.

PUBLISHED BY:
NAME: Sarah Diersing   Time: T/Th 1:00
CLASS: ART 380   Date: April 24, 2008

"Art begins with a vision-a creative operation requiring an effort. Creativity takes courage.**"**

~Henri Matisse

The Snail (1953): Three meters square gouache on paper, cut and pasted.

The Art of Henri Matisse; The Sea

Sarah Diersing

TIME: 1–2 hours   AGE: 7–9 (3rd grade)

Goals

General Goal

- The children will understand the art style of Henri Matisse.
- The children will understand color and composition from an arrangement of color paper cut-outs.
- The children will practice the use of positive and negative space (**Artistic Perception**).
- The children will measure four perfect squares with a ruler to construct background (**Connection/Relations/Applications**).

Specific Goal

- The children will understand the life and techniques of Henri Matisse art.
- Children will draw sea creatures with pencil then cut and paste.
- With construction paper the children will create their own collage of sea life creatures (**Creative Expression**).
- The children will practice their motor skills of hand/eye coordination to cut construction paper.
- Children will practice craftsmanship by cutting paper neatly without tearing.

Motivation

The teacher will excite the children by having various cut out shapes of sea creatures covering the white board. Then the teacher will go into her lesson by talking about the various sea creatures, and invite the class to help her come up with a list. After that the teacher will introduce the art project by displaying Matisse's piece, *The Sea*, recite a brief biography on his life and inspiration to art. Music of sounds under the sea will be played in the class during the project.

Vocabulary

- Collage
- Negative space
- Perfect square
- Positive space

Materials

- Per Child:
- 2 pieces of white construction paper
- Elmer's glue stick
- scissors
- 1 piece of dark blue construction paper
- 1 piece of light blue construction paper
- pencil
- ruler

Extra: Play under the sea creature sounds while student are creating their art piece (use CD player)

Procedure

1. First start by taking the dark blue construction paper and measure with ruler a five by five perfect square, and then cut out the square.

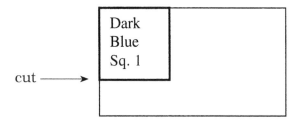

2. After you have the first perfect square, have children use that as a stencil to trace one more dark blue square and cut that one out. Now there are two dark blue squares.

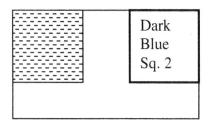

3. Using one of the cut out squares, take the light blue construction paper and trace two perfect squares and cut those ones out.

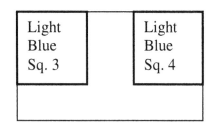

4. Now there are four perfect squares, two dark blue and two light. blue. Next take one of the large white construction papers and use it as a base to glue the squares down to form one large ten by ten square.

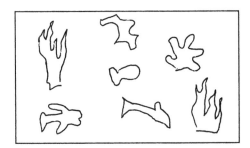

5. Next draw various sea creatures on the second piece of white construction paper.

6. Carefully cut out all creatures.

7. Take the cut out sea creature and with the glue stick, paste them onto the ten by ten blue sea background.

Evaluation

Did the child successfully demonstrate the
style of Matisse?

Were four perfect squares constructed?

Did student demonstrate good craftsmanship?

Artists: Henri Matisse 1869–1954
Romare Bearden 1911–1988

Project: Collagraph

Art Project by Melanie Vogel

Overview

In this lesson, students will observe work expressed in collage form by Henri Matisse (French) and Romare Bearden (American), both painters who focused on collage in their later years. The students will make a collagraph, which is a form of collage combined with the printing process.

Materials

- 9" × 12" construction paper (2 colors; students get one of each)
- scissors
- white glue
- pictures or photos of subject matter for student reference
- brayer (soft rubber roller)
- paten or cookie sheet for rolling out ink
- speedball water base printing ink
- 9" × 12" colored construction paper for prints
- newsprint

Objectives

Students will observe how artists work in different mediums and how collage offered a wonderful way for these two artists to express their ideas. Students will compare collage techniques and subject matter by these two artists. Students will make a collaged form that will be used as a printing plate (collagraph) and they will understand the printing process.

Vocabulary

brayer, collage, collagraph, ink, medium, printmaking, reverse image

Motivation

Show work by these two artists comparing their paintings and their collages. How are these two mediums different?

Choose a subject that would interest students. (It could be tied into a social studies, science or literature unit.) Reptiles and amphibians were the subjects for all the arts. Talk about textures and ways of layering design. It is important to note that the layering of paper in the collage creates the definition of the image for printing. Anything defined in the finished print has to be cut out of paper and glued onto the base form (explained further in *Procedure*). Talk about the printing process and how the collage will become the printing plate.

Procedure

1. Draw outline of subject on one color of construction paper.
2. Cut out design with scissors.
3. Using the second color of construction paper, cut out all details, textures, and designs for subject and glue down. (For the reptile and amphibian project, scales, stripes, patterns, eyes, mouth, etc., were glued on for detail.) More than one layer can be added, but remember, a roller must go over finished design for printing. You

now have a collagraphic plate which can be printed!

4. Set up a table for printing. Place a sheet of newsprint under collagraphic plate.

5. Squeeze some printing ink from tube onto paten or cookie sheet and roll brayer through to spread ink evenly over roller surface.

6. Next, roll ink onto plate, pressing down as you roll so low areas of design are covered. Repeat until design is covered **well** with ink.

7. *IMPORTANT!* Place fresh sheet of newsprint under inked plate so "over roll" color will not be transferred to paper!

8. Place paper on top of inked plate carefully. Do not lift up once you have placed it!

9. Rub over paper using fingertips with pressure. Feel the contours and rub over all areas well, being careful not to shift the paper. This is the most important part of the printing process because pressure is what infuses the paper with ink and defines the design.

10. Lift and separate plate from paper and place flat to dry. Remind students their prints will be a reverse image from the original plate. More than one print can be made from the collagraphic plate and plates can be reused. The paper design can be coated with shellac or varnish to ensure longer printing life if many prints wish to be made.

Extension/Integration

Collagraphy can be used to make cards or for anything requiring multiple copies. The printing plates can be inked with several colors for a multicolored print or several plates can be made and printed separately, registered one on top of another for a multiple-colored design. Animals, plants and buildings make good subject matter and could be incorporated into a social studies or science unit.

Vincent Van Gogh

Vincent Van Gogh, perhaps the most famous Post Impressionist painter was born on March 30, 1853, to a pastor of the Dutch Reformed Church. His family lived in Groote Zundert, The Netherlands. His childhood was overshadowed by the fact that his mother had given birth to a stillborn child named Vincent exactly one year previously. Some feel that Vincent always felt that he had to live up to his deceased brother, but the fact remains that each day that the family went to his father's church while they were growing up, Vincent walked by the tombstone with his name and birth date on it.

Vincent had a passionate, rambunctious personality and often clashed with his strict, religious parents. His childhood was relatively unremarkable beyond this issue. He was sent to a boarding school for two years, attended the King Willem II secondary school, and then at the age of fifteen decided to leave school.

When choosing careers, Vincent often followed in his family's footsteps. He joined his uncle's art dealer firm in The Hague and was relatively successful. At this time, he decided to fulfill a life long dream of finding a place that he felt he belonged. Vincent was never completely comfortable and suffered self esteem issues throughout his life. He was said to ask a young woman to marry him, but when she said no—she was already spoken for—Vincent flew into a fit and even went so far as to place his hand over a lantern trying to make her change her mind. He was mortified when her father reached over and blew out the flame. Van Gogh was transferred to London and later Paris, but was not as successful there.

After working as a teacher for a few months, Vincent realized that he wanted to become a preacher—like his father. He went to study theology at the university, but failed the exams. After much persuasion, the church allowed Vincent to go to the most impoverished areas and preach to the coal miners in The Borinage, Belgium. This was strictly on a trial basis; one that was to prove futile. Vincent was passionate about ministering to these people and was even said to give his shoes and money to those less fortunate. At times, he was close to starvation, but felt that his parishioners needed it more. Van Gogh's passion was not evident in his sermons, and he was not allowed to progress in his studies. It was at this time that Vincent began drawing the people around him and would later paint "The Potatoe Eaters"—a depiction of the dark, harsh living conditions of these people.

Finally, Vincent went to talk to his younger brother, Theo, and told him of his desire to paint. Theo was to become a remarkable support to his brother—both spiritually and financially. Theo told his brother that he felt he would be a wonderful painter, and Vincent would spend the rest of his life trying to live up to this belief.

Once again, Vincent attempted to find a place where he could belong. He moved to southern France and found a yellow house to rent. It was his dream that the other artists that he had come to know would move there, live together, paint during the day, and at night they could converse, learn and motivate each other. Sadly, Paul Gauguin was the only one to accept Vincent's offer. In a flurry of activity, Vincent painted numerous paintings of sunflowers that filled the fields around the village of Arles. These were later recognized as some of his greatest works. He hung what he hoped would be a bright, sunny welcome throughout the house. At first, it seemed as if this friendship would work, but Gauguin began to be increasingly critical of Vincent's work and life. During one of their constant arguments, Van Gogh had a fit with a kitchen knife, and during a fit of depression cut off the lower portion of his left ear. The police were later to find him in a pool of blood and took him immediately to the hospital.

Van Gogh spent a great deal of his life in and out of a hospital where the doctors tried to help his mental stability. Although he suffered with issues of self-doubt and depression throughout his life, his later years were extremely troubled. Many suggest that the artists' at this time suffered from lead poisoning since they often put their paint brushes (after cleaning them with turpentine) in their mouths to use the salvia to keep the bristles neat. Lead poisoning can lead to mental troubles. Van Gogh is also thought to have suffered from a venereal disease—which also could acerbate his mental state. Finally, Vincent and Theo exchanged over seven hundred letters throughout their lives. From these letters, many medical experts feel that Theo had a genetic form of epilepsy. It is very likely that Vincent, too, suffered from this ailment. After epileptic seizures the victims often experience a severe depression. All of these complications and Vincent's own lack of self-worth would continue to haunt him to the very end of his life.

Vincent became a prolific and remarkable painter, but his success was never realized during his life. In fact, it is said that he was only able to sell one of his paintings. After many years of turmoil and failures, it is believed that Vincent painted "Crows over a Wheatfield" and then proceeded to shoot himself. As much of Vincent's life, this attempt at ending his life was unsuccessful and he lay dying refusing treatment. His bother, Theo, and several of the doctors who were to become Vincent's friends were at his side when he died.

One would think that this painful story would end here, but sadly Theo would die merely six months later. It is Theo's wife who was to gather Vincent's paintings and the letters that the two brothers sent to each other together. It was a result of her work that Vincent was to become known as a great Post-Impressionist painter.

Post Impressionism was influenced by Impressionism, but the similarities were very few. Rather than focusing on light and capturing brief glimpses of life, the Post-Impressionists were centered around bright color and sharp, outlined shapes and edges. Van Gogh is known for his vivid use of color and thick, textural swirling brushstrokes. His subject matter ranged from bird's nests and old boots to portraits of the peasants that would sit and pose for him for hours on end.

Sunflowers

Lacey Kraft

TIME: Approximately 2 hours (1 Hour Periods)
AGE: 9–12 years old (4th–6th Grade)

Goals

General Goal

- Children will learn about the life and style of the artist Vincent Van Gogh.
- Children will study the famous painting "Sunflowers" by Vincent Van Gogh.

Specific Goal

- Children will create their own "Sunflowers" by cutting out flowers from construction paper.
- There will be one vase with two different colors, and the children need to sign their name on the top half, left side of the vase.
- There needs to be a minimum of five flowers and at least one flower needs to be a sunflower.
- The children will arrange the flowers so that there is a three-dimensional look to the final piece of artwork.

Motivation

Begin with a lesson on the life and style of Vincent Van Gogh. Show the children examples of Van Gogh's artwork, focusing and emphasizing the piece "Sunflowers." Let the children explore Van Gogh through the internet; have them find five facts about him that they think no one would know and present them to the class. While doing the art project, have a visual of Van Gogh's "Sunflowers" so that the children can reference back to the original piece.

Vocabulary

bold	movement
impasto	post-impressionism
color	sunflowers
contrasting	texture
expressionisn	three-dimensional
impressionism	Vincent Van Gogh

Materials

Per Child:

- Many pieces of different colored construction paper (for flowers, stems & vase!)
- 1 pair of scissors
- 1 glue stick
- 1 exacto knife
- 1 black Sharpie
- 1 12" × ~4.5" piece of colored construction paper (for the table!)
- 1 12" × 18" piece of colored construction paper (for the background!)

Extra: Have completed "Sunflowers" projects around the room so the children can see what their end artwork should look like; also, it keeps the children on the right track!

Procedure

1. Pick a 12" × 18" piece of colored construction paper for the background.

2. Put the 12" × 4.5" piece of different colored construction on bottom of the 12" × 18" to create a table for the vase.

3. Create a vase using two different colors of construction paper. First make a vase with one color, then trace the vase on the second color and only cut the top half off; glue the top half onto the original color.

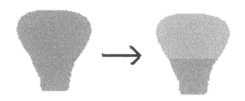

4. Sign your name on the left side, top half of the vase.

5. Now you can start making your flowers! To make the sunflower, you will need brown and yellow construction paper. Cut out a brown circle for the center of the sunflower and about 14 yellow petals.

6. Once you have all your petals cut out, you are going to glue the petals to the back of the circle fanning the petals out so that they begin to look like a sunflower.

7. Turn the sunflower over and put black spots on the middle circle with the black Sharpie.

8. You can make flowers of different sizes and different colors using the same type of pattern of petals, or you can be creative and come up with different petal shapes on your own!

9. Once all your flowers are done, you can make the leaves and stems and arrange them the way you want them to be for the final design. You need to make a slice in the vase using the exacto knife (look at picture below) because this is where the stems of the flowers are going to be placed.

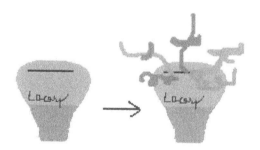

10. Once you have the stems arranged the way want, you can glue the flowers to them and then glue the vase and the flowers to the 12" × 18" piece of construction paper. The final step is to arrange the flowers and stems so that they have a 3-D look to them and aren't just glued to the paper. Bending the petals and is a good way to get the 3-D look! Have fun with it!

Evaluation

- Are there different colors for the vase top and vase bottom?
- Is the table a different color from the background?
- Did the artist sign the vase on the top, left half?
- Are there at least five flowers?
- Is there at least one sunflower?
- Did the artist arrange the flowers and stems so the final piece looks 3-D?

Thomas Kinkade

Lorraine Paredes

Thomas Kinkade, the *Painter of Light*, is America's most collected artist. As many awards as this painter has received and the countless paintings he has created, Kinkade manages to be a devout husband, father, and Christian. His journey to fame was hard, but each circumstance made him the artist he is today. The life and work of Thomas Kinkade delights people around the world. Kinkade illuminates a vision of light, peace and wholesome values. His art reflects his deep faith in God, which is the foundation of his work. Kinkade believes that art has the power to touch hearts and change people's lives.

Kinkade is considered a Romantic painter. Though Romanticism began in the late 18th century and went on through the mid 19th century, Kinkade's painting reflect the same style the Romantics did in the past. Romanticism is "a literary movement marked by emphasis on the imagination and the emotions and by the use of autobiographical material" (The Merriam Webster Dictionary, 637). Kinkade is also often compared to the late 19th century American painters, the Luminists. The Luminist emphasis was on pastoral subjects. Kinkade says he strives for the same three visual aspects as the Luminists: soft edges, a warm palette and an overall sense of light (www.tom-kinkade-gallery.com).

Kinkade is known for infusing light into his paintings. This creates a romantic and tranquil scene. It is as if the painting were glowing. Each of Kinkade's paintings affirm the basic values of family, home, faith in God as well as the beauty of nature. For the observer, his works present simpler and better times. When viewing his work, the canvas, along with its beautiful, bright colors, creates warmth. There are no outlines, all the edges are soft, as you would see it in reality. Light fills the canvas. All of these characteristics are exact characteristics of the Luminists.

Thomas Kinkade did not grow up with the same home life and values he paints about. Kinkade was considered a "latch-key" kid. He grew up in a small town called Placerville, not too far from Lake Tahoe, in the Sierra foothills. Placerville was an isolated town with a very simple lifestyle. Kinkade's parents were divorced when he was 5 years old. From his knowledge, he recollects being the only kid from a divorced family in his community. Everyone else had a mom and dad. There was no father to watch him at baseball practice. Divorce is quite common in today's society, but during his childhood, it was embarrassing and shameful. Being poor also caused him to be shameful. However, what made Kinkade stand out among all the other children was his art. From the young age of four, all Kinkade wanted was paper and paints. Kinkade says, "I was always the kid who could draw. I had this talent, and it was the one thing that gave me some kind of dignity in the midst of my personal environment, because growing up, I was very impoverished." Kinkade was 12 years old when he sold his first painting for $7.50 at a summer camp art exhibit. Ironically, Placerville and its inhabitants are a main focus in many of Kinkade's paintings, even though it was a place of struggle for him early on.

At the age of 16, Kinkade was an accomplished painter in oil under the apprenticeship of the famous, Glenn Wessels. During Kinkade's adolescence, Wessels moved to Placerville. Kinkade was thrilled to have such an admired artist as Wessels to live in his hometown. When Kinkade was 14 years old he introduced himself to Wessels and told him if he ever needed help around the studio he would love to. Wessels response was, "Thanks, sonny, but honestly, I don't have time for you. I'm just too busy" (Kinkade, 42). Though this devastated Kinkade, two years later a sad yet great situation arose. Wessels was in a horrible car accident that left his lower body crippled. Kinkade offered his help once again, and this time Wessels gladly accepted. Kinkade stretched canvases and swept his studio.

Their conversations were not just based on art, but on life too. Wessels instilled in Kinkade's mind that artists are remembered long past their lifetime, that they do impact the world. Wessels became like a surrogate father, even though he was old enough to be Kinkade's grandfather. Wessels taught Kinkade two arts: "the art of painting, and the art of making my days count" (Kinkade, 46).

At the time, Kinkade wanted to get away from the small town life and move to the big city. At 18 years old, he went to the University of Berkeley on a scholarship. There he wanted to explore philosophical ideas and expand his creative expression. One of his professors at the University spent a lecture on how artwork is all about the artist. He said it did not matter if the audience understood it or found interest in it, because it is all about you, the artist. This idea really irritated Kinkade inside. After attending an art school in Pasadena, Kinkade rejected this "pseudo-sophistication" he had learned. Kinkade wanted his art to interest everyone. Now many of his paintings reflect his "foundational values." Kinkade tries to paint images that illustrate hope, inspiration and a simpler way of life (www.satevepost.org).

Kinkade is out-going, with an incredible sense of humor. He is left-handed, about six feet tall and of Scottish/Irish decent. He is devout Christian. Kinkade acknowledges God's hand in his life and is well aware of his many bless-

ings. He is a dedicated husband to his wife Nanette and his daughters Merrit, Chandler, Winsor and Everett. In fact, Kinkade often tributes to his wife and his two daughters at the time Merrit and Chandler, in his paintings. In some of his paintings, there is a number in red near his signature that signifies how many N's, for his wife Nanette, are hidden in the painting. Some of his other paintings have other hidden images. In the paintings, *Paris, City of Lights* and *San Francisco, California Street* you can see two ways Thomas uses their anniversary date, 5-2-82. In *Rose Gate*, you will find many W's along with N's in honor of his daughter Winsor and his wife Nanette. In *Winsor Manor*, there are four N's and twenty-six W's which are representative of his daughter's birth date of April 26. There are numerous other fun trivia in Kinkade's paintings (www.tom-kinkade-gallery.com).

Kinkade paints six days a week and still finds time for church activities, reading, and extensive travel with his family, in America and abroad. His travels are very important to his paintings. Many times, the places he visits are the subject of his painting. The cottages Kinkade paints really do exist. He paints them from England's Cotswolds and the Austrian Alps. Some are homes of famous people. One is The Pine Inn in Carmel, California, others are various buildings in New Orleans and Fisherman's Wharf.

The use of light brings peace and wholesome values to life. He is known as the Painter of Light for the golden tones that are illustrated on his canvas. The subjects of many of his paintings are cottages, country sides, small towns of America or busy cities. Each of his paintings portray the radiance of light. Kinkade paints lit windows "because glowing windows say home to me" (www.christian-book.com). This is very important to Kinkade, who during his childhood, came home to an empty house. Lights in the window indicate that someone is home, waiting for you. Home is supposed to be a safe place. Kinkade wants the viewer to feel the sense of home when they look at his paintings of cottages and houses.

Many of Kinkade's paintings get transformed into books, post cards, calendars, magazine covers, cards, collector plates, figurines and other gift items. It is said that no other American artist besides Norman Rockwell has received so much acceptance and exposure (www.satevepost.org). What draws Kinkade to Norman Rockwell besides his realistic paintings is "his attitude of creating an art of meaning for people." This is something he shares with both Rockwell and Walt Disney. Each of them desire to make people happy. This broad exposure has made some of his paintings six-digit sums for his original works. A lot of his collectors include well-known leaders in politics, business and entertainment (satevepost.org, 2). A man from the Thomas Kinkade Gallery in the Brea Mall said that only museums own his original works. All the others are reproductions.

One of Kinkade's favorite subjects are bridges. Steps or grassy inclines leading upward or through a gate are also some of his favorites. Each of these is a symbol of his faith. Some are actually pictorial depictions of Bible verses. An example is *A Light in the Storm*, which is representative of John 8:12, "When Jesus spoke again to the people, he said, 'I am the light of the world. Whoever follows me will never walk in darkness, but will have the light of life'" (NIV, 1662). Other paintings are autobiographical, which is an aspect of Romanticism. *Hometown Morning* is about a boy on a bike being chased by a dog. It is a representation of himself in his childhood when he met his future wife while on a paper route. Other paintings have his hometown neighbors. Not all of his paintings have a religious connotation, but they do have a deeper meaning beyond the surface (www.satevepost.org).

In 1995, Thomas Kinkade was named Artist of the Year from the National Association of Limited Edition Dealers. He also has two Certificates of Merit by the New York Society of Illustrates and two Founder's Awards from the National Park's Academy for the Arts. He was the first artist to win twice (www.christian-book.com). He also received 1998 Graphic/Lithograph of the Year (Kinkade). These are a few among the awards he has received.

Thomas Kinkade has had an eventful life of growing up with divorced parents, working with Glenn Wessels, being compared to the famous Norman Rockwell, to becoming America's most collected living artist. Kinkade is committed to his family, God and making people happy through his art. His paintings provide viewers with an emotional sense of peace and warmth. As Kinkade puts it, "some 10 million people wake up every day to one of my paintings." It not only puts them in a better frame of mind, but his paintings allow him to reach a wide audience. His lessons of peace and tranquility in a world of stress and worry are noticed by everyone. His light not only shines through his canvas, but through his life as well. "I try to create paintings that are a window for the imagination. If people look at my work and are reminded of the way things once were, or perhaps they could be, then I've done my job" (author).

Bibliography

1. *The Merriam Webster Dictionary*. Springfield, MA: Merriam Webster Inc.; 1994: pg. 637.

2. Kinkade T. *A Village Christmas*. San Jose, CA: Media Arts Group, Inc.; 1999: pgs. 42, 46.

3. www.satevepost.org

4. www.tom-kinkade-gallery.com

House of Light

Heather Larson

Time: Approximately 2 hours

Age: 8–12 years or 3rd–6th grade

Goals

- General Goal: The main goal of this project is that the children will learn about the artist Thomas Kinkade. In addition, students will observe and identify the luminist, plein air, romantic and impressionistic style of his paintings.

- Specific Goal: The children will create an original house or cottage with one door and at least two windows. The students will use oil pastels to color their house/cottage, giving it an impressionist style. After the teacher has used an exacto knife to cut out all the windows and doors, the students will place yellow or warm colored tissue paper behind the openings to create the look of light.

Motivation

Providing examples of Thomas Kinkade's work from books or calendars as well as examples of completed projects may help to motivate the students and give them ideas. In addition, a brief discussion of Kinkade's life and his motivations for painting may evoke the students' interest. Lastly, have the students write a story about something they enjoy like painting, drawing, sewing, scrap booking, etc., and how they came to enjoy it.

Vocabulary

Luminist—An artist who uses the style of 19th-century American painting concerned especially with the precise, realistic rendering of atmospheric light and the perceived effects of that light on depicted objects.

Plein Air—A style of painting produced out of doors in natural light.

Romanticism—An artistic and intellectual movement originating in Europe in the late 18th century which is characterized by a heightened interest in nature and emphasis on the individual's expression of emotion and imagination.

Impressionism—A theory or style of painting originating and developed in France during the 1870s, characterized by concentration on the immediate visual impression produced by a scene and by the use of unmixed primary colors and small strokes to simulate actual reflected light.

Unity—Everything in a composition feels as if it belongs.

Materials

- 1 piece of 9" × 11" black construction paper
- 1 #2 pencil
- 1 box of oil pastels (if needed, 2 students can share 1 box)
- scissors
- 1 piece of yellow tissue paper
- 1 exacto knife (for Teacher use only!)
- 1 glue stick
- **Extra:** calming music/CD and CD player to create a relaxing and creative atmosphere

Procedure

1. Using a #2 pencil, create a house or cottage with at least one door and two windows on black construction paper.

2. Use oil pastels to color the house.

3. The teacher then cuts out the windows and door with an exacto knife.

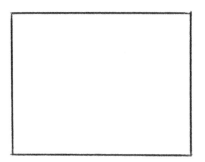

4. Once the windows and doors have been cut out, the student will cut out yellow tissue paper. The pieces of tissue paper should be just slightly larger than each opening.

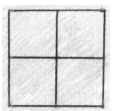

5. Once the tissue paper has been measured and cut, the student will use their glue stick to place glue around each window or door on the back of the paper. The student will then place the yellow tissue paper over the opening.

Evaluation

- Did the student create an original house with at least one door and two windows?
- Did the student use oil pastels to color their picture?
- Did the child have good craftsmanship?

Piet Mondrian

Piet Mondrian was a Dutch abstract painter born in Amersfoort, Holland, in 1872. He was the oldest son in a strict Calvanist family. He had an older sister and three younger brothers. Mondrian's father was also an artist and he taught art at a Calvinist primary school in Holland. Mondrian's strict Calvanist upbringing made him straightforward, caused him to avoid anything sensual and made him develop an almost strict spiritual devotion to his paintings. Mondrian wanted more than anything to leave home and become an artist, however his father wanted him to become an art teacher first. At the age of 22, Mondrian attended the Amsterdam Academy to please his father. While he was at the Academy, he painted in a naturalistic style of mountains and trees inspired from the surrounding landscapes in Holland.

Mondrian moved to France in 1912, and he quickly became influenced by the Cubist painters and starts painting abstract. During this period his painting are known as his "plus and minus" paintings. One of his most famous paintings of this period is his *Pier and Ocean* 1915 painting. This is one of his most famous cubist style paintings since he reduces a pier and ocean to a series of small horizontal and vertical fragments in black against a white background in an oval shape. He loved this painting and would say, "a few little lines, you might say, but I see the sea in it, waves rolling towards me under a starry sky."

In the summer of 1914, Mondrian went back to Holland to visit his dying father and, because World War I broke out, he was forced to remain in Holland. He became disillusioned about how the government was not able to prevent war or stop it sooner. The war had two effects on his art. The first effect on his art was that he rejected all art of the past and the second effect was that he searched for art free from all oppression. While in Holland, he and his friends started the de Stijl art movement that went on to influence European painting, design and architecture. He termed the phrase "Neo-Plasticism." Mondrian believed that through "Neo-Plasticism" he could somehow transform art and the quality of life. Mondrian used Neo-Plasticism as a new form of art that used pure abstraction, reduced the form to geometric shapes and used only primary colors.

Mondrian began to paint a series of paintings using his Neo-Plasticism art form called the 'diamond' paintings. His most famous diamond painting during this period was his *Composition of Red, Yellow, and Blue* 1927. In this painting, he sought a universal reality through straight lines joined at right angles because he believed this to be the perfect equilibrium. He used only primary colors of red, yellow and blue. He also used neutral colors of black, gray and white.

Mondrian returned to London; however, he did not stay long since the Germans bombed his studio during the Battle of Britain. In 1940, he moved to the United States and set up what would be his last studio in New York. While he was in New York, the abstract artists influenced him. Mondrian loved living in New York and the city influenced his next series of paintings called his 'city paintings.'

Mondrian's most famous painting in this period was his *Broadway Boogie Woogie* 1942–1943. In this painting, he increased more colors and did away with solid black lines and used color lines instead. He abandoned the severe black lines for the chain-link bright patterns. His visual inspirations for this painting were the streets of Manhattan, modern skyscrapers and illuminated signs of

Broadway. In his studio while he painted, he loved to listen to boogie woogie music that was popular at the time and so it was natural that he called this painting *Broadway Boogie Woogie.* This painting would be Mondrian's last painting that he completed before passing away in 1944. It now hangs in The Museum of Modern Art in New York.

Mondrian looked for a new truth and reality in his art. He said,

I started off a naturalist. I soon felt a need for a more severe reduction and limitation of my means, and gradually became more abstract. Each period developed logically from the previous one. My development will carry on in the same direction and not go backwards.

Mondrian's art continues to carry the viewer forward into a new reality.

Bibliography

Carmean, E. A. Jr. *Mondrian The Diamond Compositions.* National Gallery of Art, Washington D.C. 1979.

Champa, K. S. *Mondarian Studies.* Chicago Press, Chicago: 1985.

Elgar, F. *Mondrian.* Praeger Publishers, New York: 1968.

Wijsenbeek, L. J. F. *Piet Mondrian.* New York Graphic Society, Connecticut: 1968.

Create Your Own Mondrian Web Cites For Children

The Mondrian Machine: www.desire.com/2.1/Toys/Mondrian/Docs/mondrian.html

Make Piet Mondrian Roll Over in His Grave: www.kerp.net/mondrian/index.html

The Mondrimat: www.stephen.com/mondrimat/main.html

Quotes of Piet Mondrian

"Art is the expression of truth as well as of beauty."

". . . my dealer tells me I am too advanced for my time."

". . . in all art it is the artist's task to make forms and colors living and capable of rousing emotion."

"Times are hard for painters these days, not just for me and the pictures I paint, which are not meant for the masses."

"Neo-Plasticism, that's what I call my . . . direction. I want a new plasticity, a deeper realism."

"I started off a naturalist. I soon felt a need for a more severe reduction and limitation of my means, and gradually became more abstract. Each period developed logically from the previous one. . . . My development will carry on in the same direction and not go backwards."

Piet Mondrian's Compositions

Colleen Hanley

TIME: Approx. 1 hour   AGES: 6–12 years old

Goals

General Goals

- CONTENT STANDARD ONE—ARTISTIC PERCEPTION

  Children will have the ability to recognize the artistic concepts of balance, emphasis, unity, pattern, rhythm, repetition, line, shape, primary colors and nonobjective art.

- CONTENT STANDARD THREE—HISTORICAL AND CULTURAL CONTEXT

  Children will have a understanding of the abstract and nonobjective art movements through examples of Piet Mondrian's artwork.

- CONTENT STANDARD FOUR—AESTHETIC VALUING

  When the project is complete, children will have the ability to recognize the nonobjective art of Piet Mondrian. They will also have the ability to distinguish nonobjective art from abstract or realistic art. The children will be able to use art vocabulary (balance, emphasis, unity, pattern, rhythm, repetition, line and shape) to assign value and personal preference to their artwork as well as the artwork of their peers.

- CONTENT STANDARD FIVE—CONNECTIONS, RELATIONS AND APPLICATIONS

  Children will understand the math concepts of parallel lines, perpendicular lines, geometric shapes (squares and rectangles specifically), right angles, intersection and how they relate to the artwork of Piet Mondrian.

Specific Goals

- CONTENT STANDARD TWO—CREATIVE EXPRESSION

  Each child will create an original Piet Mondrian composition. Each composition will include black parallel lines that run from the top of the composition to the bottom and from the left of the composition to the right. These black lines will create geometric squares and rectangles. The children will fill in a portion of the squares and rectangles with red, yellow and blue (primary colors) construction paper to create a balanced composition.

Motivation

The day before the art project, introduce the students to Piet Mondrian. Give students a brief background of his life. Use Mondrian as a tool to introduce the students to the concepts of realistic, abstract and nonobjective art. Show the student's examples of his early realistic artwork (*Trees Along the Gein Bend in the Gein with Eleven Poplar Trees*). After discussing Mondrian's realistic artwork, show the children his abstract paintings (*Gray Tree, Trees in Bloom*). Discuss how artists like Mondrian simplified natural images. Explain that even though abstract art rearranges images, the object is usually still recognizable. Next, show the children examples of Mondrian's nonobjective art (*Composition, Broadway Boogie Woogie*). Discuss how nonobjective art is purely imaginative and that it is not derived from any image. Hang a photograph of Mondrian on the classroom wall. On the same wall hang labels that read, "Realistic," "Abstract" and "Nonobjective," and place Mondrian's artwork under the appropriate label. After the project, plan a field trip to The Museum of Contemporary Art, Los Angeles, to view Piet Mondrian's *Composition of Red, Blue, and Yellow*, as well as other abstract and nonobjective art.

Vocabulary

Art Words

balance
emphasis
unity
pattern
rhythm
repetition
primary Colors
realism
abstract
nonobjective
line

Math Words

parallel
perpendicular
geometric
square
rectangle
right angles
intersection

Materials

Per Child
1 piece of 10" by 10" white drawing paper
1 piece of 8" by 11" red construction paper
1 piece of 8" by 11" blue construction paper
1 piece of 8" by 11" yellow construction paper
1 piece of 8" by 11" black construction paper
8 strips of ½" by 11" black construction paper
1 glue stick
1 pair of scissors
1 #2 pencil

Procedure

1. Place 1 piece of drawing paper flat on the desk. Position the paper onto the desk so it makes a square.

2. Take ½" by 8" strips of black paper and make a grid-like pattern on the piece of white drawing paper. All strips should lie horizontally or vertically across the paper. DO NOT PLACE THE STRIPS DIAGONALLY. The strips do not need to go clear across the paper, as long as the line ends at the intersection of another line.

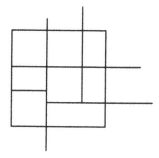

3. When you have selected an arrangement that is aesthetically pleasing, glue the strips onto the drawing paper with a glue stick. (Note: Use the glue sparingly. Big globs of glue might impede Step 5.)

4. With your scissors, cut off the strips that hang from the edges of the drawing paper.

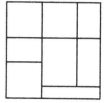

5. Once the glue appears to be dry, place the other piece of drawing paper on top of the piece of paper with the strips. Make sure that both pieces of paper are lined up so that the top piece of paper covers the bottom on completely.

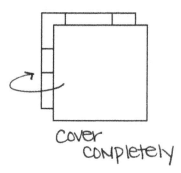

6. Using a #2 pencil, shade the entire piece of the blank white paper. (Note: This is most easily done using the side of the lead.) The drawing paper should have created a duplicate of the paper with the black strips.

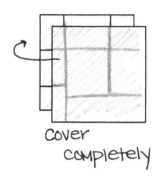

7. While looking at the drawing paper with the glued strips, have the students select which rectangles or squares they want to fill in with color. Remind the students that their composition should be balanced and include all three primary colors. The student can also fill in the rectangles with black. Warn students that the overuse of black can draw too much emphasis to one area of the composition and create an art piece that feels unbalanced. Remind them that Mondrian did fill in his shapes with black, but used it sparingly and typically used it in only one square per composition. Also remind students to leave some of the boxes white.

8. Once the students have selected which rectangles and squares they want to fill in, have each student lightly write in pencil the color the have selected for the rectangle or square. This will serve as a reminder for the students.

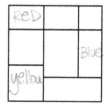

9. Next have the students find the matching square/rectangle that they selected on the shaded drawing paper. With a pair of scissors cut these rectangles and squares out.

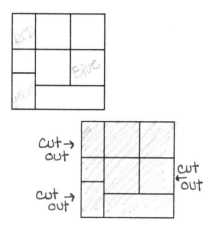

10. Trace the rectangles/squares onto the piece of color construction paper they have selected for that square.

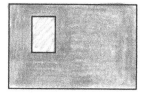

11. With a pair of scissors cut the rectangles/squares out.

12. Glue each piece of the construction paper into its designated rectangle or square (the one with its color written in pencil). Make sure that the construction paper completely fills in the rectangle/square and that it does not cover the black strips. (Note: The construction paper may have to be trimmed to ensure this.)

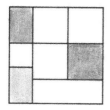

Evaluation

- Was the project done with good craftsmanship?
- Is the composition balanced?
- Do all lines end at an intersection of another line?
- Are all three primary colors used?
- Were some of the boxes left white?
- Are all lines vertical or horizontal with no use of diagonal lines?
- Does the child understand how the math concepts (parallel lines, perpendicular lines, geometric shapes and right angles) relate to the composition? (Have the children point to the parallel lines, perpendicular lines, geometric shapes and right angles.)
- Can children use art vocabulary (Balance, Emphasis, Unity, Pattern, Rhythm, Repetition, Primary Colors, Line, Shape, Realism and Nonobjective) to evaluate their own artwork? (Have the children evaluate what they like about their artwork using their learned art vocabulary.)

The Life of Monet

Oscar Claude Monet was born on November 14, 1840, in Rue Lafitte in Paris, France. In his youth he began working as a caricaturist, but began painting landscapes when he was inspired by an early mentor of his, Boudin (who was a French landscape painter).

At the age of 19, he studied at an art school in Paris, after which he spent two years serving in the military in Algiers.

In 1862, Monet entered the studio of Gleyre in Paris where he met Renior, Sisley and Bazille, fellow Impressionists.

In 1883, he settled at Giverny, about 40 miles from Paris. After experiencing extreme poverty, Monet finally began to prosper and in 1890, he was able to buy the house at Giverny. It was that same year that he concentrated on painting series of pictures of the same subject at different times of the day in different lights. Monet continued to travel a lot, but focused on his water lilies series in 1899 which became the bulk of his work. In 1914, he even built a large studio on the grounds of his house so he could work on his huge canvasses.

Many years before his death, Monet discovered that he had cataracts in both eyes; this was in 1912, two years after his wife died. Monet did not want to have surgery, because he was afraid that he vision would be changed forever. He opted for an alternative treatment which worked for a while, but eventually Monet was unable to paint in the bright outdoors that he loved so much, but he continued to paint up until his death on December 5, 1926, just four months after being diagnosed with a tumor in his lung.

Monet's Style: What is Impressionism?

Impressionism was a 19th century art movement that got its name from Claude Monet's painting, "Impression, Sunrise." Some characteristics of the Impressionist movement include visible brush strokes, an open composition (or arrangement of the visible elements in the work of art), emphasis on light and how it changed during different seasons and times of day, ordinary subject matter, illustrating movement and unusual visual angles.

Monet believed that what was most important was what the artist saw, and then how the artist transformed what he felt into paint. So that was what Monet tried to accomplish with his paintings, the feelings you get from an object or landscape and the way that the different colors mix in light.

In The Garden

In November 1890, Monet was able to buy the house in Giverny, which came complete with enough land for him to have his own gardens, water lily pond, and greenhouse. Monet wrote out daily instructions to his gardening staff for how the grounds should be planted and taken care of.

"My only virtue is to have painted directly in front of nature, while trying to render the impressions made on me by the most fleeting effects."

CLAUDE MONET

Monet loved painting outdoors in the natural daylight. His work "Women in the Garden"

(1866–1867) was painted outdoors in his own garden. The picture is about 2.5 meters high and for him to be able to paint it outside he had to dig a trench in his garden so the canvas could be raised or lowered by a pulley system to whatever height he needed. Another artist who visited him reported that Monet would not even paint the leaves in the background unless the lighting conditions were just right.

The 'Series' Paintings

In 1891, Monet began painting his 'series' paintings, beginning with 15 images of haystacks in a field. This was a turning-point for Monet, though the subject matter was simple, the thing that made these paintings impressive was the effects of lights on the haystacks themselves. So, the main focus of these paintings is the light, which shows the time of day or season. Monet said that, "Other painters paint a bridge, a house, a boat . . . I want to paint the air in which the bridge, the house, and the boat are to be found—the beauty of the air around them, and that is nothing less than the impossible." The subject matter for the different series paintings was varied: haystacks in a field, poplars, the Rouen cathedral, water lilies, the Japanese Bridge, and the banks of the River Seine.

"I know only that I do what I think best to express what I experience in front of nature . . . I allow plenty of faults to show in order to fix my sensations."

CLAUDE MONET

Bibliography

Day, Jill. *Incredible Art Department.* Princeton Online. 22 November 2008. <www.princetonol.com/groups/iad/lessons/elem/jill-monet.htm>.

Pioch, Nicolas. *Monet, Claude.* 19 September 2002. Web Museum Paris. 22 November 2008. <www.ibiblio.org/wm/paint/auth/monet Web Museum Paris>.

Tucker, Paul H., George T.M. Shackelford, and MaryAnne Stevens. *Monet in the 20th Century.* Boston: Museum of Fine Arts, 1998.

Tucker, Paul H. *Monet in the '90s: The Series Paintings.* Boston: Museum of Fine Arts, 1989.

Claude Monet. 30 November 2008. Wikimedia Foundation. 30 November 2008. <en.wikipedia.org/wiki/Claude_monet>.

Monet's Garden: Chalk/Tempera Painting

Justine Young

Time: 2–3 hours

Age: 3rd–4th grade

Goals

General Goal

- Students will learn about Claude Monet and his style of art—Impressionism (Historical & Cultural Context).
- Students will learn about color mixing, blending and different tints of colors (Connections, Relations, Applications).

Specific Goal

- Each student will create an Impressionistic landscape/garden scene in the style of Monet using white tempera paint and chalk (Creative Expression).
- Students will display good craftsmanship (Creative Expression).

Motivation

Begin the class by reading "Smart about Art: Claude Monet, Sunshine and Water Lilies," by Steven Packard and True Kelley. Have some water lilies in a bowl (if not able, then just flowers in a vase); turn the lights out (as long as there are windows in the room), then turn a lamp or flashlight, then turn on all the lights. Ask the students to describe how different the flowers looked in the different lights. How did the shadows look? Did the colors look different even though they were really the same?

Next, pass out the Monet newsletters so the students can look over them while you are talking. Have several large posters/pictures of

Claude Monet's artwork and tell the children about them—emphasize Monet's use of light in his paintings to illustrate time of day or season. Also stress how important it was for Monet to paint outdoors. Tell the students about Monet's style, Impressionism, and what that meant. Then tell the students that they are going to make their own Impressionistic painting in Monet's style.

Vocabulary

impressionism
landscape
style

Materials

1. 1 piece of textured paper (like watercolor or construction paper), at least 8½ × 11
2. 1 #2 pencil, preferably soft lead (B)
3. colored chalk
4. white tempera paint
5. 1 paintbrush
6. 1 paper plate and water cup

Procedure

1. On the paper, lightly draw a garden landscape with a pencil or white chalk.

2. Paint an area of the paper about the size of your fist with the white tempera paint.

3. Dip the colored chalk into the wet paint and begin to color in the picture, blend the different colors together. If the paint dries then paint on some more tempera paint.

4. Continue until finished; to achieve desired effect, it may be necessary to do paint another layer of white tempera paint on top of the finished drawing.

Evaluation

- Is the entire paper covered with an Impressionistic style painting depicting some kind of garden or landscape?
- Did the student use different colors and blend them together?
- Did the student display good craftsmanship?

Danielle LaPoint

Wyland's Life

He was born Robert Wyland in Detroit, Michigan, in 1956. He is the second oldest of four brothers. His father moved out when he was 4, leaving his mother to support the family. He was always mesmerized by "The Undersea World of Jacques Cousteau," which seemed odd to him because he lived nowhere near the ocean. He has always felt drawn to the ocean and its creatures.

He believes that everything happens for a reason. When he was in the 1st grade, his teacher caught him drawing in the middle of class. However, she didn't scold him. After class, she asked him about his art, she encouraged him and she told him something that always stayed with him. She said, "You could be a great artist." He feels like this gesture is what set the course of his life.

In 1971, when Wyland was just 14 years old, he and his family headed to Los Angeles to visit his aunt. His aunt decided to take him to the beach one day and drove him to Laguna Beach. He said he remembers running down into the ocean, even though it was freezing cold. He swam out and saw what he called "these huge creatures" not more than 100 yards away. They turned out to be gray whales. He watched them as they swam down the coast and out of sight. He thought to himself, "What are the chances?" He realized he had seen something he was meant to see. Because of all the whale-watching boats, the whales had stopped coming so close to the shore.

When he was 16, his mother decided he needed to see what the real world was all about. She drove him to the local day worker's office and dropped him off, expecting him to get a job as a factory worker. Three days later, he had been hired and fired three times. He wasn't trying to get fired; it was just not for him. He felt like a failure, and he was only 16. He did learn through the experience what he didn't want to do: a 9–5 job. He learned to appreciate his talents and knew he had to develop them. After that, he bore down tirelessly on his artwork and hasn't quit yet.

He moved to Laguna when he was 19, and lived off Hansen's soda and Snickers bars that he cut into three pieces—one for breakfast, lunch and dinner. He always seemed to sell a painting the day before his rent was due.

In 1980, he moved to Maui and started diving with the whales in order to paint them better. Then, in 1981, 10 years after he originally saw the whales in Laguna Beach, he painted his first mural—in no other place than Laguna Beach. He felt it was something he needed to do, for the ocean and the whales.

Greenpeace even helped him find the location. As soon as his first wall was finished, he vowed to create 100 more life-size murals around the world within the next 25 years. Everyone would be free, although expensive for him. He used profits from his artwork and galleries, as well as donations and sponsorships to help fund the program.

Wyland's Work

He is known simply as Wyland and is best known for his huge, life-sized murals of whales and other sea creatures, known as his "Whaling Walls." He is considered an environmental marine artist. He used spray guns to paint these huge pieces of art. With his personal passion for the oceans and marine life, he has created a foundation, The Wyland Foundation, to help with his programs. He also sells artwork online and in many galleries. He is a sought artist, and has been dubbed the "Marine Michelangelo." He was also named the official artist of the 2008 United States Olympic Team.

His first whaling wall was completed in 1981, in Laguna Beach, and his 100th was completed in 2008, in Beijing before the Olympics. He also completed one in his hometown of Detroit. He feels the whaling walls offer help raising consciousness about the need to save the oceans. He has also created programs like the Wyland Ocean Challenge that go out to cities around the world and offer training, school curriculums and cleanup. He says, "We talk about litter, we talk about pollution, we educate and we clean up." His credo is, "Education, then action." He believes that the education begins with children, so he focuses on the young. He feels that it is too late for his generation to change, and they did bad. He has had a tremendous impact on raising environmental awareness, and has been known to accomplish what he sets out to do. His goal is to protect the environment and water for future generations, and he wants to be someone who has actually contributed.

References

http://www.wyland.com/
http://www.wylandfoundation.org/
http://www.wylandgalleries.com/
http://en.wikipedia.org/wiki/Wyland
Yow, J. *Wyland: 25 Years at Sea.* Kansas City: Andrews McMeel Publishing, LLC., 2006.

"I first started painting whales and dolphins because I wanted to show their grace and beauty and maybe do something to help save them. I've personally grown to see a much larger picture, to save the whales is great . . . but if we cant save the oceans, we're not going to be able to save the whales and I'm driven by a dream that yet unborn children will be able to see a great whale swimming free."

—ROBERT WYLAND

Wyland was born in 1956 in Detroit. Even at a very early age, he was drawn to the ocean. And he maintains to this day that he should have been born instead on the West Coast, closer to the whales and other marine life he has come to love so well. "I was born under a water sign, a Cancer," he explains, almost as if that says it all. "The ocean is a very important part of my life, and I actually feel more comfortable in the water than out. I've always enjoyed the experience of water, whether its a stream, a lake or an ocean." As a small child, however, Wyland had to wait years before he could even step into a body of water. Born with a severe clubfoot, he underwent 11 major surgeries before the age of seven, and he was continuously hobbled by a corrective cast that prevented his swimming. Darlene Wyland became the single mother of four boys when Wyland was just four years of age. She and Wyland's father Bob divorced at that time. Wyland decided early on to be an artist and, with the support of his mom, he painted in the basement to relax after sports and schoolwork.

The Sawdust Festival is truly where Wyland's works began to sell. It was at this festival, each summer in Laguna Beach, that only local residents such as Wyland are able to display their artworks in booths along with their peers, that Wyland learned about the business of art. Wyland's idea for painting whales on the side of buildings developed quite naturally from the difficulty he was having in portraying the mammoth creatures on small canvases. In 1978, his desire to paint whales life size led him up and down the pacific coast highway from San Diego to San Francisco until he finally found the "perfect wall" in Laguna Beach. When Wyland started painting whales and dolphins in the early 1970s, the term "environmental artist" didn't exist. The whale, by virtue of its being hunted to near extinction, had become an international symbol for while-life preservation. But to Wyland, these magnificent leviathans represented even more than that—they were the icons for an entire environmental consciousness, symbols for saving the earth's oceans and everything that lived beneath them. Eventually, society began to be more aware of the environment and endangered marine animals—the result being Wyland's work began to sell. He found that the more he could tell stories in his paintings, the more impact they seemed to have.

Watercolor is the perfect medium for marine life art. Wyland believes, "What could be more natural than to pain the amazing life in the sea than in watercolor? For me, and most artists, it is the most challenging medium of all." The watercolor technique that Wyland refers to as underwatercolor was discovered while the artist was painting a mother dolphin and her calf. Wyland further explains, "having applied too much water to the painting, I was forced to pick up the entire sheet of 1,160 pound arches paper and allow the excess paint to spill off the edge. "This early mishap turned into my trademark for original watercolor paintings." When asked about his sculpture works, Wyland expresses, "I have always felt the urge to sculpt. Even in painting, I sculpt with a brush. My subjects screen for the third dimension. And while I majored in sculpture in college, it has only been in the last few years that I could afford the time to start sculpting again. I am now in the process of going back and sculpting some of my earlier paintings. I believe the next step for me will be to sculpt my subjects in their true life size. This powerful medium allows me to create my favorite subjects in the infinite realism of bronze."

The Whaling Walls evolved out of the difficulty Wyland was having painting the great whales on small canvases. He needed larger canvases so he looked at the sides of buildings to capture the true size and majesty of these huge marine mammals. Wyland concedes, "I was inspired by Jacques Cousteau in the early 1970s and the efforts of Greenpeace. I started diving into libraries to learn more about cetaceans and began drawing and painting them on many canvases. I soon realized if I really wanted to learn about these animals and share their beauty with the public I would have to paint them life-size in their natural environment." May 3, 1992, Wyland completed painting the largest mural in the world at the Long Beach Convention Center on the Long Beach Arena. Entitled "Planet Ocean," it was completed in only 6 weeks and required 7,000 gallons of paint. Featuring marine life indigenous to Southern California, the finished mural included a pod of grey whales, orca whales, blue whales, pilot whales, pacific bottlenose dolphins, california sea lions, sharks, garibaldi and a variety of other fish. The mural is over ten stories high and 1,225 feet in diameter (almost 3 acres). On Monday, May 4, 1992, the Guinness World Book of Records certified Wyland's mural as the largest ever created. In the past few years the artist has set out on a series of ocean mural tours. In 1993 he completed 17 murals in 17 cities in 17 weeks from Portland, Maine, to Key West, Florida, on an East coast Tour. In

1994, he completed another incredible tour but of the West Coast painting 13 murals in 8 cities in 8 weeks from Alaska to Mexico City. And once again, in 1997, Wyland and his team painted 7 murals in 7 cities in 7 weeks in and around the Great Lakes followed by a mural at the invitation of the Royal Ontario Museum that now hangs in its permanent collection. When asked how he paints and creates on such a large scale, Wyland explained, "I am often asked if I use grids or preliminary drawings to help me paint a Whaling Wall. I do have a grid, but its in my mind. I work from the mind's eye. I'm painting pictures in my mind's eye that will later be reflected in my art. I believe I have an 'out-of-body experience.' While my physical body is up on the scaffolding with the spray gun, my mind's eye is far away, down on the ground viewing the wall from a distance."

In 1978, Wyland opened his first Studio Gallery in the famed art colony of Laguna Beach, California. At that time, the starving artist was the only employee selling his original paintings directly to his collectors. Shortly thereafter, Wyland opened a second gallery location in Laguna Beach on the very well trafficked Pacific Coast Highway. Continuing in the growth of his entrepreneurial spirit, the artist and his younger brother Bill opened the first Wyland Galleries in Hawaii located on the North Shore of Oahu. In a few short years, the brothers had opened 14 world class fine art galleries on Oahu, Maui and the Big Island. Additionally, Wyland expanded his California locations to include a beautiful gallery in San Francisco at the famous Pier 39 and in San Diego in Seaport Village on the harbor. Today, Wyland Galleries are located throughout the United States and showcase works by Wyland and many of the galleries' artists. Wyland Galleries features original oil paintings, watercolors, sculpture, limited edition prints and other collectibles by the world-renowned artist.

When asked about his life-size legacies he's created around the world, Wyland expresses, "My dream since I was very young was to make my mark on society—I believe all artists want to leave their work for future generations to study and learn. I feel my art reflects our environmentally conscious times, and I hope the whaling walls will help future generations to understand the importance of preserving our ecosystem. I am planning to complete a series of life size canvases and sculpture depicting all the great whales and dolphins of the world and other marine life as well. It is my hope that this art will tour all of the great museums of the world and have an impact on generations to come—long after I am gone."

Wyland has enjoyed publishing a series of limited edition prints over the years. After completing the original painting in oil, watercolor or other medium, he decides what printing method would create the best possible reproduction of the original piece. Some images are created in several different print mediums and sizes. Wyland's limited editions have been enthusiastically collected throughout the United States and 40 countries around the world. Today, he is recognized as one of the the most popular and collected artists of our time. His limited edition fine art can be reproduced using processes such as cibachrome, serigraph, offset lithograph, supergloss, mixed media, giclee and repligraph.

Wyland majored in sculpture at the Center for Creative Studies in Detroit under the tutelage of master sculptor Jay Holland. The artist studies the human form and sculpted from live models focusing on anatomy. Wyland has spent many years diving alongside whales, dolphins, turtles, manatees, manta rays and other fantastic sea creatures that he later reflects in his sculptures. These experiences and his attention to detail distinguish him as the premier marine life sculptor today. As in Wyland's paintings, the eyes are the focal point of each and every sculpture. His atten-

tion to detail, dynamic motion and use of space are all the signature of this marine Michelangelo. Wyland creates fine art sculptures in bronze, mixed media, acrylic and lucite.

"A month doesn't pass when I don't get a letter telling me that one of my whaling walls has inspired someone to investigate and become active in the environmental movement. Remember—One person can make a difference."
—ROBERT WYLAND

What does the Wyland Foundation do?

Founded in 1993 by Wyland.

> Mission: To inspire people to care more about our oceans and life within them and to encourage people to become involved in ocean conservation.

> Vision: To promote, respect and protect our precious ocean resources through life-size, public art, education and awareness.

> Theme: One person can make a difference.

What is the Ocean Challenge?

The ocean challenge is an educational curriculum program designed to take students on an epic ocean journey into the underwater world of discovery. The ocean challenge is a unique educational experience that bridges the worlds of science and art. The primary objective of the challenge program is to educate students about the waters of the world and the life within them, then for the students to create a representation of their newfound knowledge through the arts. Learning through creativity is just another way to learn. Through school, parent, teacher and student participation, the Wyland Foundation has been able and will continue to inspire an entire generation to become more aware and involved in ocean conservation. This is a global educational program.

References

Foster, W., & Wyland, R. *Learn to draw and paint with wyland: a complete kit for beginning artists.* BK&Acces ed. : Walter Foster, 2002.

Martinez, A. Wyland brings whaling wall to san diego. *San Diego Earth Times.* Retrieved Nov 16, 2004, from http://www.sdearthtimes.com/et0894/et0894s6.html.

Wyland, R. *The undersea world of wyland.* Time-LifeBooks, 1998.

Wyland, R. *Wyland ocean wisdom.* Health Communications, 2000.

Wyland, R. Wyland marine artist, ocean art, whales and dolphins. Retrieved Nov 16, 2004, from Wyland Web site: http://www.wyland.com/wyland2.html.

Wyland's Pillow Fish (aka 3-D Marine Animals)

Danielle LaPoint

Time: 2 hours (Two 1-hour blocks)   Age: 2nd–5th grade

Goals

General Goals

- The children will learn about the life and style of the environmental marine artist Wyland (Historical and Cultural Context).
- The children will look at multiple works by the artist Wyland (Artistic perception).
- The children will learn about the ocean and different types of marine animals and their habitats (Connections, Relations and Applications).

Specific Goals (Creative Expression)

- Each child will draw a large marine animal or fish on a large piece of butcher paper with pencil.
- Each child will tape another piece of butcher paper onto the back of the drawing, and then cut out the drawing, making sure to cut through both pieces of paper to make two identical sides.
- Each child will then color both sides of the marine animal with crayons, colored pencils, markers, or tempura paint, while using shading techniques to make the animal appear 3-D.
- Each child will then staple the sides together, leaving a small opening to stuff the animal with paper. Then, the child will staple the animal closed.
- Each child will then attach string to the animal in order to hang it from the ceiling to create an "underwater" habitat.

Motivation

The teacher can teach the children about the ocean and its animals by reading books on marine life. She can also read the book on Wyland and his artwork. The teacher could also show pictures of Wyland's artwork and Whaling Walls. Younger kids would enjoy reading *Way Down Deep in the Deep Blue Sea*, by Jan Peck, which would introduce them to different types of marine life.

Vocabulary

marine	shading	habitat
conservation	3-D	
environmentally-friendly	Wyland	

Materials (per child)

- butcher paper (cut into 24" pieces)
- pencil
- tempura paints, crayons, colored pencils or markers of various colors
- scissors
- stapler and staples
- string
- tape
- newspaper, scratch paper or shredded paper

Procedure

1. Start by giving the child pictures of marine animals for reference. Then, allow them to draw the marine animal of their choice on the butcher paper. Encourage them to use the whole paper to make it big.

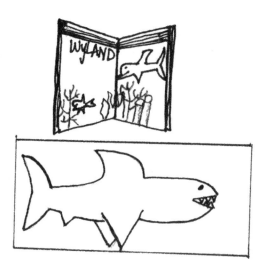

2. Place another piece of butcher paper under the first piece, while trying to line up the edges.

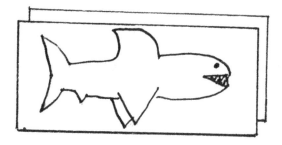

3. Use four small pieces of tape to tape the sides of the two Pieces of butcher paper together so they don't slide.

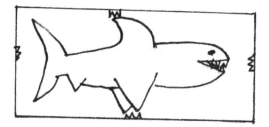

4. Next, cut out the marine animal, making sure to cut through both pieces of paper, to make two identical pieces.

5. Next, using the crayons, markers, pencils or paint, decorate both sides of the marine animal. Both sides should match, as it will be one animal. Also, use shading techniques to make the animal look more 3-D.

6. Put the two decorated sides of the animal back together, so the colored sides face outward.

7. Staple the outsides of the two pieces together, along the outside edge. Make sure to leave an area open for stuffing.

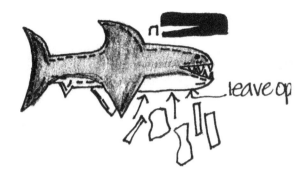

8. Fill the entire inside of the animal with torn newspaper or shredded paper.
9. Staple the last opening closed.

10. Lastly, attach a piece of string to the top of the animal for hanging.
11. Now all the animals can be hung from the classroom ceiling to make an "underwater" habitat.

Evaluation

- Did each child make a marine animal pillow?
- Do both sides of the animal look identical?
- Did the child decorate and color the animal?
- Is the animal filled with paper to look 3-D?
- Does the animal have string attached so it can be hung?
- Did the child use good craftsmanship?

Paul Gauguin

(June 7, 1848–May 8, 1903)

Eugene Henri Paul Gauguin was one of the leading Post-Impressionist artists. His artwork was focused on bold colors and the subject matter of his artwork combined people, objects, and landscapes in unique and original ways. He was most well known as a painter, but also created prints, wood cuts, ceramics, sculpture, as well as writing.

Born in Paris, Gauguin's family soon was forced to move to Peru as a result of his father's political activities. Paul's father died on the ship on the way to Peru; his mother was forced to move in with her great uncle in Lima. Paul joined the French Merchant navy at the age of seventeen; upon the death of his mother. Paul settled down and lived with his wealthy guardian who was to introduce Paul to the world of art. Paul later became a stock broker, and was able to buy work by Monet, Pissaro, and Renoir. He was married and had five children. At this time he began painting as a hobby. Approximately ten years later, the bank where he was working failed. Gauguin decided to move to an artists' colony and soon developed his own style of painting.

Paul Gauguin left France and moved to Panama where he worked for the Panama Canal Company, but was fired two weeks later. He moved on to Martinique and continued on with his painting. At this point in his life, he decided to move back to France and moved in with Vincent Van Gogh. This was to be a traumatic time for both artists, yet proved to motivate Paul to be a prolific painter. Being deeply depressed, Gauguin left his family and moved to the South Pacific Islands—away from the stresses of day to day living. He lived in Tahiti periodically from 1891 until his death. His work evolved to reflect the primitive forms and vivid colors of the local area. His paintings depicting the Polynesian women are considered true masterpieces of the Post-Impressionist era—several which were of the young girls that he took on as *wives*. Gauguin died from a heart attack brought on by drug use and poor living conditions.

# The Tropical Rain Forest

Inspired by the Art of Paul Gauguin
by Melanie Vogel

Overview

In this lesson the students will learn about the art of Impressionist artist, Paul Gauguin, and create a rainforest scene using permanent marker and soft pastel.

Materials

- pencils and erasers
- white drawing paper (9" × 12" or larger)
- black Sharpie marker
- wide, chisel point (*Marks-a-lot* or similar brand) black permanent marker
- soft pastel sets
- visuals of Paul Gauguin's art, specifically Tahitian paintings appropriate for children's viewing
- visuals of tropical rain forest plants and animals
- newsprint to cover working surface
- artist's fixative or aerosol hair spray

Objectives

What students will learn:

- about the life and work of artist Paul Gauguin
- about the structure and life found in the tropical rain forests of the world
- about line, shape, space, value, emphasis and pattern
- to blend soft (chalk) pastels

Vocabulary

tropical rain forest: warm forests which are located near the equator around the world

temperate rain forest: cool forests of conifers where moisture is high

understory, canopy, emergent forest layers: rain forest structure: middle layer, treetops and new growth

emphasis (element of art): the subject or focal point within a work of art

value (element of art): the lightness or darkness of a color

Background/Motivation

Introduce the life and work of artist, sailor, stockbroker and world traveler, Paul Gauguin (1848–1903). Focus on the paintings of his life among the Tahitian people. You will need to be selective in your choice of visuals for the elementary student. Point out and discuss the plants and animals of the tropical environment where he lived. Show maps where the world's tropical rainforests are found and describe the type of flora and fauna found there. This can be easily correlated to a unit on rain forest habitat. Provide pictures of tropical rain forest animals from different countries that the student can use for inspiration.

Procedure

Distribute rain forest animal pictures. Have students choose one animal as the emphasis in their drawing. They need to draw (in pencil)

the animal large and suggest an asymmetrical composition with the animal extending beyond the visual space of the paper. Next draw other animals, insects and plants behind the subject. Suggest exotic leaves and flowers—fill the background and foreground with foliage and create depth by overlapping images. Next outline all pencil using both permanent markers. Make bold wide lines in some areas and thinner lines for detail. Variety in line width adds visual interest to the drawing. Next add the color using the chalk pastels. Color lightly and blend with the index finger. Shake accumulated dust onto table covering. Encourage blending one color to another and light to dark for value. Color all parts of the drawing. Spray lightly and evenly with aerosol hairspray or artist's fixative to set the pastel (some pastel will still rub off).

Assessment

Have students evaluate their drawing to the procedure requirements: Is my animal the emphasis and did I draw it large enough that my eyes see it before anything else in the drawing? Did I create value and blend and mix colors? Did I overlap the images to create a sense of depth? What is the mood, temperature and action in the drawing?

Integration (Applications/ Connections)

This project could correlate to literature and science as it relates to the study of the rain forest. Play rain forest sounds as children are drawing. Take a natural history museum field trip and focus on the rain forest environs of the world. Research endangered plants and animals of these regions. Learn about medicines, foods and products we receive from rain forest plants. Learn about the life of human rain forest inhabitants. Hawaii, our 50th state, has tropical rain forest. Research plant and animal life there.

Self Portrait

Using Warm and Cool Colors for Light and Shadow
by Melanie Vogel

Overview

In this lesson, students will view a variety of famous artist self-portraits and compare artistic styles. Students will learn about facial structure, facial features and proportions and then draw their self-portrait. They will learn about light and shadow and be able to use warm colors in place of the light or highlighted areas of the face and cool colors in the shadow areas of the face within their drawing.

Materials

- 9 × 12 or larger black or brown construction paper
- soft (chalk) pastels
- mirrors (one for each student)
- newsprint to cover desk surface
- prints or reproductions of famous artist self-portraits
- anatomical drawing or 3-D head for discussion of facial features, structure and proportion.
- color wheel

Objectives

Students will become familiar with different styles in self-portraiture in work by famous artists. Students will understand the structure of the human face, basic proportions of facial features and become keen observers of detail in their own face. Students will learn the warm and cool colors and complimentary colors on the color wheel. Students will learn blending in the use of soft (chalk) pastels.

Vocabulary

anatomical

blend

complimentary color (colors opposite one another on the color wheel)

cool colors (blue, green, violet)

facial features

portrait

proportion

warm colors (red, orange, yellow)

Motivation (into)

Show a variety of famous artist self-portraits. Discuss the use of color, light, shadow and technique. Point out each artist's unique style. Look closely at artist's choice of colors in the highlighted and shaded areas of the face. Have students point out what colors they see. Look at color relationships on the color wheel. Identify the warms and cools. Explain how complimentary colors are opposite on the color wheel and that when used together in a work of art, they enhance one another. Refer to famous artist portraits and see where artists have used complimentary colors. Next, demonstrate blending chalk pastels: overlay two warm colors for example and then blend with fingertip until smooth. Remind students that complimentary colors will enhance each other when used in adjacent areas. They will *mix* to a neutral gray brown when blended! Talk about the shape of the head and how eyes are approximately ½ the distance between the top of the head and the chin. The nose is approximately ½ the distance between the eyes and chin, and the mouth another ½ distance. Observe that the ears line up with eyebrow area and space above upper lip when viewed from the front. The distance between the eyes is about the same width as one eye. Have students look in the mirror and make observations about their own face. Have them also observe where they see light and where they see shadow on their face. Explain that they will use warm colors for the lighter areas and cool colors for the parts of their face in shadow.

Procedure

Background information and motivation is important for success in this project. Have students observe their face in the mirror. Draw outline of head (oval shape) first with a light color of chalk pastel. Next draw in facial features. Start blending in warm colors in areas of the face where they see more light. Blend in cool colors in shaded areas. Draw in details with darker colors. Hair should be drawn last over the head. Remind them to look at the details of their face carefully and often. The students get a likeness of themselves fairly well, even when they don't think so. Background color should compliment the hair color, not camouflage it. Remind them to have fun, be observant and not to worry if the portrait isn't a real likeness. It is important for them to have the experience of observation, blending color, looking for areas of different value (lightness and darkness), etc., and for drawing what they see!

Assessment

Ask the students how their portrait compares to other artist's work in terms of color, style, etc. Ask them what they like about their work. Ask them what they would do differently next time. Did they use warm colors in the lighter areas of their face and cool colors in the shadows? Did they blend the colors? Is the background complimentary to the hair and skin tones?

Extension/Integration

Portraits can be done in a variety of mediums. Young children can talk about their faces and the shapes they see in the features. Remember to compliment, not criticize. If the child asks for advice on a shape (nose, for example) draw on another paper but never on theirs! This project can be extended to mask designs in paper, paper mache, clay, etc., for three-dimensional design. Have students illustrate reports on famous people by drawing their portrait. Investigate artists who have painted the presidential portraits or the governors of the state. Portraits can be done at different times of the school year. Have students compare their own drawings.

Pinch Pot Lesson Plan

Lesson Introduction

Pinch pots were the first form of pottery there ever was; many theories of discovery and creation surround these crude little artifacts dating from the Neolithic period 10,000–3,000 BC. Because of their simplistic structure as well as the spontaneous and resourceful use of natural clay materials, it is theorized that nomadic hunters and gatherers were the first creators of these crude yet functional vessels, possibly being inspired by a simple desire to heat food and/or eat more of it with less waste in the cooking process. The earliest known functional pottery artifacts are from about 5,000 BC. Serendipitously, these little crude bowls also seemed to have coincided with the discovery of firing clay, which many believe was a happy coincidence occurring when man attempted to cook the food inside the vessel. This crude firing process made the clay hard and permanent or "fired." Within the next couple of hundred years, we start to see large changes in the societal organization of these nomadic hunter and gatherers; many bands will begin to settle in what is called the fertile crescent—what we recognize as ancient Mesopotamia—and start to make small farms. The pinch pot and its ability to provide functional food and water containers for the hunters and gatherers as well as the early farming socialites; this is suggested to have played a pivotal role in the advancement of today's civilized world. Later ceramic storage vessels would provide the means for secure storage and the ability to pack goods for shipping allowing for trade with other communities when there was a surplus. Advancements in vessel creation began to take into consideration form and function; coil building and the development of the potter's wheel further allowed "craftsmen" to provide a useful way

tool for their now agrarian society. The pinch method quickly went by the wayside for the more successful and refined advancements in pottery creation ensuring that pottery became one of the earliest trade industries with skilled craftsmen. These craftsmen would later become part of the craft guilds with a skilled hierarchy of labor division: master potter, workshop master, journeyman worker, and apprentice or trainee. Many workshops were family owned and trade secrets were passed from one generation to the next.

Presently the pinch pot still survives. Contemporary ceramic artists such as Paulus Berensohn, Mary Rogers and Jane Perryman still utilize the same thumb and finger pinching techniques to make these humble little pots yet elevating them into an appreciated art form. With simple functionality, delicate thinness that defies the physical limitation of a clay and the aesthetic pleasure of a vessel formed as pure sculpture, these artistic pots are no longer disposable castoffs for the next hunter and gatherer to use, but highly regarded works of art selling from $200–$2,000 for a single pot.

Objectives and Standards

Artistic Perception

Students will view historical examples of Neolithic pottery.

- Students will examine a variety of actual artist-made pinch pot examples.
- Students will become aware of Paulus Berensohn's *10 tools* and how to use their alligator pinching fingers with their thumb on the inside only.

Creative Expression

Students will create a pinch pot using the traditional pinching method.

- Students will decorate their pot with a textural impressed pattern. (Drawing scenes on pots did not come until much later in the history of man.)

Historical and Cultural Context

Students will become aware of the role that the pinch pot played in the development of mankind's civilization.

- Students will learn the difference between the Paleolithic (Old Stone Age/stone tools) and Neolithic (New Stone Age/use of clay along with stone) periods.
- Students will view where the Fertile Crescent is on a map of the world and learn why it is referred to as the *cradle of civilization.*

Aesthetic Valuing

Students will discuss the differences between ancient potters and contemporary potters and the differences of why they would make pinch pots.

- Students will discuss their use of texture and the variety of tools they used to create the variety of patterns they made.
- Students will discuss the technical qualities of their pot: the wall thinness-thickness, lip smoothness, bottom flatness, as well as whether each piece contains ornate or simplistic patterns.
- Students will discuss the difference between functional and nonfunctional pottery and what role each plays in our society.

Integration
Social Studies

Students will be introduced to the idea of discovery and its importance. For example, how the discovery of firing the clay would lead to the permanence of a piece.

Students will learn the major differences between hunting/gathering societies and agrarian societies; students will also be introduced to modern day versions of these societies.

Language Arts

Students will read excerpts from Ling Po's *A Single Shard.*

Math

Students will be introduced to ceramic math. For example, if clay is measured in tons and sold in 25 lb chubs, how many chubs in a ton?

Science

Students will be introduced to the clay cycle and how clay is created through the erosion process. They will also be introduced to what geographic areas are more clay rich and why.

Materials

25 lbs of clay will be enough for 25–30 students

(A small ball of clay is better for pinch pots)

wooden pencils for textural pattern making tools and/or other impressing tools—nothing fancy though. Think Neolithic—maybe sticks?

newspaper to cover desk

Note—do not add water or allow students to smooth surface with water, which will weaken the pots. Cracking is part of the prehistoric look.

Procedure

1. Roll clay between hands into a ball.

2. Place ball in left hand. Press thumb from right hand into the center. When your left hand feels the pressure of the right thumb, stop and that will be the bottom of your pot.

3. Take your thumb out of the ball and practice using your alligator fingers—keeping all your fingers together clamp them shut against your thumb. *Be sure to keep all your fingers together. Put your thumb back inside the ball all the way to the bottom and evenly pinch the sides of the wall of your pot. Gently rotate and continue pinching until you get the desired thickness of your walls. Your pot should have grown from the original ball size and you should now have a small pot that fits neatly inside your hand.

4. Stop when the walls start to feel as though they could collapse. Impress your textural pattern in the walls being sure to go completely around.

5. Take time to smooth out the lip, or rim, of the pot. This will be an important part of the structural integrity of the pot.

Evaluation

1. Did students successfully utilize the traditional pinching method?

2. Did the student create an ornate textural pattern or a simple textural pattern?

3. Did the student create a lip (the top of the pot)? Did they smooth it or leave it rough?

4. Did the student create a functional or a sculptural pot? Can they state the difference?

5. Did the students use good craftsmanship? Was the pot structurally sound?

A note about firing and materials can be obtained from Aardvark Clay and Supplies. They have a fantastic online catalogue at http://www.aardvarkclay.com (714-541-4157); 1400 E. Pomona St., Santa Ana, CA, 92705.

Laguna Clay Co., www.lagunaclay.com (612-330-0631); 14400 Lomitas Ave., Industry, CA 91746

Muddy's Studio, http://www.muddysstudio.com (714-641-4077); 2610 S. Halladay, Santa Ana, CA 92705.

Reptile Ceramic Sculptures— What Is a Reptile?

A **reptile** is a creature that is cold blooded and breathes air; they lay eggs. Reptiles have skin that is covered with patterned scales, which are specific to their environment and/ or part of their camouflage. There are 6,800 reptile species spread around the entire globe, but being that reptiles are cold blooded there are no reptiles in the arctic regions of the world, but are found in areas that do freeze forcing them to hibernate during the winter. The Rocky Mountain Rattler is a perfect example of a North American snake (reptile) that lives in a climate that freezes during the winter.

Reptile classifications consist of the snakes, lizards, alligators, crocodiles and tortoises. Dinosaurs are extinct reptiles.

Sculpture pre-dates pottery in creation in the timeline of mankind. The earliest known sculptures are from the Paleolithic period dated from about 30,000–10,000 BC and were found in the now Northern European Continent. Some of the eeriest sculptural representations of reptiles were found in Egypt in 2,500 BC. Ancient bronze sculptures from Africa in 500 BC from the Nook culture and by the Australian Aborigines around the same time. These ancient artists utilized basic yet effective decorative elements to create these animal effigies; many of them arranged the sculptures in life-like poses.

Vocabulary

Pattern—any shape or design repeated over and over

Texture—a surface that we can feel (actual)

Or a picture of a surface (implied)

Camouflage—to hide or disguise by changing appearance. Blending in with the surroundings, the **shapes** and **color** of the **patterned** scales are the camouflage of a reptile.

Lesson Objectives

Artistic Perception—Students will view images from the Nook culture in Africa (alligator), Aboriginal shield (cordial that ate a turtle) and Artist created snake, lizard, tortoise and dinosaur sculptures. Students will become aware from the difference between actual and implied texture as well as how to create a textural pattern.

Creative Expression—Students will create a reptile sculpture that will imply some kind of movement, which will be achieved through arrangement choices. Students will create a textural pattern as well as represent physical features, i.e., scales pits, fangs, or shell on their piece.

Historical/Cultural Context—Students will become aware of the cultural role reptiles and humans have had with one another in these ancient cultures i.e. respect, spirituality, fear, mythology, medicine, food and clothing that reptiles provided. Students will compare and contrast that with modern knowledge of reptiles.

Aesthetic Valuing—Students will visually compare and contrast their sculpture with that of the ancient Nook people, the ancient aboriginal people, Mayan expressions of the serpent. Students will discuss the sense of movement that their sculpture expressed by its arrangement and compare and contrast that with the ancient sculptures.

Integration—Students will become aware of reptile physical characteristics, geographic regions, the differences between reptiles, mammals, and amphibians. Students will discuss what is extinction and why the dinosaurs became extinct. Students will become aware that humans and dinosaurs were not on the earth at the same period of time and that eons separated their time on the earth and that is why we only are left with their fossil remains.

Procedure

1. Between your hands (not on the table) squeeze and roll a thick coil. This is for the body, unless you're making a tortoise.

2. Bend it into a shape. The position of the head suggests the mood of the piece; for example, a coiled snake with the head down means sleeping. S-shape means moving forward, coiled with head raised is striking. Tortoises have angular heads and take large strides with their legs. Alligators and crocodiles can be laying still, but their features will aid with creating a mood— s-shaped tails mean moving, open mouths mean striking. These sculptures of dinosaurs must portray movement and their heads should have an angular placement.

3. Now using your wooden pencil start to impress details for the physical features i.e., eyes, pits, fangs, shells, scales. Be sure textural patterns are reticulated. (Overlapping like shingles.)

4. Put vent holes or hollow out if thick so that the piece will fire correctly.

Material list—25 lbs of clay for 25–30 students
Wooden pencils for making texture and scales
Newspaper for tables

Evaluation

Did students create a sense of movement with the arrangement of their sculpture?

Did students create a textural pattern to represent their reptile species?

Did students include anatomically correct physical features?

Can students name the species included in the reptile family?

Did the students use good craftsmanship and take pride in their work?

Lesson Extension

Visit the American Museum of Ceramic Art (http://www.amoca.org), 919-865-3146. Open: Wednesday through Sunday, 12 p.m.– 5 p.m. and second Saturday of the month from 12 p.m.–9 p.m. Cost: Adults—$5, Students & Seniors—$4, Children under 12— Free. Make advance arrangements for groups larger than 10 and docent-lead tours. There are great teacher resources on their website. Go to "About AMOCA" on the toolbar and select the collections. Feast your eyes. Then go to "Education, Events and Exhibitions" to see what fits your class's needs. But this amazing resource is right here in Southern California, 399 N. Carey Ave., Pomona, CA, 91767.

by Jennifer Oh

I will be teaching my students about the difference between warm and cool colors. I am going to incorporate science into my art lesson and talk about color changing of the leaves according to the seasons. First, I will talk about the primary and secondary colors. Primary colors are red, yellow, and blue, and they cannot be mixed but are found only in their pure form. Secondary colors are made when mixing two primary colors. For example, if I mix red and blue, I would get purple. Purple and the other colors made by mixing red and yellow, or yellow and blue, would be known as secondary colors. Then, I will ask them how to group the colors differently; according to how the colors make them feel. As the students are thinking of their response, I will introduce warm and cool colors. Warm and cool colors are also tied into the analogous color family. Analogous colors are the colors that are next to each other on the color wheel, and they complement the neighboring colors. I will also address monochromatic colors; also known as tints and shades. I will tell them about the characteristics of warm and cool colors, using the color wheel as my reference, and they will have a more clear idea of which color goes into which group. Red, yellow, and orange are considered warm colors because of the psychological and physiological response they generally evoke; and blue, green, and purple are considered cool colors. The same but opposite response is usually evoked by the cool color family. The students and I can make a list of different objects in nature that contain the colors we are going to talk about.

In understanding color theory and season, I will now introduce the leaf families that will be our project subject matter. Leaves are part of a plant and are also in charge of making food for the plant; this is also known as photosynthesis. Plants use carbon dioxide and water to make oxygen and sugar. Plants use glucose as food for energy and to grow. A chemical called chlorophyll helps make photosynthesis happen. Chlorophyll is what gives plants their green color. As summer ends and autumn comes, the days get shorter and shorter, and plants are less exposed to sunlight. During winter, there is also less water for the plants to take in. With less supply to continue photosynthesis, the plants know that it is time for them to prepare for winter. They begin to use the stored food they saved during the summer and shut down the food-making factories. When the food is not made, green chlorophyll disappears from the leaves. As the green fades away, red, yellow, and orange that was covered by the bright green starts to appear on the leaves. The bright reds and oranges we see in leaves are made mostly in the fall. In some trees, like maples, glucose is trapped in the leaves after photosynthesis stops. Sunlight and the cool nights of autumn cause the leaves to turn this glucose into a red color. The brown color of trees, like oaks, is made from wastes left in the leaves.

Objectives

Artistic Perception: Students will see the different types and shapes of the leaves. They will also become aware of warm and cool colors and how they affect humans' psychological and physiological response. Students will be practicing how to draw different lines such as zigzag, wavy, horizontal, vertical, and diagonal lines. They will also draw in patterns they choose to fill in the sections.

Creative Expression: Students will draw lines and patterns, according to their own style, on the leaves. There are many patterns students can choose to create, and they will show and represent their originality through the process of creating their own leaves.

Historical and Cultural Context: Colors were widely used in art since the Renaissance, when the artists incorporated a greater sense of light and colors. Josef Albers came up with the Color Theory, and it was widely taught for better understanding of how the colors work together, the illusion of depth and space, and different effects.

Aesthetic Valuing: Students will be aware of how warm colors bring the object forward, and cool colors push back the object. They will create their leaves according to whether they want them to have a more pulling effect with a warm background, or a pushing away effect with a cool background.

Integration: Students will become aware of the science behind why and how the leaves change color according to the season. They will also discuss how the color changing of the leaves make them feel throughout different seasons.

Materials

- Paper
- Watercolor paint
- Paintbrush
- Pencil

*NOTE: You can always change the coloring materials according to the age of the students.

Procedure

1. Draw a leaf on the paper with a pencil.

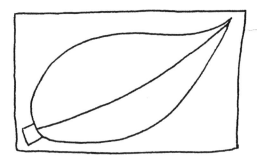

2. Divide the leaf into different sections.

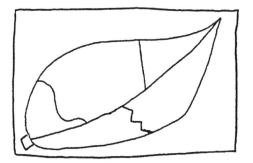

3. Draw different patterns inside the divided sections.

4. Using warm or cool colors, color in the background.

5. Using warm or cool colors, color in the patterns.

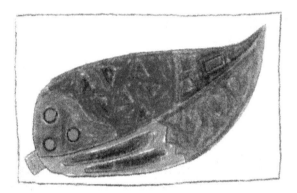

*NOTE: The background and the patterns should be painted in different color families. If the background is warm colored, then the pattern should be in cool colors. This applies to the colors being other way around.

Evaluation

1. Did the students understand why leaves change color according to the season?   Y/N

2. Did the students understand the difference between warm and cool colors?   Y/N

3. Did the students use their creativity to draw different patterns?   Y/N

4. Did the students use various lines to create their lines?   Y/N

Clouds and Winslow Homer

by Brittany Hudson

Introduction (Background/History)

I will be teaching my students about the weather, specifically on clouds. Clouds have a tremendous influence on the weather, because they block sunlight and they cause rain, snow, lightning, and rainbows. Clouds are suspended in the atmosphere and are made up of tiny water droplets. They are classified into four main groups based on their appearance and height off the ground: stratus, cumulus, cirrus, and nimbus. Stratus means layer in Latin, so the cloud form is going to be sheet-like. Cumulus means heap, so it is going to be puffy. Cirrus means curl of hair, and the cloud form is wispy. Nimbus means violent rain, which is obviously a rain cloud. Each of these clouds resides at a certain altitude. Stratus clouds are low-altitude clouds, so they will not go any higher than 6,500 feet. Cirrus clouds are high-altitude clouds, where they reside higher than 20,000 feet. Nimbus and cumulus clouds both reside in middle- to high-altitude (6,500 and higher), because they both can develop vertically.

Temperature and humidity of a certain place rely on air masses. Air masses form when they stay over a place for a while; they retain the same temperature as the area, because the heat and moisture transfer from the ground to the air. For example, air masses over the ocean are moister than air masses over a continent. When the air mass leaves its spot to a new location with its different temperature and humidity, it results in changes of weather. A stormy place where warm and cold air masses collide is called a front. As a front moves over a location, one air mass replaces the other. Warm fronts are where warm air takes over the place of the cold air, and advances slowly, so you get clouds and precipi-

tation. Cold fronts are where cold air takes over the place of the warm air, and pushes it upward, advances faster, and are associated with thunderstorms. Clouds form in three different ways, and all involve the rising of warm air. The first way is when warm air rises from the ground that exceeds its dew point. A dew point is the temperature at which air is so saturated with water vapor that the vapor begins to condense. This would create a cumulus cloud. As the rising warm air cools, it moves away from the cloud back to the ground, which would change the cloud's shape. The second way is when warm air is pushed up a mountain or mountain range. Clouds will form if the humidity is high enough. The third way is where warm air is pushed upward by a gust of cold air. This would create clouds that can cover hundreds to thousands of square miles.

An artist who painted clouds was Winslow Homer, 1836–1910. He was born in Boston, Massachusetts, where his family lived by the sea. As he grew up, he became an apprentice at a Boston lithography shop. His father owned a company that bought and sold merchandise from across the ocean that came by ship. His mother was a watercolor artist. Both parents were very encouraging toward Homer, who wanted to be an artist. While his mother did help her son, he basically taught himself how to become an artist. Homer didn't go to college. He wanted to live on his own and earn a living. Fortunately, his father had a friend who owned a printing company in Boston, so Homer agreed to be an apprentice for two years at the company. While under the apprenticeship, he was taught many different techniques, but he did not care for the job. After his two years were up, he left to be an illustrator for Boston's *Ballou's Pictorial*. He then moved to New York City, because magazines needed more illustrators, and started working for the *Harper's Weekly*. People who read *Harper's Weekly* really enjoyed Homer's illustrations, because he showed everyday people doing normal things rather than using the popular style of the time where they copied Europe's stiff and royal themes. In 1861, *Harper's* sent him to the front as an artist-correspondent at the start of the Civil War. While he did illustrate some battle scenes, he preferred to show the soldiers in camp. A few years later, he debuted as a professional painter at the National Academy of Design's annual exhibition. By the end of his life, Homer tended to be by himself; not that he did not like people, but that he preferred to paint by himself.

Objectives

- Artist Perception: Students will view watercolor examples by Winslow Homer; i.e., *Osprey's Nest*, *The Blue Boat*, *Boys on a Beach*, *Tinemouth Priory*, etc. They will become aware of the techniques used to create watercolor images.

- Creative Expression: The students will paint, with watercolor, their own personal interpretation on how clouds look to them. They will be learning how to use different watercolor techniques like variegated wash, gradated wash, layers, dry brush, and stippling to create a better representation of their clouds. Students will represent their own Homer feature in their art. Students can also represent their feelings through the colors they used throughout the piece.

- Historical and Cultural Context: Students will become aware of another artist who may not be as famous as Vincent Van Gogh, but still relevant to them, by expand-

ing their knowledge, and it would show them that there are other amazing artists out there besides the ones that are usually taught in school. Students will be introduced to the basic concepts of cloud types and watercolor techniques.

- Aesthetic Value: Students will discuss their choices with color value within their painting. They will also discuss their choice of a Homer feature and how it relates to them in some way.

- Integration: Students will become aware of the four types of clouds, air masses, and fronts, along with Winslow Homer. Students will be able to recognize and gain understanding in the differences between the clouds that they see almost daily: cirrus, cumulus, stratus, and nimbus.

Material List

- 8 ×10 sheet of watercolor paper (one per person)
- Watercolors
- Brushes
- Water Cup
- Ruler
- Pencil

Procedure

1. Draw an outline of the clouds and the horizon line.
2. Paint the sky layers in order to give the sky character.
3. Paint the cloud layer in order to show the value of the cloud.
4. Paint the ground and a feature in the painting that Homer would have put into one of his own paintings.

Evaluation

- Did the student try to make the clouds look as realistic as possible?   Y/N
- Did the student put in a Winslow Homer feature?   Y/N
- Did the student use at least two of the techniques?   Y/N
- Can the student respond to a question about Winslow Homer or clouds?   Y/N

Musical Art Lesson Plan

By Jennifer Strasheim

Introduction

I will be teaching students the history, culture, technical, and visual information about painting to musical styles. One of the first artists to create abstract art with the major influence of music was Wassily Kandinsky. "Kandinsky saw himself as a prophetic figure, whose mission was to translate the most profound human emotions into universally comprehensible symbols and visual sensations. He saw music as the most transcendent form of non-objective art, and strove to produce similarly object-free, spiritually rich paintings" (Griffin). Kandinsky was born in Russia where his upper-class family encouraged his gift for expressing sensual experiences by enrolling him in cello, piano, and private drawing lessons. Yet, he did not pursue art until his thirties; instead, he studied law and became a very renowned lawyer. He was inspired by his traveling, and trips to Vologda, Munich, Moscow, and around Europe and France. He moved a lot due to WWII, and went to Switzerland and Moscow, then was forced out of Russia. He returned to Germany and began to settle down some. He became the director of an avant-garde group at Phalanx School, where he taught and arranged exhibitions for other members of the school. He soon showed his interest in distorting figure-ground relationships and the use of color to express emotional experience instead of reflecting nature. He familiarized himself with the increasing Expressionist movement, as he started to develop his own style inspired by folk and children's art, like he had seen in Vologda. He was also extremely inspired by Monet. He organized artist groups like The New Group of Artists, which did exhibitions that promoted modern art and spiritual experience through symbolic associations of sound and color. He published a few works about his artistic philosophy that later turned to geometric elements: especially circles, half-circles, straight lines, angles, and curves. Near the end of his life, he changed his style once again, and his biometric forms appeared more organic. He had a major impact on forming the philosophic foundation for Abstract Expressionist artists. "Kandinsky developed a pictorial language that only loosely related to his subject matter, seeking to depict the tones, rhythms, and spiritual resonance of nature as opposed to the onward appearance of objects. His emphasis on spontaneous activity and the subconscious had great effect on action painters like Jackson Pollock and his analysis of the sensorial properties of color was influenced on the Color Field painters." (Wassily). Kandinsky was believed to have synaesthesia, a harmless condition that allows a person to appreciate sounds, colors, or words with two or more senses simultaneously.

Wagner's *Lohengrin*, which had stirred Kandinsky to devote his life to art, had convinced him of the emotional powers of music. The performance conjured for him visions of a certain time in Moscow that he associated with specific colors and emotions. It inspired in him a sense of a fairy-tale hour of Moscow, "The violins, the deep tones of the basses, and especially the wind instruments at that time embodied for me all the power of that pre-nocturnal hour. I saw all my colors in my mind; they stood before my eyes. Wild, almost crazy lines were sketched in front of me. I did not dare use the expression that Wagner had painted 'my hour' musically." Kandinsky was also very inspired by the work of Aleksander Scriabin, whose innovations he found compatible with his own objectives in painting. What especially intrigued Kandinsky were Scriabin's researches toward establishing a table of equivalencies between tones in color and music, a theory that Scriabin effectively applied in his orchestral work, *Prometheus: A Poem of Fire* (1908)." (Ku).

Objectives

a. Artistic Perspective: Students will view images of artwork painted by the artist Wassily Kandinsky. Students will be informed about emotions and expression through music and art. Students will learn about shapes, lines, and forms to create artwork.

b. Creative Expression: Students will create their own piece of art based on their interpretation of four different types of music. Students will demonstrate listening, drawing, painting, and musical interpretation skills. They will use a variety of colored oil pastels and choose from watercolors.

c. Historical and Cultural Context: Pre-Modern, Modern, and Post-Modern Art. Movements will be time-lined and briefly described. Students will get a brief biography of a well known Abstract Expressionist, Wassily Kandinsky. They will learn what inspired him and about his artwork.

d. Aesthetic Valuing: Students get the opportunity to mimic the artists' style and type of painting, but put their own creative twist on it. Students are encouraged to express their emotions and reactions to different types of music. Students are asked to display and explain/describe their painting to the class and what the colors and designs mean to them.

e. Integration: The students are encouraged to make connections and use concepts of shapes, colors, emotion, musical instruments, and different genres of music.

Students are asked to interpret their feeling and emotions from music and share with their peers.

Materials List

- 9 in × 12 in white sheets of paper (one per student)
- Oil Pastels: 5–7 varying colors for different expression and emotions
- Watercolor paint
- Mixed CD or iPod playlist with a variety of music: classical, rock, piano, familiar (children's song), orchestra

Procedure

1. Have all materials set up on each student's desk. Then, direct students to close their eyes and listen to the music for 5 seconds.

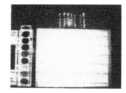

2. Stop the music and ask the students to pick one colored oil pastel that reflects how the song made them feel.

3. Start music again and instruct students to draw lines and shapes that reflect the movement of the song and how it sounds to them.

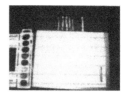

4. Stop music and instruct students to listen to the next song and select a different color that makes them think of the new song.

5. Have students draw lines and shapes to the new song. (Repeat steps for a total of 4 songs.)

6. Instruct students to choose one watercolor that reflects the overall mood and feeling they got from the music that was played. They should lightly paint over the pastels until they feel they are finished representing the music.

Evaluation

Did students follow directions?

Did students reflect the mood of the songs played?

Did students use creative expression to make artwork they are proud of, and are they able to express this to their peers?

Bibliography

Griffin, Eve. "Wassily Kandinsky Biography, Art, and Analysis of Paintings by TheArtStory." *The Art Story.* N.p., n.d. Web. 20 Oct. 2012. <http://www.theartstory.org/artist-kandinsky-wassily .htm>.

Ku, Oleg. "Wassily Kandinsky—Biography, Paintings, Books." *Wassily Kandinsky—Biography, Paintings, Books.* N.p., Apr. 2008. Web. 20 Oct. 2012. <http://www.wassilykandinsky.net/>.

"Wassily Kandinsky." *Wassily Kandinsky.* Famouspainter.com, 7 Nov. 2002. Web. 20 Oct. 2012. <http://www.famouspainter.com/wassily.htm>.

Dada Portrait—Hannah Hoch

by Melis McNeill

Introduction

Students will be introduced to Dadaism (Dada) and how it transformed the art world, creating a cultural movement that broadened the thought processes and perceptions of expression. Dadaism is defined as *"the style and technique of a group of artists and writers from 1916–1922 who created a movement of satirical works, protesting the ideas, thought processes, and decisions executed by society and government, where greed, arrogance, and prejudice ruled the day. Their artistic mode of expression purposely violated the natural laws of nature and civilization."*

In 1916, a man by the name of Tristan Tzara was discussing with a group of friends in the Cabaret Voltaire, a local theatre in Zurich, Switzerland, the devastating atrocities of World War I and the bourgeois capitalist society that inspired it. According to Tzara, *"We had lost confidence in our culture. Everything had to be demolished. We would begin again after the 'tabula rasa.' At the Cabaret Voltaire we began shocking common sense, public opinion, education, institutions, museums, good taste . . . ".* Dada's intent was to become a revolution and destroy traditional culture and aesthetics, to offend and appeal to the people's sensibilities. Tzara took the first step in a poem.

World War I ended in 1918 and most of Zurich's Dadaists returned to their homelands and pursued their agenda. The movement flourished in Berlin, Cologne, Hannover, Paris, and New York. The Berlin-Dadaists were extremely active in Germany during this period. Grosz, Hausmann, Hoch, Baader, Huelsenbeck, and Heartfield became the voice. Their focus was on the political and social issues that plagued the nation.

They attacked with corrosive manifestos and propaganda, biting satire, public demonstrations, and overt political activities. Hoch and Grosz also used Dada to express their post-war communist sympathies.

The art of the period was innovative and demanded a freedom contrary to the already established law and social order. Chaos and irrationality was the mantra. It was during this period that photomontage: the manipulation of photographs found in publications, postcards, and photographs, came to be the new medium of expression, along with the help of another technique known as collage, where the random piecing of cut or shredded photographs was applied. Grosz and Heartfield are credited for the development of photomontage, but it was perfected by Hannah Hoch, whose compositions were highly unified with elements grounded by good compositional structure. The works of the male Dadaists lack this quality. Grosz and Heartfield were against her participation in the 1920 Dada Fair, and the other men in the group never accepted her as an equal. While she embraced the political and social agenda of Dada, she distanced herself from her male colleagues and found support from other artists involved with the movement.

Hoch (1889–1978) was a designer and avant-garde artist in Germany. She worked for Ullstein Press, designing dress and embroidery patterns, which gave her a source for her earlier montage works, and financial support during the lean Dada years. Hoch loved to experiment and explored numerous themes and artistic techniques of the movement. She was well known for her works in outright abstraction, intimate portraiture, manipulation of photomontage, and surrealist fantasy. She had a lifelong preoccupation with gender identity and relationships between the sexes. Her focus on the female identity reached a peak during the 1930s, where she expanded the concept to include racial and gender ambiguity. Her exploration of the emotional element of the time was a key element in all of her works. Her first piece after the war titled, "Androgynous Woman," represented the female desire to be considered equal to men and their rights to ownership of themselves, property, and political involvement. She consorted with the communists of the day and sympathized with their cause. Later, Hoch created for an exhibition 17 montages, which depicted the "primitive cultures, inferior/ underdeveloped people, and female alien-ation." She believed what was classified as primitive was being carried away and de-stroyed by modern civilization, this including the subjugation of the female identity. Hoch's placement of female heads on male bodies and combining African art and primitive imagery was her means of protesting the desecration of the woman herself. She was a strong advocate of women's rights and equality. She resented the prejudices of the day regarding racial integration and mixed society. Her best work represents these themes, illustrated with the images and mediums of the day, mixing them up to create a new idea, form, and/or reality.

While all of the artists during this movement were affected by the rise of Hitler to power, nuclear science, and the wealth and greed of the church, investors, financiers, and govern-ment; the Berlin-Dadaists dared to look at their surroundings and how it influenced the individual.

They dared to challenge the conventions of the time and its thought process. A few lost their lives in Hitler's concentration camps, while others fled to the United States. The Dada movement greatly influenced a changed world. Their principles were modified and became the basis of the Surrealism movement in 1924, and continued to find a sound footing in other future movements such as Abstract Expressionism, Conceptual Art, and Pop Art.

Artistic Perception

Students will be introduced to art works of the Berlin-Dada movement, focusing on the works of Hannah Hoch. They will become familiar with the inner thoughts and modes of expres-sion of this period, where tragedy, transforma-tion of the individual and society, along with political changes in government and society become the subject matter of protest. Intro-duction to the inventions of the time, such as collage, photomontage, and assemblage, as well as their influences within the art form will be represented as well.

Creative Expression

Students will create their own collage-photo-montage based on the theme of "The Modern Woman." They will search through magazines and photographs to find illustrations to depict their concept of how they define to-day's female: mother, teacher, doctor, soldier; or their perception of how society defines the modern woman: beauty, identity, success. Students will create this person(s) on a collaged background made from various materials, along with objects, if desired, onto a poster board.

Historical and Cultural Context

Students will become aware of the history and mindset of society during one of the most innovative, industrial, and brutal periods in mankind's history (1916–1924). Prejudices, individual greed, and demoralization of the female identity will be illustrated by the works of Hannah Hoch and her frustration within the period. Students will be able to under-stand the psychological and emotional effect World War II had on the world, and why it was necessary to change society and break the mold of the Victorian era. Associations be-tween the past and the present will be ex-plored to determine whether anything has really changed at all. Students will take their observations and further explore the influence of other cultures, and determine whether the world has become more inclusive or nationalistic.

Aesthetic Valuing

Students will discuss their choice of images cut from the magazines and/or photographs collected and state how it defines their perspective of the modern woman and her role within their worldview. Their choice of background materials will also be addressed in how it supports their intent:

- Does it bring their woman to the foreground or background of the piece?

- Does this approach continue to illustrate their intent of their perception of the woman?

- Do the objects placed within the picture represent something in contrast or in support of their theme?

- Was there a purpose in the colors chosen for the piece, the mediums used, and the layout of their pieces?

- Is the piece eclectic and random, or is it following the traditional form of proportion, balance, and beauty?

Integration

- Students will be able to perceive and comprehend the concept of 2D and 3D in their surrounding world.

- Students will be aware of the power of influence others' actions and thoughts have had on the future due to prejudices, biases, fear, and greed in comparison to what we share in common, and the value of acceptance and respect of the differences between us.

- Students will begin to recognize the influences within their environment, and how their own thought processes are affected; for example, how we define a woman and her role in society.

- Students will be introduced to the freedoms and influences the Dada movement had on literature (poetry) and music (jazz).

Materials

- Magazines, photos—people's faces/bodies **and** objects

- Paper—scrapbook, tissue, construction, newspaper, comic strips

- Fabric—cotton or blends, felt, doilies

- Wallpapers, borders

- Trinkets, buttons

- Tacky glue (trinkets and fabrics)

- Elmer's Gel Glue (papers and magazines)

- White poster board (8" × 11")

- Scissors

Students are to choose various mediums to create their background collage and support their theme.

Procedure

- Stage 1
  - Choose materials and images from magazines or photographs needed to create an eclectic background and support theme
  - Cut, rip materials in desired shapes and sizes and create layout

- Stage 2
  - Create background: Paste materials on poster board in random order
  - Create theme: Paste images on top of background to support theme

- Stage 3
  - Add trinkets or other 3D objects to picture for dimension or further theme support

Evaluation

- Did the student use a variety of materials to create a collage background?

- Did the student cut out images from the magazines that defined their idea of the modern woman?

- Were the pieces strategically placed to illustrate clearly their perception of the modern woman?

- Were there other influences or lack of influences represented in the picture that supported the theme?

- Is the student's perspective of a modern woman any different than the perspective of Hoch's women?

- Did the student create the traditional composition with the use of a foreground and background, or did they create an alternative composition contrary to traditional layouts?

Vocabulary

- **Dada (Dadaism)**
  - The style and technique of a group of artists and writers from 1912–1924 who created a movement of satirical works, protesting the ideas, thought processes, and decisions executed by society and government, where greed, arrogance, and prejudice ruled the day. Their artistic mode of expression purposely violated the natural laws of nature and civilization.

- **Collage**
  - The pasting on a single surface of various materials not normally associated with one another, such as newspaper, photographs, wallpapers, etc.

- **Eclectic**
  - Selecting from different sources and combining to create an effect.

- **Photomontage**
  - The piecing together of photographic and typographic sources for artistic effects.

- **Portraiture**
  - The art of creating a graphic and/or detailed description of a person.

- **Cubism**
  - A school of modern art developed during the early 20th century (1908–1912) concerned with the analysis of form by means of abstract and geometric representation, rather than with a realistic interpretation of nature. Influenced the Dada movement.

- **Futurism**
  - A style of art, music, and literature developed around 1910 in Italy, where Cubism forms were used to represent rapid movement and dynamic motion.

- **Surrealism**
  - A style of art developed during the 20th century (1920–1930) that attempts to express and exhibit the workings of the subconscious mind, especially as manifested in dreams and uncontrolled by the reason or any conscious process; characterized by the incongruous and startling arrangement and presentation of subject matter.

- **Pop Art**
  - An art movement developed within the United States (1950–1960), where the subject matter chosen represented the everyday and standard icons of American life, such as comic strips, billboards, commercial products, and celebrity images.

- **Avant-Garde**
  - A group of individuals whose art work is characterized by unorthodox and experimental methods.

- **Art Manifestoes**
  - A new visual language developed by art movements where what is expressed in visual form transcends the day's current mode of perception: visionary.

- **Art Theory**
  - Concerned with the nature of art and its mathematical composition of all forms relative to the mind, emotions, and sense of beauty.

- **Graphic Design**
  - The art of visual communication, which combines images, words, and ideas to produce a special effect and convey information to an audience.
- **Assemblages**
  - The organizing or composing into a unified whole "objects" that are unrelated, fragmented, and discarded.
- **Memorabilia**
  - Matters or events worthy to be remembered.

Bibliography

Boswell, P., Lanchner, C., & Makela, M. (1996). The Photomontages of Hannah Hoch: Minneapolis: Walker Art Center.

Esaak, Shelley (unknown). Dada-Art History Basics on the Dada Movement—1916–1923 Retrieved from http://arthistory.about.corn/cs/arthistoryl0one/a/dada.htm

Finger, Missy. (1996). Book Review: The Photomontages of Hannah Hoch. Retrieved from http://www.dallasgoethecenter.org/Hannah. htm

Funk & Wagnalls New Comprehensive International Dictionary, Encyclopedic Edition, includes the Funk & Wagnalls Standard Dictionary, International Edition (1978).

Hager, Liz. (2010). Hannah Hoch: The "Quiet Girl" with a Big Voice (Part I): Venetian Red Art Blog. Retrieved from http://venetianred.net/2010/0l/16/hannah-hoch-the-good-girl-with scissors-part-i

Krieg, Susan. (unknown). The History of Collage. Retrieved from http://www.krieg artstudio.com/nesting_cranesfsusan_kieg history_collage.htm

Source: Leland, N., & Lee, V. (1994). Creative Collage Techniques: Chapter One.

Handouts

Name _____ Date _____

"Self Portrait"

Semester_____Year _____Hour _____

Name: _____

Campus ID _____

Address: _____

City and Zip Code: _____

Telephone: Home_____ Cell _____

E-mail: _____

Major _____ Year at CSUF _____

What is your experience in art from elementary school to the present?

How do you view your creative self?

What art museums have you visited?

Any special needs or concerns that you would like me to know?

Evaluating and analyzing a work of art using the framework standards

Questions to ask when looking at a work of art:

- Title of work? Who is the artist? Date and time period?

- What appears to be the center of interest in the work? (Emphasis)

- What elements and/or principles of art does the artist use to lead our eye to the center of interest?

- What color groups do you see? (complimentary, analogous, intermediates or neutrals, warms, cools, etc.) Does the artist change the value in the work? (areas of dark and light or tints and shades of one or more colors)

- Are there repeated elements like line, color, pattern, shape or form?

- Where are contrasts in the work of art? (large and small shapes, textured and plain areas, light and dark colors, etc.)

- Does the artist use overlapping, linear perspective and/or atmospheric perspective?

- Does the work seem unified and harmonious? Why or why not?

- If not stated, what would you guess the artist used to create the work? (medium or materials)

- What do you think the artist was trying to say to the viewer? Is there symbolism? What is the mood? How does the work make you feel? What do you like or dislike about the work and why?

Aesthetic Scanning

Although there is not one correct way of looking at a piece of art, a teacher may enlist several different options that will help the children focus and become more involved when looking at a piece of art thus making the experience more memorable and rewarding.

As suggested by Harry S. Broudy in "The Role of Imagery in Learning," a teacher or parent wants the child to become involved in the critical thinking process and attempt to analyze and talk about the sensory, formal, technical and expressive properties of a particular work of art. He suggested that their approach be explored through the four stages of looking at art.

Sensory (descriptive) Properties

Remind the children of the Elements of Art. What colors do you see? Are there any lines? What type of lines? What objects do you see? What is the biggest shape? Are the geometric shapes? Or just organic shapes? Is this piece flat or does it look 3-dimensional?

Formal (analysis) Properties

This section is based on the composition of the piece, or discussing the way the artwork was organized. You may want to remind the children of the Principles of Art: Was the artwork balanced? Does one area or object have more emphasis than the others? Is a color, shape or line repeated? Is there good contrast?

Expressive (interpretation) Properties

How do you feel when you look at this piece of art? Happy, sad, scared, angry? What do you think the artist was feeling when the artwork was created? Is the artist telling us a story? Would you like this hanging in your room? Can you tell a story about what you feel is happening in this piece?

Technical (judgment) Properties

How do you think the artist made this piece of art? What media do you think that the artist used when he/she created this work? What type of tools did the artist use? Do you think that the artist drew several sketches first before making this piece?

Name _____ Date _____

Community Service Rubric and Evaluation

Location _____ Grade(s) _____

Contact Person or Supervisor _____

Art Project: _____

Objectives (What did you want students to learn and/or accomplish?):

Background/Motivational Info (What did you do to get students interested and excited about the project?):

Assessment: What did you observe as they were working? What was successful about your lesson? What would you do differently next time? What was the student response to the project and what did they learn from the objectives?

Supervisor evaluation of lesson and process:

Supervisor Signature _____ Date _____

Lesson Plan Guidelines

When writing a lesson plan, make sure that it is so clear that a person with little or no experience with art could follow your directions.

Title of Lesson Plan

Appropriate Age
Time needed to complete the project
List the standards that will be addressed in each.

Overview of the Lesson

This section is the information that the children will be expected to understand after completing the project. It will go closely in hand with the California State Content Standards: Artistic Perception, Historical and Cultural Component, Aesthetic Valuing, and Connections, Relationships and Applications. Make sure to add all areas that will aid in the integration of other subject areas. The project is not to be discussed here.

Specific Goal (the project to be completed)

This will tie in with the California State Content Standard of the Creative Expression. It should include a description of the project including the media used and will be in direct correlation to the evaluation.

Motivation

What activities, books, videos, or posters will you use to grab the students' attention? You must be specific and use titles or give websites if appropriate. This often makes the difference between a good and great teacher.

Vocabulary

What vocabulary words will each child be expected to learn—may be related to art and other subject matter.

Materials

What materials will each child need to complete this project? Be specific and note if it is something that will be provided by the teacher. You may also wish to add teacher supplies if you are planning a separate demonstration for the lesson.

Procedure

This should be a step by step description of the project. Make it short and clear, but include enough information that the students will be able to have a successful experience.

Evaluation

This may be a rubric or a list of areas or responses that each child will be graded on. These should tie in with the goals so that children know what they are to be graded on at the beginning of the lesson.

Giving Your Art a Finished Look
Matting and Mounting

A **MOUNT** is attaching your work to the front of a precut board. Measure the perimeter of your artwork, add 2 inches to *each* side, then cut your poster or matt board those new dimensions. Attach your artwork to the board with a GLUE STICK so it will dry flat. It is always a good idea to place some heavy books on top for a few hours to prevent curling, rippling or detaching. Your mat or poster board should be CLEAN and EVENLY CUT on all sides.

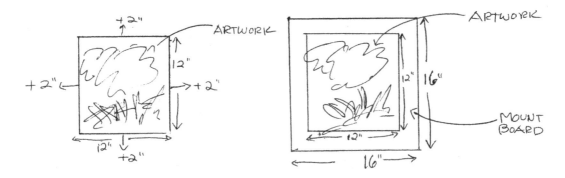

A **MATT** is a "frame" over and around your artwork. It looks like a window. Cutting a matt takes a some practice (practice on some scrap board first) because you have to use a knife against a straightedge. First, you measure the perimeter of your artwork. Next, add 2 inches to *each* side. These new dimensions will be the finished size of your matt. Cut the perimeter of your matt. Turn it over. All measured marks are made on the backside so they won't show. On the backside, measure 2¼ inches inward from the edge on all sides. (The ¼" is the amount you need to overlap your finished art. Draw your window. Next, line your straight edge along one of the lines, and holding it steady, cut downward and against your straightedge with your X-acto or utility knife. Overcut the corners slightly so the centerpiece falls free. Tape your artwork in place on the back side of the matt. Make sure edges are *NEAT* and *CLEAN!* Points will be deducted for work that is not matted, mounted or if the board is dirty and sloppily cut.

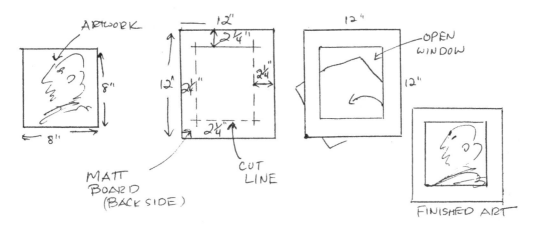

Art Resource Notebook

This notebook is intended to be a reference for teaching art to elementary students as well as a compilation of course hand-outs, projects and research. *This will count as one art project grade.* Set up and add to your notebook throughout the semester. It should be neat, organized with a table of contents and dividers. Due at semester's end.

Materials Needed

3-ring notebook (3"), dividers, page protectors (*optional*)

Sections to be Included

1. *ART HISTORY TIMELINE*
2. *VISUAL GLOSSARY*: Art Elements, Principles and Color Theory
3. *CALIFORNIA DEPARTMENT OF EDUCATION VISUAL ART FRAMEWORK AND CONTENT STANDARDS*: Download grades K through 6th from web address: www.cde.ca.gov/ be/st/ss/vamain.asp
4. *CLASS HANDOUTS, QUIZZES, MIDTERM EXAM*: Include all printed information handed out in class and exams as well as class notes.
5. *FIVE EXAMPLES OF CHILDREN'S ART*: Have five children of different ages (2 to 13) draw the same subject (draw your family or draw your house, or draw your favorite animal). Label back of drawing with **artistic development characteristics** as stated in the text. Take note of how individual children fit the developmental characteristics for their age or if they seem to be advanced or delayed. This is to be an observational period requiring patience and time. Do not wait until the day before the notebook is due to get these drawings. *Do not download any drawings or copy any drawings from another source.*
6. *ARTIST BIOGRAPHIES*: Keep all artist biographies you receive from fellow classmates, including your own, in this section.
7. *LESSON PLANS*: Include ten lesson plans. Can include ones from the Internet or classmates.
8. *ARTICLES AND IDEAS*: (Minimum of 10) Anything that might pertain to integrating art into the elementary and middle school curriculum (A newspaper article talking about elementary kids painting a mural based on space exploration, or information on writing a grant for an arts festival, etc.). Also include anything that supports art education. Sources can include art magazines, web sites, periodicals and newspapers and museum brochures and newsletters.
9. *NOTEBOOK COVER:* Original and aesthetically pleasing—add your name, class/period, and date.

My students from past semesters have considered this a valuable resource. They especially liked having the artist biographies and lesson plans for setting up their classroom art curriculum.

California Gane
Standards
235-237, 239

California State Framework
Content Standards for Visual Art

Artistic Perception *Processing, analyzing and responding to sensory information through the language and skills unique to the visual arts*

1. **Develop Visual Arts Vocabulary:**
   - Describe the world using art terminology.
   - Identify and discuss the elements and principles of art found in the environment at appropriate age and grade levels.

2. **Develop Perception Skills:**
   - Illustrate what is seen in the natural world using a variety of techniques and media.
   - Employ the five senses to respond to the environment and to stimulate the imagination.
   - Use symbols to reflect understanding of world environment.

3. **Focus on Art Elements and Principles of Design:**
   - Explore expressive qualities of elements such as: color (warm and cool, analogous, etc.), shape (geometric or organic), space (positive and negative), etc.
   - Distinguish between representational and nonrepresentational artwork (Rembrandt vs. Picasso).
   - Identify and discuss art elements: line, shape, color, form, pattern, texture, space.
   - Compare and contrast use of elements.
   - Identify artist's choice of media.

Creative Expression *Creating, performing and participating in the visual arts*

1. **Skills, Processes, Materials, Tools**
   - Employ a variety of media to explore the variations in the elements and principles of art.
   - Create original works of art that include:
     - Compositions that reflect a sense of unity and rhythm.
     - Artworks that reflect a study of a culture.
     - Images that show real objects in new ways.
     - Convey emotions in an assigned medium.

2. **Communication and Expression Through Original Works of Art**
   - Respond to and discuss own artwork.
   - Identify the elements and principles of art in own artwork.
   - Demonstrate combinations of elements and principles in own artwork.
   - Respond to the work of other artists.

Historical and Cultural Context *Understanding the historical contributions and cultural dimensions of the visual arts*

1. **Role and Development of the Visual Arts**
   - Recognize variety of artwork and artist's styles from various cultures.
   - Identify art and artists in home, school and community by:
     - contrasting art from various regions and historical periods.
     - discussing how art is used in events and celebrations from past, present and in various cultures.
   - Identify characteristics of art forms from different cultures

2. **Diversity of the Visual Arts**
   - Describe how art galleries and museums contribute to conservation of art.
   - Identify and discuss major works of art produced by women or members of diverse ethnic groups.
   - Use a variety of sources to report on various civilizations or cultures from ancient to modern times.
   - Identify and discuss the artwork of a particular artist.

Aesthetic Valuing *Responding to, analyzing and making judgments about works in the visual arts*

1. **Derive Meaning**
   - Observe art and discuss reasons artist had for creating artwork.
   - Describe likes and dislikes about a particular artwork. Explain why you feel this way.
   - Identify and discuss the message, meaning and/or mood (expressive properties) of specific works of art.
   - Discuss ideas about literal and expressive content of art.

2. **Make Informed Judgments**
   - Describe what artists do and discuss elements artists use to create a work of art.
   - Identify broad categories of art (e.g., ancient, Byzantine, Modern, etc.).
   - Apply four steps of art criticism to own artwork and that of others:
     (1) Describe work
     (2) Analyze work in terms of elements and principles of art
     (3) Interpret work in terms of ideas and emotions (expressive properties)
     (4) Judge work as to its success both technically and in communication of an idea and/ or fulfilling a purpose

Connections, Relationships, Applications (Integration) *Connecting and applying what is learned in the visual arts to other art forms and subject areas and to careers*

1. **Connections and Applications**
   - **Integration** of art to other subject areas including, math, social studies, science and language arts.

2. **Visual Literacy**
   - Develop competencies and creative skills in problem solving, communication and time management which will enhance lifelong learning.

3. **Career and Career Related Skills**
   - Learn about careers related to the visual arts.

Integrating the Visual Arts with Core Curriculum"

"Neither life nor art happens in a vacuum." Progressive art educators like Frank Wachowiak and Robert Clements, authors of *Emphasis Art,* set the national standard of integrated art lessons and art experiences for children in the United States for the last 63 years. As the traditional classroom continues to change, educators are constantly looking for new ways to effectively reach out and teach today's students. Other respected educators and their methodologies have long supported the use of integrated arts curriculum in the classroom. Benjamin Bloom and his theory of the three domains of learning naturally integrates the experiential nature of art making in the classroom with recognition of the three different types of experience for the child: cognitive, affective and psycho-motor. Art affects all learning domain areas. More recently and an ongoing support for the use of integrated visual arts lesson in the classroom is Howard Gardner's research on the multiple levels of intelligence. Gardner has identified 8 primary learning modalities/intelligences with which integrated arts curriculum will enhance the learning experience for your students. Utilizing the visual arts is an effortless way to become familiar with and recognize your student's learning modality/intelligence. Research is ongoing—see www.Harvard UniversityProjectZero.org for further information.

Integrated arts curriculum opens learning opportunities for all learners. Understanding the classroom instructional potential paves the way for all art lessons to be fully integrated with not only core curriculum, but life experiences as well. Explore the possibilities; ask the question, "So just how does my art lesson fit in with core curriculum areas?" "How will I tie all this info together into a cohesive lesson?"

The following are guidelines that will help you narrow the information down and help you create original lesson plans that will make your lessons rich with core information, artistically expanding and creatively meaningful for your students.

1. Remember—Visual Arts is also a core subject. California state teachers are required to teach an art lesson for 45 instructional minutes per week.

2. Know your grade level art curriculum requirements according to the State Standards. You'll be amazed by the range of creative experiences the standards state as well as suggestions for material exploration. If your school stock room does not have the necessary supplies, try the district warehouse. If they don't have it try the county. If they don't have it, call the state. Keep trying. A good teacher should work tirelessly to get the materials necessary for his/her students.

3. Review all other curriculum standards areas. I look for logical application of the art skills and materials that I will be teaching for that grade level. I always review one grade below and one above. It's good to review and it's even better to introduce new ideas and concepts.

4. Know the resources in your area. For example, museums, zoos, libraries, historical sites, parks, arboretum/botanical gardens, art supply stores or retailers with art supplies all often offer support in a variety of ways. It can't hurt to ask.

In conclusion I often go through my classroom textbooks themselves; many of them include art extensions with images of historical and cultural artifacts, famous works of art and photographs of social events that celebrate the creation of art and its purpose within the cultural context. Simple Google searches often result in additional discovery of historical and contemporary works of art whose images are specific to the subject that I want to teach how to draw or paint. It's great when the students are learning and so am I. Look at historical artistic illustrations of bugs. Amazing and beautiful! Visit museums. All museums not just art museums and remember most of them have educator discounts on memberships and special perks like expert advice and lending trucks come with those memberships. They also are very generous with your students and many have admissions reimbursement; don't be shy about asking. Museums are great resources; I've been struck by learning lightning more than once in a museum.

Give it a try; I'm sure you'll surprise yourself. There's a reason you went into education in the first place. Celebrate the joy and academic success that art and integrated art lessons will bring to your classroom.

Name _____ Date _____

Artist Biography

Choose an artist from the list or one you are especially interested in. You may choose a local artist. ***Please do not copy a web page and turn it in for credit. I expect research from at least 2 sources (only one from the Internet) and the essay written in your own words.*** The essay needs to be typed (*three-page minimum not including sources or work of art*), must show one famous example of the artist's work, and contain a bibliography. Please check for spelling and grammatical errors before turning in your paper!!

Your artist biography should contain the following information and any additional material that would be of interest to children:

- Artist's name, birth, death and country of origin.
- Information about childhood and family.
- Schooling and apprenticeships, interests and hobbies.
- Influences leading to an interest and study of art.
- People the artist studied with and places where the artist lived and worked.
- Development and style of the artist's work (*ex. work evolved from realism to abstract expressionism*). What medium(s) does the artist use and what makes his/her work significant from that of other artists?
- Emphasis in work (*ex. artist painted mainly landscapes and portraits, etc.*). Was the artist's work influenced by his/her culture, events or politics from the era?
- Significant quotes, ideas and personal philosophy from the artist.
- Artist's later years
- Bibliography (works cited). This must include at least one book.

***Include an example or examples of the artist's work. A copy in black and white from an art book or from a web site would be fine and can be placed on the same page as your biographical information. (If you were doing an oral presentation for children, in a classroom setting, you would want large examples of the artist's work like slides, prints, posters or a movie about the artist.)*

Please make copies of your artist biography for the class. (1 for each student, including yourself, and one for the instructor.) These are to go in your *Art Resource Notebook* for future reference.

Art Museum Field Trip

(Report due mid-semester, date will be announced)
One scheduled class will be devoted to this trip during the semester

Choose a local museum from the list. Find the museum's website and get all pertinent information regarding hours, current exhibitions, admission prices and directions. This will be part of your research. Plan to spend some time there and really absorb what you see! For those of you who have limited or no experience going to art museums, perhaps this opportunity will provide a new area of personal interest and enjoyment. For you future teachers, art museums may well be high on your list for class field trips since they span history and culture across a broad spectrum. If the museum is large, like the LA County Museum of Art or the J. Paul Getty Museum, I don't expect you to tour the entire museum, but I do expect you to know what is there and make choices based on personal interest. Take notes on what you see. Your report must include the following information and should be written in an essay style:

1. Date and time of your visit (attach a ticket stub, brochure or something from the museum that proves you were there).
2. The name, address and hours of museum.
3. Kinds of art found in the museum's permanent collection (*ex. Egyptian art and artifacts 2000 B.C. to 800 A.D., Renaissance and Baroque painting and sculpture, 19th century period furnishings, 20th century painting and sculpture, etc*). In other words, you will list what the museum features or what it is known for.
4. Choose a favorite work from that period or style and write the title, artist, medium and brief description of the work. Analyze the work using the Elements and Principles of Art to describe it: *how does the artist use line, color, shape, form, space, value, texture, balance, emphasis, movement, pattern, rhythm, contrast, variety, unity, etc?* Describe how the work made you feel and what you think the artist's intent was in creating it. (*Plan to spend some time just sitting with the artwork to observe and "experience" the piece.*) Remember the four stages of looking at art.
5. Additional areas or galleries you visited within the museum.
6. Your overall experience at the museum. Be descriptive. Tell about impressions feelings, mood, layout, architecture, gardens, etc., both positive and negative.

Local Art Museums

Los Angeles County Museum of Art (LACMA) (Los Angeles)
Norton Simon Museum (Pasadena)
Huntington Library and Art Gallery (San Marino)
J Paul Getty Museum (Los Angeles)
Orange County Museum of Art (Newport Beach)
Laguna Beach Museum of Art
Bowers Museum (Santa Ana)
Long Beach Museum of Art
Latin American Museum of Art (Long Beach)

Name ______________________________ Date ______________

How Do You See Line?

STRAIGHT

CURVED

DOTTED

BROKEN

ANGLED

CURLY

BOLD

THIN

HEAVY

SOFT

ANGRY

ZIGZAG

DYNAMIC

MEANDERING

WISTFUL

WAVY

ARCHED

UNEVEN

FLOWING

LAZY

EXPRESSIVE

TANGLED

Art 380 Final: Written/Oral/Visual Presentation Instructions

1. Research a lesson plan on line or from the many available in the CSUF library or the text. Some websites are listed under "art lesson plans" and include Crayola.com, Kinderart.com, ArtsEd.net, Princetononline.com, Getty.edu, Teachnet.com and Artsedge.kennedy-center.org.

2. Sign up for what you want to teach (no duplicate projects, first come, first served).

3. Sign up for a presentation date for your class (no more than 7 per day, first come first served).

4. Your art lesson presentation must:

   a. Feature an ARTIST (ex: Pablo Picasso or Frida Kahlo), OR art from a CULTURE (ex: Hopi pottery or Australian Aboriginal paintings).

   b. Be INTEGRATED with a CORE ACADEMIC SUBJECT other than visual art (e.g., language arts, math, science, social science) AND/OR one of the other arts disciplines: music, dance or theater.

   c. Must be designed for a specific GRADE LEVEL so you can include that grade level STANDARDS in your written lesson plan.

   d. Must be written in the LESSON PLAN FORMAT style.

   e. Must have VISUAL PRESENTATION BOARDS that include the following:

      • at least three (8 × 10 or larger) color reproductions of the artist's work or examples of art from a specific culture.

      • 3 or more visual steps for the project.

      • an example of the finished project.

      • vocabulary words with definitions.

      • BRIEF instructions plus an example of an integrated subject (example: how to write a Japanese haiku poem to integrate with an art lesson on Japanese ink painting).

5. Your visuals must be *high quality*: creative, colorful, outstanding craftsmanship in lettering and design. (**No hand written lettering on the board**!!) You may also include background music, a Power Point, a video clip, a reading or a demonstration in your presentation. Bring in artifacts and anything visually exciting to enhance the lesson—think about what would be of interest to kids.

6. You will be presenting biographical info about your artist or cultural art and explaining your project to the class, not actually doing it. Expect to be in front of the class for approximately 15 to 20 minutes. Dress professionally (dress as if you are going for a job interview).

7. Make a copy of your lesson plan for each person in the class, including instructor. Hand them out before you start your presentation. (You do not have to present in the order you signed up.)

Name _____ Date _____

Lesson Presentation Boards

Lesson Presentation Boards are visual aids to enhance an art concept, artist, art movement in history, etc. and to explain an art project. They are designed to give information, be aesthetically pleasing and provide stimulus for creative expression. Video, performance, music, storytelling and artifacts are additional enhancements to a lesson.

Your presentation boards will accompany a lesson plan and will show examples of art from an individual artist or artists, an art movement, style, or culture. These examples can be from art prints that can be purchased from a museum gift shop or gallery. (The National Gallery of Art, at the Smithsonian in Washington D.C., sells beautiful prints inexpensively.) Art calendars and magazines provide good size images to use in your display. You may also use art postcards and art book reproductions as your source, enlarging and reproducing them as a color copy. You must have a minimum of 3 examples no smaller than 8 × 10.

Keep in mind that you are making this for children ages 5 through 13. The display needs to be eye-catching, interesting, easily viewed and read (uncluttered), aesthetically pleasing and view-able from a minimum distance of 12 feet.

Your presentation boards will be graded on the following elements:

1. Size: Use a triptych display board (can be purchased at Staples, Office Depot, or CM School Supply), Foam Core Board, Mat or Poster Board(s). Nothing smaller than 22 × 28, preferably larger. Multiple boards can be used to display each part of the lesson, if you wish.

2. Must have three or more examples of the artists work no smaller than 8 × 10. Title and date should be included in ¼″ type below the artwork. You must have a photo or self portrait of the artist as well. If the art is from a culture or time period then include a map of the region or photos of a cultural activity related to the art.

3. Must have five important facts about the artist shown as bulleted points (type can be no smaller than a half inch high). You must have vocabulary words on the board.

4. Must have a title with letters 2 or more inches high. Must have subheadings for areas of the board no smaller than an inch high. All lettering must be printed, die-cut or cut out with craftsmanship. You may not have anything handwritten on your board!

5. Must have a step chart with three or more steps shown with a brief description of each (more detail is in your written lesson plan). Your final step must show a finished product.

6. Must have an integrated lesson for a core subject such as language arts, math, science or social studies as related to the art project. Example: for science integration, your board could show the parts of a plant, the skeleton of a mammal, the species of fish along the California coast, etc. For language arts, your board could show the written instructions for writing a poem to accompany the art with a sample included. Integration images could include photos, maps, timelines, species, etc.

7. All text, prints, photos must be backed with colored paper or enhanced creatively with paint, decoupage, etc. You may have 3-D and interactive items on your boards. **Everything must be neat, cut evenly and glued on straight!**

These are some suggestions for making a quality board:

- Use glue stick or spray adhesive for flat gluing results. Place a heavy book as weight on top of areas you have glued to insure flatness.
- Laminating (optional) the visual examples or boards that are thin enough can extend the life of the display.
- Using fadeless papers (available at the art or teacher supply stores) helps to keep the displays looking fresh and bright.
- Identify the visual examples (artist, title, date, etc.) on your display.
- Pant hangers can be used to display the boards from the top of a whiteboard or can be hung from various points in the classroom so you are hands-free during your presentation. More rigid boards can be placed on a railing or on a flat surface which has a wall or support behind it. Triptychs are free-standing.

Lesson Plan Final Presentation Evaluation/Score Sheet

Section _____ Semester _____ Score _____

Did the **written** lesson plan include:

_____(5) Title of lesson

_____(5) Overview

_____(5) All materials needed

_____(5) Objectives (*must include visual art standards for one grade level*)

_____(5) Vocabulary

_____(5) Motivation/Background Information (*include some key components about the artist, culture or historical period. What are you having the kids do to get them excited about the lesson? Lecture, story, skit, slides, movie, preactivity?*)

_____(5) Procedure

_____(5) Assessment

_____(5) Integration/Extension (*how would you integrate this lesson into the other core subjects and did you modify or expand the lesson for gifted learners? Developmentally challenged learners?*)

_____(5) Source (*did you write the lesson, modify it or does it belong to someone?*)

_____(5) Neatly and clearly written so anyone could do the lesson easily from the plan?

_____(5) Were copies made for the class?

_____(60)

Did the **presentation and board** include:

_____(5) **Title** of lesson (*needs to be bold and eye-catching and 2" minimum*)

_____(5) **Bulleted information about the artist or culture (5 minimum)**

_____(5) Large **visual examples** of the **artist**'s work or art from the **culture** presented (*at least 8" × 10" in size*).

_____(10) **Visual integration** to a **core subject** (science, math, language arts, etc.). (information should be on the triptych or a separate board in the form of pictures, maps, diagrams, directions or sample writing, depending on subject)

_____(5) Is the **text** neat, organized and easily read? (Subheadings must be at least an inch high)

_____(5) **Step-by-step instructions** and examples for the project *(should be at least 3 steps with a brief description under each.)*

_____(5) An **example** of the finished **project**

_____(15) **Creativity** in display and presentation *(think exciting, fun and interesting for children. Think of this as a creative art project!)*

_____(15) **Craftsmanship** *(thought, care and effort in putting the board together.)*

_____(20) **Presentation:** *(well prepared with biographical info presented on the artist or culture, strong voice projection, good eye contact with audience, project explained well, professionally dressed)*

_____(90)

_____ **Bonus points:** Additional lesson enhancement tools such as a Power Point, costumes, artifacts, demonstration, storytelling, dance, etc., to enhance your presentation.

Total points: _____   (Perfect score is 150 points)

Comments: (see back for additional)

Art 380 Teaching Visual Requirements and Rubric

1. Lesson Title size 1½"–2".

2. Visual Steps: How to images 7" × 9" or 8" × 10" (clarity and quality). Brief written instructions ¾"–1" font size.

3. Example of finished project.

4. Graphic Communication: Can we see it? Can we read it? All written support material must be ½"–¾" with ¾" bold title. Legible font.

5. Graphic Layout: Logical and correct sequence to the lesson. Professional image quality, no pixilation. Visual balance with use of synthesis space, professional use of color families, professional use of visual support material. (No felt pom-poms)

These elements make up the overall craftsmanship and effectiveness of your teaching visual. The next section is the creative application of your ability to make connections between subjects.

6. Integration/Lesson Support: This can be achieved by a combination of interrelated ideas as it pertains to your lesson (minimum of 3).

   - Vocabulary list with brief definitions
   - Map correct size 7" × 9" or 8" × 10"
   - Movement Summary, with dates
   - Artist list
   - Images of famous works of art or examples of works of art correct size
   - Artist portraits with names correct size
   - Historical photos as it pertains to the lesson correct size, i.e., celebrations, travel photos, landmarks
   - Actual materials or tools or photos of materials that are culturally specific correct size or material essay or facts
   - Scientific diagrams, illustrations or photos
   - Cultural timelines, drawings or photos
   - Artist biographies or facts with dates

Art 380 Teaching Demo Evaluation

- All material prepared y or n _____

- Professional appearance y or n _____

- Class attention/close y or n _____

- Greet class and introduction y or n _____

- Eye contact and posture y or n _____

- Voice projection and pronunciation y or n_____

- Explanation(E)/demonstration(D) of lesson:
  overview:
  steps:
  history:
  techniques:
  cultural:
  materials:
  vocabulary:

- Use of examples and or visual y or n _____

  _____

- Interaction with students y or n _____

 *Recipes:*

Homemade Play Dough

3 cups of flour
1½ cup of salt
6 teaspoons of cream of tartar
3¼ cup of water
3 tablespoons of oil
food coloring or Kool-aid

Combine all dry ingredients together in saucepan. Mix liquids and gradually add into the dry. When mixture is smooth, cook on high for 3–4 minutes stirring constantly until a ball of dough forms. Remove from heat and, as soon as possible, knead until smooth. Separate into several portions and add drops of food coloring or Kool-aid kneading until uniform in color. Note that the Kool-aid will also make the play dough smell great, but also may promote sampling with some children. Store in airtight containers. Note: an excellent tool for improving a child's ability to cut with scissors is to use play dough instead of paper. Everyone experiences success and the muscles used for cutting will be developed.

Goop

2 cups of salt
⅔ cup of water
1 cup of cornstarch
½ cup of cold water

Mix cornstarch with ½ cup of cold water and set aside. Mix salt and ⅔ cup of water together in saucepan and heat for 3 to 4 minutes. Remove from heat and immediately add cornstarch mixture. Stir quickly. Return to heat if too goopy. Add food coloring before cooled.

Puffy Paint

Shaving cream
Glue (such as Elmer's)
Food coloring
Bowls and objects to use for paintbrushes

Mix equal amounts of shaving cream and glue. Add a drop or two of food coloring until desired color is achieved. Mix. Allow the children to use paintbrushes, hands, spatulas, pine tree branches to paint. A vinyl tablecloth may be an excellent addition to this project.

Silly Putty

Elmer's glue
Liquid starch

Mix equal parts of Elmer's glue and liquid starch together and knead. Don't stop until the desired consistency is reached. You may have to add more glue and continue kneading. If too sticky, add more liquid starch. If too stringy, add glue. Food coloring may be added. Store in air tight containers.

Sun Clay

2 cups of salt
1 cup of cornstarch
⅔ cup of water

Mix the salt and water together in a saucepan. Cook over medium heat for 4 to 5 minutes stirring constantly until salt is completely dissolved. Remove from heat. In a separate bowl, slowly add ½ cup of water to the cornstarch. Stir until smooth and then add to salt mixture. Return to low heat and cook until smooth stirring constantly. Store in sealed container or plastic bag.

Clay may be used in any sculptural manner. Let the children add small rocks, leaves, or twigs to their artwork. When finished, place the finished objects in the sun to dry. When completely dry, this clay will not crumble.

Web Links to Museums—Check for Current Show before You Go!

(* means smallish—** means large)

** J. Paul Getty Museum http://www.getty.edu

  * Laguna Art Museum http://www.lagunaartmuseum.org

  * Long Beach Museum of Art http://www.lbma.org

** Los Angeles County Museum of Art http://www.lacma.org

** Museum of Contemporary Art (MOCA) http://www.MOCA-LA.org

  * Geffen Contemporary http://www.MOCA-LA.org

  * UCLA Hammer Museum http://www.hammer.ucla.edu

** Bowers Museum http://www.bowers.org

** Huntington Library http://www.huntington.org

  * Japanese American National Museum http://www.janm.org

  * Museum of Latin American Art http://www.molaa.com

  * Norton Simon Museum http://www.nortonsimon.org

  * Pasadena Museum of California Art http://www.pmcaonline.org/

  * Bergamot Station Arts Center http://www.bergamotstation.com

  * CSUF Grand Central Art Center http://www.gradcentralartcenter.com

  * Los Angeles Municipal Art Gallery [aka—Barnsdall Park Museum]
   http://www.culturela.org/lamag/Home.html
   See also the site of Los Angeles Dept of Cultural Affairs:
     http://www.culturela.org/

More museums—can be found at: http://www.artscenecal.com

  * Museum of Tolerance, LA http://www.museumoftolerance.com

** Museum of Modern Art, NYC http://www.MOMA.org

Pointillist Painting Project and Classroom Museum

Preparation: Show works from Post-Impressionist Painters Georges Seurat and Camille Pissarro. Compare and contrast the formal aspects of each, content and meanings.

Discuss: how the dot method uses additive effects of adjacent colors to produce the perception of a unified visual image through **optical mixing**.

Making the picture involves the Creative and Expressive Standard 2.0

Discuss: **Simultaneous contrast**. [1.0 Standard Perception] Adjacent colors tend to force the appearance of their complements. For example, placing greenish colors next to any color tends to make it appear more red. This effect also works with value too. The eye perceives and emphasize relative values between colors. Simultaneous contrast may be perceived as a glow of the contrasting color at the juncture of two colors.

Discuss: The process of looking at paintings as a novice in art.

See Efland's concept of the novice to expert continuum in arts awareness, attached to this document.

[4th Standard]

Making the Paintings

Select pictures from art reproductions. Choose works that have a wide selection of local colors in a relatively small space. We used old calendars with Impressionists, Post-Impressionists and Early 20th Century Artists.

Look for a variety of **local** color so the pictures appear lively.

- Have students identify the name of the artist, time period, type of media, scale of painting; other factoids such as location of painting, etc., may be useful for the Classroom Museum Project.

- Cut a window from paper to frame a part of the picture. If the artwork is not very complex, or the same size as the painting surface, consider adapting the whole piece, or dividing the project into sections for multiple students to paint.

- On a sheet of paper or suitable board draw a graphite sketch of the color boundaries to be painted. Keep this sketch very light. In more complex works it may be necessary to complete a grid of the image and carefully transfer the image square by square. [5 × 7 Index card stock works well.]

- Prepare a palette with a small amount of pigment. Tempera or acrylic can be used. Each student will need 5 cotton swabs, a towel and paper to blot excess pigment. Also students benefit from a second sheet of paper to test mixed colors. A simple palette of primaries only or more complex choice of colors is possible. Black and white should be available for mixing tints and shades.

- Painting process involves building up layers of colors that are carefully placed next to each other. It will take several "dots" to build up local color. In some instances it is easier to block out areas with premixed colors, then go back with dots on top of the tone underneath. Remember that the effect of simultaneous contrast will "force" colors to make adjacent colors appear like the complement. For example blue will make any color next to it appear like orange, and vice versa. The effect also works with neutralized colors. Simultaneous contrast works for neutral colors, and for tints and shades of colors too.

- Mix colors by applying layers of pigments. It will take some time to complete the process carefully.

- Allow paintings to dry. (Curling may happen to any thin board with a thick layer of paint on one side. Flatten excessive curling by applying a layer of paint to the backside.)

Classroom Museum

- Once the paintings have thoroughly dried they should be mounted within a small matte window.

- **The mattes can be decorated** to resemble ornate frames, using string, or corrugated board. In this project we adapted the Post-Impressionist's technique of painting the frame to heighten color contrast within the pictures.

- These works can be presented as a classroom museum. *Have the students make labels* to identify the works original maker, title of the picture. The original reproductions can be presented alongside the interpretations. If students are going to sign their pointillist versions, they should use the words, "after (name of artist)" then their own name.

- Students can present "docent tours" of the artworks, or conduct additional investigation into artist biographies.

The Classroom Museum concept can apply to any body of cultural artifacts students choose to study.

Assessment

Students will benefit from the opportunity to deepen looking at artworks as they make a painting. What they say or write about what they see is important. This should be evaluated on their communication about the works in Elements and Principles Language, sharing of meanings found in the works, in writing or orally.

Lifelong Learning in the Arts: Relating Change in Visual Arts Knowledge to a Subject in Formation

The idea of artistic growth stems from efforts to reason through the evolution of thinking during the lifespan. By learning about development, one begins to comprehend the complex transformation that education intends, and the meaning of the phrase *lifelong learning*. It is beyond the scope of an introductory course in artistic growth to elaborate a connection between arts learning and potential for evolutionary advantage. Nevertheless, one may recognize intuitively that stages in artistic growth reveal a procession of adaptive abilities that lead towards more complex states of differentiation and to a deepening of social skills needed for survival. (Gardner 1990, Arnheim 1954, Dissanyake, 1992). By understanding that artistic growth is potentially a lifelong experience, educators move beyond simply valuing art education for its own sake; changes in arts knowledge become an aspect of understanding the changes in a maturing conception of self.

Lifelong learning in the arts depends upon adequate opportunity to elaborate meanings of art in experiential practices, both art making and social interactions through art. Growth in selfhood means progress through "balances," stages as tension between ways of knowing. A balance generalizes and objectifies—"makes an object of"—the subject's awareness of desires, powers of mediation and social situations. A given balance or stage makes sense of a given situation through the thinking patterns and abilities that are features of the stage. Manipulative age children try out media. Schematic children use symbols. Early adolescents stretch categories of knowing, often beyond what adults consider acceptable. Each stage draws upon forms of knowing constructed in previous stages to reflect upon or to advance growth. Thus, aspects of each stage persist in balances of subsequent stages.

For example, as children experience pre-schematic mark making they bring meaning to random movements of hands, or notice the pleasure of making marks with a tool. Gradually, with the support of attentive caregivers, the meanings of marks coalesce toward symbolic forms. While an adult may see all marks as effort to tell a story, children in the pre-schematic phase experience art as the movement embodied in the media. In the course of development, it remains possible to understand prior awareness, and teachers also recognize how to support transitions.

This chart describes development during the manipulative phase as an effort to achieve balance of self as an "I am" in the world. "I am" implies a knowledge of the self as distinct from the (m) other-caregiver. As children grow through schematic phase they work toward "mastering" of durable categories, and they continue to recognize common or shared meanings.

By middle childhood a rich store of information and experiences prepare the child for complex changes in adolescence.

As noted, mastery of new information or experience that challenges a balance is first understood in the framework of the prior stage. *Growth* means that the individual evolves towards a new balance whose artistic forms represent a change in subjective understanding of the forms. Second-order consciousness—graphic equivalent of schematic drawing through Lowenfeld's "gang age"—implies an expanding awareness of durable symbols, and knowledge that others of like mindedness exist. For example, as Wilson and Wilson describe (1979), children draw "quests ranging from space odysseys to mountain climbing; trials; conquests and conflicts. Mastery of denotative knowledge—the facts and "how to" of art making—requires a sense of the self able to make sense of what one sees and experiences in the world. Children with second-order consciousness adapt their symbol systems to portray their experiences[1] of the larger world. Each of these theorists illuminate ways second-order subjectivity seeks to make sense of the an expanding view of and competence in the larger world as a new self-balance.

Movement on the ladder is possible when subjective balances complete or with support by a teacher-caregiver-tutor. There is also a frequent observation of apparently untutored synthesis without teaching. In a rich environment children do naturally learn up to a point. In both models a subject still has to advance through categorically different forms of knowing that follow a notion of stages.

Vygotsky's *zone of proximal development* (1934, 1978) based upon constructive learning theory, models growth possible through teachers and students' interactive relationship. The zone of proximal development is the potential area for new knowledge that the teacher contributes through learning activity. This further supports teacher framing of a developmental mindfulness in their work with children. Teaching dialogues, motivations, and curriculum design anchors to the *zone* because the teaching creates a space for the child to extend their understanding or ability to the next level.

In this theoretical organization artistic development relates to the process of individual meaning making through art experiences. Notice how the point of view of the self changes through successive grammatical forms of self-awareness, and how each order of consciousness not only builds upon the prior phases, but also implies wider awareness of social networks and increasing artistic skill. Notice also how conflicts and difficulties often reflect the efforts of the subject to apply knowledge gained in mastery of prior balances to current situations. For the manipulative age child, the opportunity to experience a broad range of media and time for elaborating many concepts provides a base for innovation during schematic phase. With a greater range of mark making ability a larger repertoire accumulates. Moreover the child who is accustomed to the trial, error and reflection process builds the ability to persist at problem solving.

The growth of third-order balances implies awareness of cross-categorical structures—knowledge that similar connotative meanings may be present in multiple forms, and that meanings have a social context that involve common experience. Of course shared experience may still be centered upon peers and like-minded people. There is a new capacity for recognition of friendships based upon mutuality of purposes, and great strengthening of age group-related awareness. ["I and thou," grammar form, and the cliquishness of early teens.]

Emerging critical ability quickly sees the contradictions inherent in social contexts. Adolescents frequently point out the distinctions between their experience and the expectation for following the rules. This involves a process of "inference" founded upon the idea that meanings endure. There is also the potential for emerging critical ability to negate any aspect of knowledge formation. Many pre-adolescents may "over-think" or attach too much significance to the meanings of

---

[1]See Alex's Winter Olympics drawing, *Children and their Art*, Hurwitz 8th Ed., p 52.

structures. As Burton (1980) observes this emerging ability is often intent on pointing out flaws and contradictions in the adult world. The term "cognitive conceit" implies knowledge, which should determine meaning, yet adults misunderstand an adolescent context or recognize it but desire to focus "more appropriately." Results on art making at the third order of consciousness may either be far below an individual's real ability (apparent at age 10–11) or represent a sustained effort at establishing new skills. Either way, if a child is left to experience frustration with symbol making that is an inadequate representation of their world, they will most likely end up giving up on art altogether.

Hence the importance of good art instruction for early adolescents cannot be overstated, as the growth of critical ability is applied to the perception of self and to social experiences. As with all balances, there will be great diversity in how the balances are experienced, and it is not necessary to have art experiences across the totality of possible human art. Rather an individual need only have experiences meaningful to them, or those, which have inherent meaning, such as a well organized, subject centered, and developmentally appropriate learning program.

Fourth-order consciousness in art can only be achieved through the work of comprehending gathering experience about art as systems for aesthetic knowing. The process involves generating art, looking carefully at it, evaluating the work, and making inferences about possible meanings. "Art experience" is the *body of rules* for making and experiencing art. These are complex systems in which the subjects "knows" through relating of ideas and purposes of the institution to their aesthetic thinking. This may involve ideological identification related to shared identity as a "role" defined by an institution/social ideal. An example of this might be selection and activity towards a professional goal for art such as a major in college

In fourth-order balance the subject recognizes that an aesthetic experience depends upon, not merely the reenactment of art, but a living through it according the regularities of the system, and a person who is able to undergo the experience. This subjectivity or perception of selfhood, is bound up with valuing the self in a social context usually through building or participating in shared ideology. The subjectivity may take all grammatical forms, yet identity is perceived *through* these forms, not *despite* these forms.

Art instruction for this age group 1) continues to develop new capacities for media mastery 2) makes sense of art as an aesthetic system 3) must share meanings for form and content in conversations or in shared documents.

Fifth-order consciousness implies that all the forms of consciousness from the fourth-order contribute to subjectivity. This subject, recognizes that though they may associate with the concepts of a particular context and share ideological perceptions, the sense of self endures beyond an a communal or institutional experience. For example, the self is not only an art major, they are a person whose major is art. Art is both a durable category and a lived experience in a social world. An inter-individual consciousness demands a thinking through related meanings, recognizing others' understandings of meaning, even where different.

Transformational learning theorists (Belenky 1986, 2000) suggest that moral thinking is no longer tied to rules, but instead the process of thinking relates across categories towards support of others who may be either like-minded or contrary minded. Belenky thus looks less at the excellence of individual evolution of artistic experience and more towards the notion of building a shared network of "knowers."

What Does This Mean for Visual Art Experience?

Critical experience of the arts ties [or unties] disparate art experiences into meaning structures. The fifth-order balance tolerates experiences that are not compatible with ideology. This may result from certainty or confidence in one's ideology, or from awareness that the self endures or has in many "roles"—individual, family member, social network, professional life in which ideological points of view vary. In other words the person with fifth-order balance comprehends multiple contexts for understanding the self.

(Based upon the educational theorist Kegan, R. (1994) *In Over Our Heads*, Table 8.1, Chapter 8, p. 291)

Curricular Form	Appropriate Audience	Cognitive Operation	Claim on Mind Subjectivity; "Balance"
Material exploration	Early childhood after infancy; Pre-K and K.	Sensory Motor Experience/ enclosure making—"paper is the target"; kinesthetic of movement and tool usage.	Separation and individuation; toward imperial balance—the "I" first-order balance.
Elementary Art Making	**K–6**	**Data**	**Evolution toward Second Order**
The stories of art making and how art has a context in social life.	Grades 1-3 a stretch; grades 4-6 elaborating on emerging capacity.	Data of how to make. Learning about symbols/ meaning (Denotation)	Evolution toward second order of consciousness; (durable categories of self in the world) "I and me" and others related to me.
Elementary Artistic Theory	**Adolescents**	**Inference**	**Transition toward Third-Order Consciousness**
How art is made; its dependence upon the perspective of the artist; the themes and values expressed by art, artworks and culture.	Junior High a stretch; High School elaborating and emerging capacity.	Recognizing that the symbols, images and media have meaning, *and* that *meanings* both endure and communicate. (Connotation)	Cross-categorical structures. Personal needs to express versus acknowledgement of social context for meaning. The "we"; the "I and thou"[1] (Interpersonal, mutuality balance).
Artistic Theory	**Adults**	**Formulation**	**Fourth-order of Consciousness**
The discipline's system or systems for creating *aesthetic* knowledge, generating, regarding, evaluating, and relating inferences.	Any higher educational setting (a stretch for many since there may be few artistic experiences to frame a "system").	Generative with awareness of system regularities. Art is the body of rules for making art.	(Complex systems) Relating ideas and purposes. Identity with *institutional* logic of art making, and aesthetic thinking. Ideological identification. (Role playing versus connectivity) Use of all grammatical forms of subject.

Curricular Form	Appropriate Audience	Cognitive Operation	Claim on Mind Subjectivity; Balance
Critical Theory	**Adults**	**Reflection upon Formulation**	**Fifth Order of Consciousness (Trans-system Structures)**
Critical reflection on the discipline itself; subjecting its prevailing theories to analysis not just from the perspective of another contending theory, but also recognizing paradox or contradiction within valued systems.	Any higher education setting (a stretch for most); graduate programs in art, criticism; theory: professional life of artist/art writer, art educator (a stretch for most since criticism demands making an object of ideological structures).	Reflection means consideration of how structures interrelate; how paradigms interconnect or through critical reasoning have no relationship to each other, to self.	Interindividual: Subject more than ideological perception of self. Subject connected with system knowledge, and people in the system, yet balance held distinct from the forms of knowing in the arts. Multiple institutional settings and meaning making schemes.

Art Education History: Personalities, Issues, and Topics

Jean Jacques Rousseau—Swiss-French enlightenment philosopher. Active during second half of 1700's. Idea of *natural* education, an origin of developmental theory as the study of children's growth in stages. A contrast with concept of personality and emergence of "soul."

Pestalozzi—Swiss, founder of modern idea of public education. Early participatory-constructive learning methodology directed towards happiness in new social conditions.

Frederick Froebel and invention of kindergarten: "The Gifts and Occupations" 1835–1850. Include investigation of **Kindergarten Movement** in America during 19th century, or emergence of learning materials and games produced by private enterprise, such as Milton Bradley Corporation.

Benjamin Franklin: described art education as part of full education needed for democratic system. Predicted many contemporary aspects of arts learning and proposed programmatic curriculum for schools.

Walter Smith, Supervisor Public School Drawing—1871 State of Massachusetts passed the Drawing Act of 1870. A first public curriculum in art making based upon observation and imitation of Greek and Roman plaster casts in a sequence of increasingly challenging arrangements.

Arthur Wesley Dow—*Elements of Art and Principles of Design* (1890–1930's NYC). Noticed design in Japanese art. His interest in Japanese art inform ideas of teaching. Modern social conditions in America drive need for technological understanding of objectivity and beauty.

Marion Richardson—a great art teacher and inspector-supervisor of London Schools; drawing from imagination based upon listening to evocating language and seeing abstract lighting/projections. (England 1920–1940s).

Picture Movement 1920's. **Royal B. Farnum**, a faculty member at Rhode Island School of Design, leading role in publication and distribution of an art appreciation program. Utilizing modern printing methods the posters were widely circulated for school programs. Works tended to show images of moral, patriotic, religious importance, and introduce artistic masterworks to the public.

Franz Cizek and child-centered art movements in early 20th century Vienna, Austria. Deeply connected to naturalism and support of children's free expression. See also connections to Art Deco; Viennese art movements—Klimpt, etc. Printmaking to represent ideas encouraged as means of emotionally expressive artworks. Psychic growth more than learning of form and culture; learning involves the an expressive, complex self.

Viktor Lowenfeld, adapted Piaget's philosophical orientation and Cizek's child-centered approach to education in relation to the child's need for personal self-expression through stages of thinking. Research can be about the works of VL or may describe the stages applications to school art lessons. Note: the entire class should be aware of L's concepts of stages of artistic growth. A project to present his work should briefly outline these, but also relate some of the biographical connections of his experiences to teaching of visual art. Text: *Creative and Mental Growth.*

John Dewey *Art and Experience,* 1934—an influential book by this leading education philosopher and writer on progressive education. The brochure can be a reading of *Art and Experience* selections: Live creature and Having an experience, or an overview of Dewey and progressive education movements, nationally or internationally. Other texts include: *Child and the Curriculum,* 1902; *Democracy and Education,*1938.

Herbert Read, *Education through Art* 1947. This author was an influential mid-century arts educator and critic. Read articulated values of art education as link to human cultural inheritance. *Education through Art* was composed during WWII when the very foundations of the West were under attack from fascism and totalitarian communism. He extended Jung's concept of collective unconscious as the basis for the common core of worldwide culture, diverse yet comprehensible through understanding of one's own culture.

Outline ideas on visual art and culture. He relates teaching of the visual arts to classroom as an active learning environment. The arts enliven a healthy social experience through participatory connection to all humans through art and art history, artifacts, and cultural experience. Read extensively wrote art criticism.

Victor D'Amico *Creative Teaching and Art*, 1942/1953; New York 1930–1940's. Director of Art Education at the Museum of Modern Art taught NYC schools using modernist concepts of representation, innovative 20th century media, such as collage, to schools. D'Amico established an influential art school on a literage barge docked on Long Island.

Howard Gardner—*Multiple Intelligences,* 1983. Gardner is not an art teacher, although his educational interests consistently relate to describing learning in through the arts as development and as mastery of content experiences in the Arts. His works have had a great impact on education through Harvard University Project Zero—an innovative think tank devoted to advancing and applying aesthetic thinking to classrooms.

Arthur Efland—*A History of Art Education,* 1990. Arthur Efland did extensive research on the history of art education serves as a wonderful resource for students, professors, and researchers. His book, is one of the few texts of its kind.

Recent Movements and Conceptual Approaches to Arts in Education

Reggio Emilia—(A school not a person); A dynamic method of teaching similar to Montessori, in which the child learns through self-direction under the guidance of teachers for projects. The school program founded in Italy has spawned an international movement of schools that connect art making with learning through student experiences in social contexts.

DBAE (1990s) overview of this educational reform program in Art Education. Discipline Based Art Education—art education through 4 disciplines in art world:[1] Essentially a reform of traditional, academically oriented versions of Art from a technical-rationalist point of view. In practice it provides an assessable and challenging curriculum in four domains: art making, art history, art criticism, aesthetics. Aesthetics is a branch of philosophy that deals with issues about feelings, sentiments, and perception in the experience of the arts.

Visual Thinking—a developmental approach to arts learning relating growth in aesthetic ability and critical thinking in cognitive domains. Abigail Hausen's concepts are now a full-fledged program available for use in the schools. Visual Thinking Strategies is a not-for-profit corporation that applies developmental concepts to education in the arts and critical thinking. http://www.vtshome.org

Marion Diamond Brain Research—find her lectures on YouTube! Her concepts describe a scientific basis for connecting constructive, experiential learning in the arts to the brain. These are particularly valuable in relation to articulating a vision for "brain-based learning." This presentation will involve understanding what aspects of art teaching support learning in a way the brain utilizes the best.

Daniel Pink—*A Whole New Mind*—the book that adapts right brain-left brain concepts[2] to an argument that U.S. business community needs to comprehend how learning through creativity enables a more effective work structure to remain globally competitive. 2010. His recent book, ***Drive, the Surprising Truth about What Motivates Us***, examines the three elements of true motivation—autonomy, mastery, and purpose—and offers smart and surprising techniques for putting these into action.

Sir Ken Robinson an author and public speaker reasserts the connection between the arts and commerce, creative problem solving and newly evolving understanding of their interaction in emerging global world. Notice that the concept of the Arts and Creativity is not merely a craft discipline of art making, but includes contributions from the Visual and Performing Arts (dance, music, visual art, theater). Another contribution of this influential figure is his reminder that the Arts have had a dynamic alliance with progressive interests in commerce and science since the Enlightenment; he offers a critique of the basic learning model an realignment of aesthetic learning with current historical trends.

http://www.ted.com/talks/ken_robinson_says_schools_kill_creativity.html
http://www.choralnet.org/view/268945

Edwards, Betty, 1999. *The New Drawing on the Right Side of the Brain.* New York: Penguin Putnam.

A very readable book connecting Edwards' version of how the brain works to ideas of being creative. Essentially Edwards presents a series of exercises that put into practice the use of both hemispheres of the brain to encourage greater visual awareness and drawing ability. Developed from her years as a high school teacher, these ideas and techniques lead to competent drawings and strengthen skills in making art.

---

[1] The critic Arthur Danto, coined the term "art world" to indicate the varied social communities and interrelations of the art world in an essay in the late 70's.
[2] Betty Edwards, extensively cited by Pink prepared an excellent art teaching book *Drawing on the Right Side of the Brain* in the early 1980's. The current edition, *The New Drawing on the Ride of the Brain* (2003?) updates her teaching ideas.

Brookes, Mona, 1996. *Drawing with children*. New York: Putnam.

Brookes designed a very specific sequence that teaches how to draw. It is useful for teaching oneself to draw too! This is a great guidebook for beginning students. An excellent chapter on teaching supports for students who have disabilities.

Smith, Nancy, 1998. *Observation Drawing with Children*. New York, Teachers College Press.

This might be the best connection for teachers to observation drawing and developmental processes. Unlike Brookes and Edwards who have found functional training techniques that work in a classroom, Nancy Smith works from a research based, developmental perspective. She orients lessons to growth in cognitive ability and the new kinds of seeing they experience as they mature.

Movements in Visual Art and Art History

Modernism—Refers the art historical pathway of the arts aligned with a concept of progressive change and growth. The Bauhaus in Weimar Germany was the first school devoted to teaching through modernist precepts. Author instructors include: Paul Klee, *Pedagogic Sketchbook;* Wassily Kandinski, *Point and Line to Plane, Concerning the Spiritual in Art.*

Many resources can be found on this subject, especially the recent show at the MOMA.org in NYC.

For writing on teaching of modern art in general see **Harold Rosenberg's** writings. His terse evaluation—Art Education = craft + inspiration—summed up the classroom approach in Post WW II America.

ISMS in ART HISTORY—These may be more relevant for lesson development, although some of these contribute to art education.

Realism: Courbet, Manet Monet, Renoir, to Thomas Eakins in America.

Post-Impressionism: Seurat—Pissarro
Nabis Movement,

Cubism: Picasso, Braque, Gris.

Russian Constructivism—Rodchenko, Tatlin, El Lissitsky, Malevich, Luibov Popova.

Futurism: A lyrical graphic approach to glories of machines, movement, style. Visually stunning, many futurists in Italy supported policies of the Fascist Dictator, Mussolini.

Surrealism: More of an art education phenomenon for high school, in context of art education.

Mondrian and Visual Modernism.

Pop Art.

Robert Rauschenberg, Jasper Johns, Andy Warhol.

Post-Modernism and Art Education Overview—Po-Mo has had extensive impact on art education because of socially proactive in educational settings, community work, large museum installations, art fairs—the expanding network of aesthetic international arts and engaged art making.

Relationships of Art are positioned as critique of status quo in consumer world (Frederick Jameson) to issues related to the experiences of culture and language. The context for active, contemporary approaches lies outside traditional history of great works, yet also includes museum patronage and community applications.

Michael Apple's 1971 deconstruction of educational practice traced formation of hegemony of dominant class ideas. **Post-modernism** draws upon **semiotic** interpretation to contextualize visual meanings in relation to their settings (Roland Barthes). Since the meaning of art depends upon the kinds of interpretive understandings the viewer brings to the art experience, study of the arts develops an understanding of sign systems that mediate an experience.

De-constructivism—A method or process of analysis that carefully studies language and images of cultural experiences or art objects. Deconstruction as creative production is sometimes represented in "bric-collage," or assembling through juxtaposition of contrasting elements. Deconstruction is also a method for the literary analysis of narratives of contemporary experience in an issue responsive, multi-cultural, feminist, philosophical criticism, and viral conditions in hyper-reality. In art education deconstruction creates broader contexts for learning through interdisciplinary problem solving. Relating, describing contemporary architecture is valuable, visually rich approach to deconstruction.

Architectural Approach to Teaching Po-Mo: Peter Eisenmen and Jacques Derrida. Deconstructivist Architecture Exhibition at Museum of Modern Art 1988, organized by Phillip Johnson and Mark Wigley. Works of Frank Gehry, Daniel Libeskind, Rem Koolhoas. By looking at the concepts and forms of these architects one can see postmodernism in context of living space.

Three interrelated philosophical systems inform contemporary art education.

1. **Marxism**—Critical perspective on privilege of dominant groups; **hegemony—a concept described by Marx elaborated upon by** Gramsci, an Italian philosopher/theorist in the 20th century developed the concept that thought is mediated through perception of power.

   An excellent resource for preparation of learning: John Berger's (1972) *Ways of Seeing.*

2. **Feminism**—Lucy Lippard, scholar-critic-educator, see especially Linda Nochlin's essay, "Why have there been no great women artists?" the critique of artistic experience as traditionally dominated by masculine-centered, patriarchal perspective. Or chose an artist, such as **Judy Chicago** to discuss feminist issues in the works. Or explore feminist artworks by **Martha Rossler** (construction of identity in images), or explore how the goal of equality of the sexes has influenced art teaching.

3. **Multi-culturalism**—Looks at the traditional art world claim for "universality" and observes that this means the absence of artists of color. [Banks] Authentic representation of cultural experience demands presentation of diversity of cultural and artistic expression. Artists: Kara Walker, Juan Sanchez, collections of MoLAA in Long Beach. Suggested review text: *Contemporary Art and Multicultural Education*. Note that multi-cultural contexts in art education are not simply valuing indigenous cultural artifacts; multi-cultural concepts confront global *hegemony* of western culture.

Environmental Art—Donald Krug article highlights this burgeoning orientation to teaching the arts.

Popular Culture—Visual Culture connects educational practice as enhancement of knowledge of common experiences in contemporary society where visuality is key component. Different from, but related to Pop Art as a historical movement from the late 1950s to mid-1970s. Suggested artists: Stuart Davis, Roy Lichtenstein, Murakami.

Useful resource: *Teaching Visual Culture,* by Kerry Freedman (2003).

New Conditions for Art Education—The web enables new type of knowledge holding. The group can represent ideas in common sites. Groups have ability to link with other interests across the network.

Viral growth of ideas—spreading exponentially—a diffuse yet worldwide experience.

Rhizome growth—spreading through clusters of roots; local perception.

Problems: Technology is expensive and must be updated to reflect current software. Use of technology still requires basic art education practice to prepare for thinking in any media.

Instrumental Benefits[1] and Intrinsic[2] Benefits Private and Public

PRIVATE VALUE	Intersection Private Values with Public Benefits	PUBLIC VALUE
Education generally improves test score of individual.	Education improves self-efficacy; learning and communication skills	Education provides populace with knowledge and skills for economic growth (social capital).
Captivation;[3] Interests in special forms of knowing; curiousness to experience through perception.	Expanded capacity for empathy and understanding[4] across culture(s)	Building of social bonds; expectation for social experiences[5]
Pleasure;[6] self-esteem through mastery of new knowledge areas,[7] or pleasure experience through media manipulation	Cognitive[8] growth	Expression of communal meanings;[9] shared awareness of connotation and value

[1] "Instrumental" means purposes or functions for social policy, education, specific application for knowledge for practice of an art project by individual.

[2] Intrinsic benefits are internal processes, which improve thinking or contribute to making thinking more complex, dynamic, nuanced or interrelated. Thinking becomes "meta-cognitive" in the sense that it is thinking about or speaking about the process of thinking and doing. Meta-cognitive practices—reflections, dialogues, sharing with a group indicate an agency present in the thinking process who 'makes an object of the concept' [Kegan, Robert, 1982, *The Evolving Self*, and 2001; *In Over our Heads*] and relating ideas to the self through systems of mastery/self-repertoires.

[3] A remarkable feature of Arts experience is the engagement of interest. It is related to the human capacity to "make special" [Ellen Dissanayake, 1995 *Homo Aestheticus*], and the concept of "flow"—described by researcher Czikszentmihalyi as the experience of happiness through meaningful activity [Czikszentmihalyi, M. 1990 *Flow: The Psychology of Optimal Experience*].

Capacity also implies potential for an assessment. The visual arts reveal the potential for evaluating intelligence and forms of knowing through practices in the arts.

[4] This can only occur if the dynamic for art experience is a social one. Where art is modeled upon the notion of perfection, the formal properties of art as imply recognition and acceptance of the expert-authority position. Where the aesthetic emerges through discussion of experiences, involves sharing of points of view and acknowledgement of differences between viewpoints, there is the potential to model art social experiences as an aspect of living democratically.

[5] This can only occur if the dynamic for art experience is a social one. Where art is modeled upon the notion of perfection, learning the formal properties of art involves recognition and acceptance of "exemplars from the canon." Thus the expert as authority determines what to know. Where the aesthetic emerges through discussion of experiences, involves sharing of points

of view and acknowledging of differences between viewpoints, there is the potential to model social experience of art as a democratic practice.

[6] The connection of the arts to affect is well known. Brain research tells us that affect is not a separate kind of cognition but is part of the rich associations one has with cognitive experiences. Self-esteem is not simply feeling good about oneself; it also means understanding of capacity for handling situations which are not clearly defined, which demand adaptive thinking and transfer of knowledge from one area to another.

[7] Mastery implies a continuum of novice to expert practitioner. For children mastery may mean an emerging ability that grows more elaborate because the child enjoys investing time to improve, or because of well-ordered, supportive learning curricula. A good example of this is found in gifted children who make considerable efforts to improve their art about specialized imagery. Internal processes which contribute to making thinking complex, dynamic, interrelated are called **meta-cognitive** because these forms of learning experience involve thinking through or speaking that the individual expresses their sense of the knowledge. This indicates an agency doing the thinking process.

[8] Cognitive growth; see Bruner, Jerome, 1979, "After John Dewey, What?" On Knowing: Essays for the Left Hand.

[9] Meanings" also refers to experiencing of social values, not simply knowing the connotations of the symbols used by a given group.

Art History Brochure Project: Tips on Making an Outline

1. Tell the story of your topic in as brief a means possible.
2. You are basically collecting information to make a visual presentation that is truthful without being overly detailed. We are making posters for display.
3. You can post your outline and completed project to the Blackboard.

Is Your Topic a Person?

- Focus upon the accomplishments that are discussed in the Hurwitz text and references.
- If the person is particularly famous for an idea, you need to outline the concepts of their idea.
- Find a picture, painting or image of your person.
- Are there famous quotations that summarize the concepts?

Is Your Topic an Idea?

- Gardner's Multiple Intelligences, Froebel's Kindergarten, Marxism—How does this kind of thinking influence art education? What institutions relate to this idea?
- How is the idea represented in artworks related to the idea?
- What are the basic precepts of thinking in this idea?

Some ideas, such as Modernism in art education need to be contrasted with other ways of thinking about the arts, such as Post-Modernism.

- Examples of the ideas as seen in visual arts, or artist who typically represent the period in history are ways to manage the large "ism" topics.
- Be alert to other locations in the text where you may find images.
- A chart of characteristics might be the best here; contrast of concepts in each e.g.

Modernism	Post-Modernism
Believe in "correct" interpretation of art through forms	Believe in multiple interpretations relating to point of view, social class, gender, interest in object as expert/ novice
Progress in art through a succession of styles and artistic ideas improving upon universal themes	Progress is a phenomenon best described as evolving dominant forms, always changing and differentiating

What else is happening in education at the time of your topic?

- For example at the time of Dow, American society was influenced by "social Darwinism"—the best ideas and people would tend to be successful. Part of the success of Dow's teaching methods is that the elements of art and principles of design provide "objective" means of discussing the arts.
- The receptivity of U.S.A. Lowenfeld's expressive education occurred partly from the advances in psychology (Piaget's stage theories) and the post-World War II beliefs in personal expression and freedom of the individual.
- Be alert to other parts of the text where images might be found.
- Look carefully at the references at the close of the chapters.

Provide Citations at the end. You must have a bibliography someplace on the poster. It can be in small type.

Keep track of the locations of your resources. Most of this project can be accomplished by careful mining of the Internet, CSUF library or Hurwitz text. Where you gather information from other sources, such as the web or library resources provide citations for others to retrieve the info, if needed.

Assembling the Poster/Brochure

If you are proficient in digital design programs, go for it. Create your poster using the data, images and information you have gathered! Make it colorful, readable.

If you are better at creating a collage with the outline, use the cut and paste collage.

Size and Paper: You may select a format for your size. The obvious choice would be standard 3-fold 8.5 × 11 brochure, but 8.5 × 14 may be necessary to have additional space. Both sides of the page should be utilized.

Poster: The minimum size should be 11 × 17. The poster should have information with sufficient depth and visuality to intrigue and inform a diligent student.

Your display should not only have information and citations for sources, it should also be visually intriguing, show a designed, organized space, and images relating to the topic.

Strike a balance between a fun visual and content that you want to convey.

If There Is a Design Motif in Your Topic, Use It!

- Adapt artwork to your poster/page. Change the scale to suit your needs.
- For Example: A poster on the Bauhaus should look modern, the way modern looked in the 1920s.

 Observation Component—Art 380

The purpose of this project is to observe and describe children in the process of making art and make connections between what you see in their art making process and relevant theories of artistic development. Students who do not have access to young children making art can complete Option Two. Please read both Options. Notice that we are using class texts for literature review in both options.

A. *Observe and describe the range of activity you see children perform as they complete a particular project in a classroom.* This involves looking carefully at the lesson, how children respond to each part of the lesson, and formally evaluating what you see in the artworks that connects with growth concepts found in the readings. Collect samples of the artworks by using a digital camera to record the range of student works. You do not need to photograph students for the project—you will need permission to use their photo if you do. Nevertheless, you should be a witness to the making process so that you can describe how the child-subject made the work. In the write-up section you will compare and contrast the children's approaches to art making in relation to your understandings of artistic growth in the readings.

B. *Case study of an individual artistic growth.* If you have contact with a child or extended family, consider collecting or reviewing one or two children's artworks, possibly interviewing the child about their experience of the works, and writing a case study. This option may also involve observation of the child making visual art and discussions with them on the meanings or process of their works. Where relevant you can incorporate conversations with parents or care givers. A review of literature appropriate to the age group or developmental level is also required.

C. *No Kids?* Prepare a more detailed review of the literature and relate it to lessons in our classroom. Discuss particularly how a given lesson is "developmentally appropriate."

How Do I Write a Literature Review?

The literature review is a summary of the main points of the topic, which other authors have already identified. A good review will identify these points and describe in your own words the ideas of the authors. This is not an effort to summarize everything. It is also not appropriate to simply quote the article at length. Using your own words to relate main ideas, especially ideas you expect to find in your observation, will enable you to make these ideas your own.

We are using a limited number of texts for the review, and we are limiting the topic to children's artistic development Pre-Kindergarten to 8th grade. If you have already found a child or children you can select to review articles appropriate to the age. Have a good understanding of all the readings, however.

Looking at *The First Visual Symbols* as an Example for Review

In each of the Burton articles we are using for our review practice, she provides a broad, general description of the core experience children have as they develop in art. She is careful to connect this growth in thinking with an experience of art making, and to link her background understandings to literature herself. Moreover she provides also a general description and many examples of children's artwork that show an aspect of the stage. Burton is careful to relate what kinds of thinking children must engage.

Look carefully at the articles to inform your own understanding of *how* children grasp the concepts. The *how* of each stage is the developmental change in the thinking of children. That means you have to describe where the child has come from and where the child is going. [A bridge is anchored on both sides.] It does not mean that children all behave the same way. Rather, the examples provide variations on the main insight.

For example in "The First Visual Symbols," Burton explores how children who already have an extensive repertoire of mark making gained through "pre-representational preparation (scribbling), adapt this knowledge to a new ability to represent ideas.

In Rodney's painting the lines not only "go fast" like the action of a speedy brush, they also re-present graphically the idea of a car that goes fast. This is an important difference for the child because the process is not only anchored in the *sensory logic* of paint, it is also put into service of Rodney's idea—the car that goes fast. She also carefully situates Rodney's ideas about cars into context of play and awareness of cars. The car painting [Figure 1, "First visual symbols"] demonstrates how Rodney connects his car knowledge with knowledge of materials. It also relates a conversation with his teacher, through which Burton clarifies the concept of representation as a connection between perception and how to fit it with an understanding. For most children the connection arises from an awareness of "common characteristics" between an idea and a certain material. In this instance the ideas relate to Rodney's expertise with toy cars and his awareness [gained through opportunity for art making] that lines have different properties.

Setting the Stage for the Observation

Notice how through understanding this summary prepares the reader for your own observation of a child in similar circumstances Burton's other examples in the "First Symbols" article bring us closer to the idea of making a symbol that is even more visually like the object it represents.

Notice how in all of the examples insights into the material provide the connection to an idea or experience. These early symbol making discoveries have not yet hardened into the form known as "schemas," which connect to representing ideas recur in the child's expanding world.

The Observation Process: What to Gather

When interacting with children most researchers do not have the opportunity to record notes during the process. Even if you could, the pace of interaction with a child may be rapid. Write down the activity you have witnessed as soon as possible. Record what a child tells you during the process, and any behaviors they have as they make work. If you are observing a classroom record conversations, prompts, etc., from the teacher/parents. These all contribute to your insights into the process of arriving at the finished piece. If permitted you can also collect or photograph the artworks. It is **not** necessary to include a picture of the child. In some observations the conversation is recorded if students are responding to specific questions about a work of art, such as an investigation of how children converse about visual art. Any actual picture contributes a potential visual example to include in the paper. If you can, repeat the same process with other kids. It is not uncommon to collect 5–8 representative works from a whole class of students.

The Write-Up—Post-Observation

1. Describe the processes and people that are specific to your observation. This will be a representation of your notes from time with the kids. Include information about the child or children, how they made the work, instruction you observe, outcomes of the work—a formal description of what you see in the pieces you have collected and/or the kind of growth you may have observed. For example, use the language of elements and principles, and/or use the developmental vocabulary describing children's artworks such as: scribbles, bang dots, fast lines, fold-over views. Another outcome of the work besides the drawing or artwork may be conversations, or even descriptions of an activity or movements you observe during the making of the work.

2. As a transition to your analysis you may need to identify or elaborate upon the appearance of the works, if you have not already provided a brief description during the observation section.

3. Discuss how what you see agrees with, contradicts, or adds to growth concepts introduced in the Literature Search. If you have conducted an interview describe how the child's understanding of artworks relates to the ideas you are highlighting about developmental growth.

4. Relevance to art education section. How does the lesson or activity you witnessed provide insight into artistic growth? Some common questions researchers consider: Are there differences between boys and girls? Have you gained any insight into how to teach developmentally? What modifications would you suggest as an activity to support or continue growth? What might be next steps/design for developmentally appropriate activities for this child or group?

5. What have **you** learned that augments your awareness of teaching the arts? How are your observations relevant to your emerging practice as an educator?

6. Bibliography in APA-like format, a complete citation: Author, date of publication, title, publisher and city.

7. Illustrations—gathering or experiencing these should occur before you even write the paper! Use a digital camera to record or make copies of the artworks. These may be inserted into the body of the paper, or placed at the end of the paper with appropriate identifications that link pictures to your text. Ideally you will be present for making of the whole work, and even participate in conversations, notice various behaviors, etc. The pictures are compelling evidence in the paper; they are also only part of the story of a holistic view of development.

Suggested Outline and Reasoning Process (5–7 pages, about 1,500–2,000 words)

8. **Introduction**—State clearly the ages, the context, lesson and purpose of your writing. When did the observation occur, how old, what did the teacher say, how did they respond? Can you see parallels between your investigation and growth theories? This is the introduction—an opportunity to paint the broad strokes of the intentions, background and discoveries of the project.

9. It is not necessary to conduct extensive additional research, although you should at least be familiar with the outline of child development in Chapter 2 of the *Creative Classroom* text and the method of connecting visual analysis of children's drawings with developmental stages and understandings. In *Creative Classroom*, this means knowing Lowenfeld's stages

from his famous textbook, *Creative and Mental Growth*. Recognize that other researchers, such as contemporary visual culture ideas may provide an alternative to stages and phases of growth models.

Your literature review should acknowledge sources of commentary. It should summarize in your own words the authors' ideas. Two or three pages are usually sufficient!

10. **Discuss and reference literature with brief description of concepts of growth for the age or ages discussed by the authors.** The discussion from the literature serves as a platform for your observation. Identify what behavior or art-making concepts or patterns you expect to see in the field. For example, children may have completed a series of scribbles, or be showing examples of transition between stages. I am not expecting you to conduct extensive research outside the required texts and handouts, but it is necessary to specify what you see in the forms of artworks, behaviors and comments, which you identify in the literature discussion. You should cover the related age groups for your subjects. If you have an eight year old, you will need to reconstruct an outline literature on scribble to schema, as well as their current phase as a schematic drawer. What does the literature describe as the norm for this age of child? The bibliography will list sources of your arguments. Cite in foot or endnote sources you quote from directly.

11. **Describe the processes and people that are specific to your observation.** This will be a representation of your notes from time with the kids. Include information about the child or children, how they made the work, instruction you observe, outcomes of the work—a formal description of what you see in the pieces you have collected and/or the kind of growth you may have observed. For example, use the language of elements and principles, and/or use the developmental vocabulary describing children's artworks such as: scribbles, bang dots, fast lines, fold-over views. Another outcome of the work besides the drawing or artwork may be conversations, or even descriptions of an activity or movements you observe during the making of the work.

12. **Discuss how what you see agrees with, contradicts, or adds to growth concepts introduced in the Literature Search.** If you have conducted an interview describe how the child's understanding of artworks relates to the ideas of developmental growth.

13. **Relevance to art education of this observation.** How does the lesson or activity you witnessed demonstrate or provide insight into artistic growth? Are there differences between boys and girls? Have you gained any insight into how to teach developmentally? What modifications would you suggest as an activity to support or continue growth? What might be next steps/activities for this child or group?

14. **What have you learned that augments your awareness of teaching the arts?** How are your observations relevant to your emerging practice as an art educator? Similar to #6, except that it asked for a more personal reflection of value applied to you.

15. **Bibliography** in APA-like format, a complete citation: Author, date of publication, title, publisher and city.

16. **Illustrations**—Gathering or experiencing these may occur before you even write the paper! Use a digital camera to record or make copies of the artworks. These may be inserted into the body of the paper, or placed at the end of the paper with appropriate identifications that link pictures to your text. Ideally you will be present for making of the whole work, and even participate in conversations, notice various behaviors, etc. The pictures are compelling evidence in the paper; they are also only part of the story of a holistic view of development.

OPTION TWO—Alternative to Observing—*"No Kids to Write About"*

Write a 5–8 page (about 1,500 words) research overview relating core understandings of child development in class readings.

The Howard Gardner article provides a scholarly overview of the role of art education in all human development. I am not expecting you to conduct extensive research besides these texts and recommended readings. However I do expect a bibliography of sources and citation of sources if you quote from them, or summarize ideas. You may use endnotes or footnotes to reference quotations.

If you are observing a multicultural, contemporary art activity or interdisciplinary activities please augment your research with some of the additional readings available online. If you draw upon other research, such as found in CHAD or Liberal Studies courses, the concepts should apply to visual art. They need citations just as any of the documents found in our readings!

Suggested Outline—OPTION TWO

1. **Introduction**—State what you are up to in the broadest sense; specify the purpose of writing. What do educational theorists mean by growth through the visual arts? Describe how these understandings may be useful for art education. Is this a natural phenomenon or does culture play a dominant function? This will set the attitude of the paper. If you are comparing and contrasting growth phases describe the epistemology of the child during the phase, preparations for transition and how these appear in their art experiences.

2. **Review of relevant literature**—Provide a succinct overview of how the readings have contributed to your knowledge of development. What do these authors say artistic growth is, and how do children show it? What is the logic of growth in stages? This might be a comparison and contrast of expressive growth with those who look at cognitive growth through the arts.

3. **What have you learned that augments your awareness of teaching the arts?** How are your observations relevant to your emerging practice as an art educator?

4. Bibliography in APA format, a complete citation: alphabetical; author last, first, date of publication, title, publisher, and city.

5. **Survey of sequence possible in art.** Describe how a child might traverse stages. Trace this experience in a medium such as drawing or painting, sculpture or even visual culture, e.g., games, movies, comics, television, coloring books. [See Nancy Smith text or Judith Burton readings.]

6. **Describe the relevance for your art education practice of your current understanding.** How would you apply these ideas to the developmental rationale in a lesson, such as a drawing lesson for 3rd grade, for example. Include a description of how the frameworks and Standards relate to what you describe and understand about artistic growth. What does "developmentally appropriate" mean in context? Use the Nancy Smith book, *Observation Drawing with Children* for a lesson, or apply to Art 380 activity.

7. Illustrations are an option, although visuals you collect from readings, et cetera, are suitable documents for visual demonstration.

Author Bibliography—Articles by these researchers are posted on Blackboard. You do not need to read additional texts to prepare this project. Appropriately cite and recognize the ideas you paraphrase or quote.

Burton, Judith—All six articles, especially the 4th–6th apply to art camp observation.

Devine, Kay and Judd, Marsha—This is the course textbook; it is not online.

Gardner, Howard—provides a context for development in society.

Hurwitz, Al and Day, Michael—*Children and Their Art*, 8th Edition—any edition 5th–9th is appropriate.

Smith, Nancy and the Drawing Study Group—Useful to study the dialogues and structure of learning activity if you are observing during a school lesson.

Museum Visit—Los Angeles County Museum of Art

Why Do This in the First Place?

What we are encouraging is the value of discovery, the interest in things beneath the surface, the joy of looking and thinking. It is here that meanings are made, that one's own life illuminates a work of art and a work of art in turn illuminates who we are and what we do. It is an experience that is powerful and personal, and it makes the view alive in a way that no amount of information can. But if you don't stop, you won't see anything.

Rika Burnham 1994. "If you don't stop, you won't see anything." *Teachers College Record, 95, 520–525, p. 524.*

Assignment Selection:

1. Treasure Map for one room or exhibition
2. Learning Brochure
3. Compare and contrast two works of art.

Plan to spend additional time for your project. I strongly suggest you prepare this project as soon as possible after visiting.

Bring sketchbooks or something to take notes with. Remember graphite, not ink allowed in the museum. Unless specifically prohibited, you can take photos. [Check with the guards if in doubt.]

Prepare a Written Response to the Museum

Our written response will incorporate the experiences you have with works of art. This experience will deepen to the extent you prepare through reading and visiting the website. If you are going to the museum for the first time, be ready to bring yourself to perceiving the art objects. We will be selective in our viewing, even though the museum is an encyclopedic excursion in the arts. While at the exhibitions take careful notes on several of the artworks. Use the 4-step method of looking carefully, describing, and rendering careful judgment, then your opinion. These notes will become the basis for your responsive paper or brochure. 2–3 pages, typed please.

We will also draw briefly if permitted. Pencils and charcoal pencils only can be used in the galleries. Ink pens are not permitted. You can also purchase reproductions available at the museum, if they can assist with creating meaningful descriptions.

If you use references, such as the website for the museum, credit in a brief bibliography.

Choose a Project

A. Compose a dialogue that you could use while guiding children through the museum. Assume that the children have completed some investigation of the subject prior to their visit. Yet share what they know in context.

The dialogue may focus on the formal aspects of the artworks, and include guiding questions that call upon students to consider through seeing and describing the relationships of the work. What do you say, what kinds of answers do you expect? How will you respond? Questions should include your expected answers. It is a dialogue you are composing. "Let's compare" should be the emphasis. Some factual questions will be necessary, although don't let these get in the way of guiding looking for meaning. Remember to include your expected responses, not just questions.

B. Prepare a museum treasure map that will lead students through the museum. This can take the form of a brochure, short essay, detailed lesson plan, illustrations and actual map. [How will it look for the children?] A set of questions that guide looking and discovering aspects of objects in the exhibition. Write **open-ended** questions that guide looking, or help students find a theme in the work. The treasure map works well within a limited area of the museum. You can include puzzles that students solve through looking at the works, drawing stations, factoid assemblies—provided they contribute to seeing meaning in the whole, following a pathway to other meaningful artworks.

Describe a holistic experience of discovering the museum as an institution. [Who is doing what? What kinds of things can one learn at the museum? What are details of artworks or placements of work that your students can notice, which indicate meanings or contexts or use? What are some of the ways that we can experience the museum? Examples include: looking for architecture in other cultures, the theme of light in art, relationships in art; spirituality; nature/nature transformed by humans, unusual materials or use of materials. Objects in the museum will demonstrate high-level use of materials.

For both of these writing projects, Hurwitz provides many suggestions. You should also consider Standards that may apply to your project. In other words how is activity which meets the content idea of the Standard embedded in your project? (What specific standard? How do students perform the activity?)

C. While at the museum, take careful notes on several works of art. Return later to see if you notice anything new to your eye. Then compose a compare and contrast discussion of the two works. You should base this discussion upon a thorough description of the works, along with pertinent information you have discovered in research about the art. But do not let the essay become a trip to the library or mining of the web. *Respond to what you see* in the works. What compels you to consider these works, besides the assignment? Suggestion— some of the pieces may have reproductions for sale in the museum store. If you can purchase small reference copies, please do so. Notice the differences between the reproduction and your experience of the artwork. Include any photos in your submission; it helps the reader to see what you have seen.

Final Notes

How is the museum trip related to the rest of the course?

The visit to the museum should inform your preparations for the lesson presentations with the class due in the last weeks of the term. This lesson should incorporate cultural ideas, aesthetic understanding and studio art activity. The basic idea is to describe and perform an interdisciplinary lesson that exemplifies a full understanding of California Visual Arts Standards. The visit to a museum and preparation should make this connection more possible. Many students discover artists or cultural examples they had never considered previously.

I strongly suggest you prepare this project as soon as possible after visiting.

Color Images

Visual 2:1

Visual 2:3

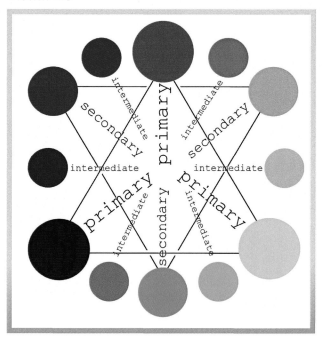

Visual 2:2

Visual 2:4

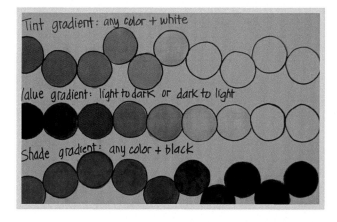

Visual 2:6

Visual 2:7

Visual 2:9

Visual 2:10a

Visual 2:8

Visual 2:10b

Visual 2:11

Visual 2:12

Visual 2:13

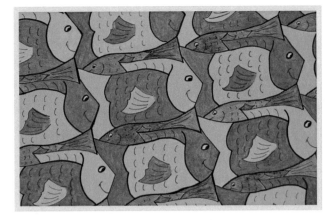

Visual 4:9

Visual 2:14

Visual 4:10

Visual 2:15

Visual 7:7

Visual 7:13

Visual 7:10

Visual 7:15

Visual 7:11

Visual 7:26

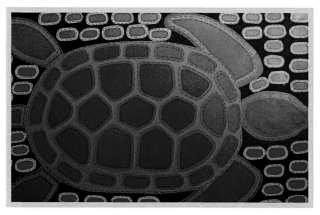

Visual 7:27

Visual 8:1

Visual 7:28

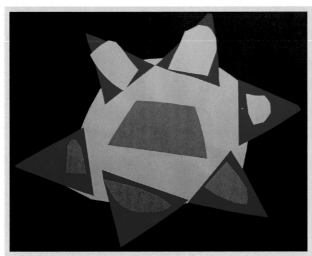

Visual 8:2

Visual 8:3

Visual 8:4

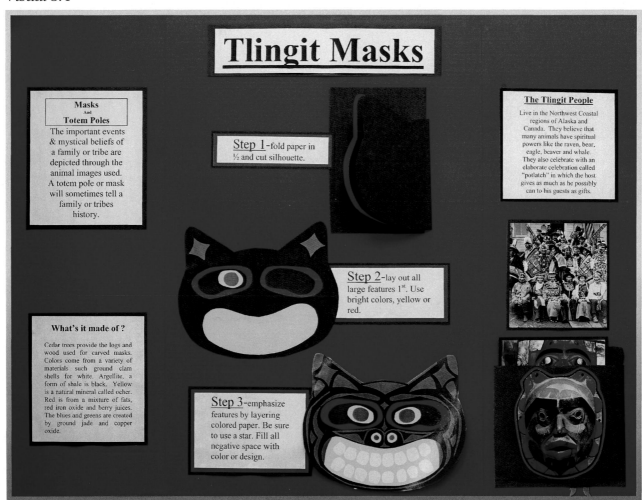

Tlingit Masks

Masks
And
Totem Poles
The important events & mystical beliefs of a family or tribe are depicted through the animal images used. A totem pole or mask will sometimes tell a family or tribes history.

Step 1-fold paper in ½ and cut silhouette.

The Tlingit People
Live in the Northwest Coastal regions of Alaska and Canada. They believe that many animals have spiritual powers like the raven, bear, eagle, beaver and whale. They also celebrate with an elaborate celebration called "potlatch" in which the host gives as much as he possibly can to his guests as gifts.

Step 2-lay out all large features 1st. Use bright colors, yellow or red.

What's it made of ?
Cedar trees provide the logs and wood used for carved masks. Colors come from a variety of materials such ground clam shells for white. Argellite, a form of shale is black. Yellow is a natural mineral called ocher. Red is from a mixture of fats, red iron oxide and berry juices. The blues and greens are created by ground jade and copper oxide.

Step 3-emphasize features by layering colored paper. Be sure to use a star. Fill all negative space with color or design.